# RECENT TRENDS IN PUBLIC ADMINISTRATION

## Other Books by the Same Author

1. Principles and Philosophy of Cooperation, 1970.
2. Rural Development Administration in India, 1970.
3. Strategy of Cooperative Development and Other Essays, 1970.
4. Economics, Planning and Public Administration, 1976
5. Planning in India, 1976.
6. The Profession of Public Administration, 1980.
7. Grammar of Planning, 1983.
8. Essays in Public Administration, 1985.
9. Policy and Performance, 1986.
10. Essays in Development Administration, 1987.
11. Delivery System, 1987.
12. Administrative Reforms, 1986.
13. Prestroika in Cooperation and Other Essays, 1993.
14. Grammar of Administration, 1994.
15. Economic Thought of the 20th. Century and Other Essays, 1996.
16. Essays on Rural Development.

# RECENT TRENDS IN PUBLIC ADMINISTRATION

**Dr. P R Dubhashi**

**Kaveri Books**
**New Delhi - 110 002**

Edition 2017

ISBN-10: 81-7479-003-9
ISBN-13: 978-81-7479-003-3



*Published by*
**Kaveri Books**
**4832/24, Ansari Road**
**New Delhi-110002 (India)**
Tel: 011-23288140, 4707 2321
E-mail : info@kaveribooks.com
kaveribooks@gmail.com
Website: www.kaveribooks.com

*Typeset at*
Delta Book World, New Delhi - 110 002.

**PRINTED IN INDIA**

# CONTENTS


**Introduction** vii

**Part I—General**

1. Trends in Public Administration in South Asia 3
2. Excellence in Administration 13
3. Can We Make India Smooth Running ? 17
4. Work Ethic in Government 23
5. Administrative Challenges in Development 33
6. Public Adminstration for 21st Century 35
7. Importance of Field Administration 45
8. Promoting Efficiency in the Civil Service 53
9. India's Political Administrators 59
10. The ICS and the IAS 65
11. Civil Service Yesterday and Today 71
12. Role of Administrator in the Changing Environment 77
13. Transplanting British Administrative Institutions 83
14. Whither Indian Bureaucracy ? 87

**Part II—Policy Making**

15. The Concept and Importance of Policy Formulation in Government 95
16. Policy Making in India 125
17. Policy Making in India — Three Case Studies 137
18. Jawaharlal Nehru and Public Administration 143
19. Indira Gandhi and Public Administration : Some Reminiscences 177

**Part III—Bureaucracy**

20. Bureaucracy 187

21. Bureaucracy—The Challenge of Change 191
22. The Decline of the Civil Service 197
23. Generalist vs Specialist 203

**Part IV—Training**

24. Training System of Civil Servants in India 209
25. Training for Transformation : Tasks Ahead 223
26. New Dimensions of Training in Public Administration 229
27. Training of Trainers in Public Administration 235

**Part V—Politics, Administration and Public Interest**

28. Role of Bureaucracy vis a vis the Political Executive 243
29. Public Accountability and Ethics in Administration 255

**Part VI—Administration of Public Enterprises**

30. Politico-Social Environment and Public Sector Enterprises 261
31. Public Enterprises— State Policies and Managerial Improvement 263

Annexures-I 281
Annexures-II 283
Index 285

# Introduction

In the collection of my thirty one papers brought together under the title "Recent Trends in Public Administration", I have dealt with a whole range of issues related to public administration which has a crucial role to play in every modern society. These are classified into six parts viz. General, Policy Making, Bureaucracy, Training, Politics, Administration and Public Interest and Administration of Public Enterprises.

The tone is set by the first paper, which deals with important administrative changes that have taken place in the SAARC countries relating to five aspects viz. planning and its impact on administration, changing relationship between politicians and civil servants and between administration and the citizens, decentralisation and peoples' participation.

In the second paper, I have dealt with the seven attributes of "excellence in administration" viz. quickness in dealing with public business, promptness and punctuality in operation, sensitivity and concern for the hardship of the citizens, courtesy and consideration, proper maintenance of public assets, fairness and objectivity and high degree of competence, knowledge and skill among the administrators.

The third paper "Can We Make India Smooth Running ?", answers the question by giving examples to show that we could do so if we change our attitudes, organisations and procedures with the sole aim of making the ordinary business of life smooth and convenient to all our fellow citizens.

The fourth paper deals with work ethic in Government. It starts with the proposition that the roots of work ethic are in the culture of the people. The Indian culture is not inimical to work ethic. But it has to be nurtured through a systematic effort to promote morale and motivation and that is the task of leadership.

The fifth paper formulates the administrative challenges in development viz. stopping the tide of population increase, increasing food production to cope with the rise in population, providing gainful opportunities and income generation specially to the weaker sections of the community and maintaining national integration and social cohesion which are the *sine qua non* for development.

The sixth paper, entitled "Public Administration of the Twentieth Century" outlines the tasks the administration should undertake in order that India of 21st century should be politically strong and stable, economically, scientifically advanced, socially cohesive and just and culturally rich.

The seventh paper deals with the importance of field administration. It makes the point that only the field administration clothed with prestige, recognition and high morale can ultimately deliver the goods which the government and administration are expected to deliver.

The eighth paper deals with the important question of promoting efficiency in administration. It calls for a qualitative change in administration—almost an "internal administrative revolution".

The ninth, tenth and eleventh papers compare the role of the IAS officers with that of the ICS in yester years. The ICS traditions survived in the form of IAS but the range and content of the development work which the IAS is called upon to undertake is indeed way beyond the scope of work of the ICS and requires innovative approach, specialist expertise and responsiveness to local demands. And yet some of the good features of British administration as laid down by the ICS officers such as personal interest in the training of juniors, appreciation of good work of juniors, importance given to the "man on the spot", intensive touring in the countryside, and upholding the rule of law are still relevant and the IAS officers of today should see that they are retained.

The twelfth paper analysing the role of the civil servant in the changing environment in India says that to play a proper and an effective role, the civil servant has to be a combination of a bureaucrat, a manager, a social worker and a social scientist in action.

The thirteenth paper on Transplanting British Institutions compares the character and the role of the civil service in Britain, the white colonies of Australia and Canada, India and the erstwhile Colonial countries of Africa and concludes that the different pattern of administrative institutions can be understood only through a historical perspective and analysis.

The fourteenth paper under the title "Whither Indian Bureaucracy?" analyses the changes in political and economic set up and policy approaches after independence and concludes that while the role of bureaucracy envisaged at the dawn of freedom has undergone a change, the nation needs good bureaucracy for objective administration and orderly development of the country and its stability.

Part two devoted to policy making begins with a conceptual paper on scientific policy analysis and then in the next two papers makes a critical analysis of several policies adopted in India after independence viz. policies relating to law and order, defence, external affairs, economic management, agriculture, education, and science and technology and brings out several shortcomings in policy making in India and gives suggestions as to how these could be overcome.

Next two papers in this part deal with approach to administrative problems of Jawaharlal Nehru and Smt. Indira Gandhi. Jawaharlal Nehru the first Prime Minister of free India was at the helm of administrative affairs for 17 years and his daughter for 14 years. Both left a strong foot print on the sands of time. Jawaharlal Nehru laid the foundation of the Indian administration and evolved basic policy approach. The paper Jawaharlal Nehru and Public Administration is a comprehensive presentation of the basic ideas and outlook of Jawaharlal Nehru on public administration as also on specific subjects like law and order, linguism, press, freedom, judiciary, the role of governors, foreign policy, defence policy, economic policy, food and agriculture, rural development, land reforms, industrialisation, planning, education, health, welfare of backward classes and science and technology. The paper on Indira Gandhi, and Public Administration, though not equally comprehensive, gives a more intimate and first hand account of her ideas since they are based on what she said in course of two memorable visits of the administrators participating in two advanced courses on public administration in the Indian Institute of Public Administration.

The third part is on Bureaucracy, the basic institution of public administration. The twentieth paper in this collection and the first in this part recapitulates the essential characteristic of Bureaucracy as defined by Max Weber who called it the rational legal institution of the twentieth century. To live up to its ideal type Bureaucracy has to maintain high standards. It should be efficient, honest, fair, just, objective and responsive. Unfortunately, in practice it has been identified with redtape, delay, circumlocution, lack of imagination, excessive rule mindedness, lack of responsiveness to the people, internal jealousy, etc. Hence the need is for bureaucratic reform. In the 21st paper, the discussion is carried further in the context of challenges of development and democracy in India after independence. Bureaucracy has betrayed several defects in the functioning but these are defects betrayed by the nation itself. The twenty second paper entitled "The Decline of the Civil Service" carries the discussion further. The subordination of the civil service to the politicians in power has made it subservient. The doctrine of neutrality of the civil service has given way to a committed civil service. The commitment of public service to public interest has been compromised. There is a need to restore the independent functioning of the civil service. The twenty fourth paper on generalist vs specialist states that the services of both are necessary for the fulfilment of the goal and objectives of public administration.

Papers in the fourth part are on the subject of training of civil servants. The twenty fourth paper deals comprehensively with the training system of civil servants in the country. The next paper on Training for Transformation draws attention to specific areas in which training would be needed in the wake of development and transformation of the economy viz. disparities in development, demographic pressure, urbanisation, science and technology and environment. Training will have to be focussed on better implementation, eliciting popular participation, microplanning and provision of social services. Regarding the training programmes there should be greater exchange of experience between the developing countries. In the same vein the next paper draws attention to new dimensions of training viz. project monitoring and evaluation, microplanning, new techniques of administration like PERT & CPM, management of public sector enterprises, management information system, use of computers in administration, material management and financial management including performance budgeting. The twenty seventh paper deals with the training of trainers in the state level institutions of training and the need for close nexus between the State and national level training institutions.

The twenty-eighth paper deals comprehensively with the delicate issue of the relationship between the civil servants and the political executive in the context of the wider concern for public interest. It begins with the issues raised by the Ponting case in UK and the Amstrong Memorandum and Parliamentary Committee enquiry that followed. It then turns to the position in India. It defines the code for civil servants and their accountability. It broadens the discussion to the relationship between administration and politics. It concludes by saying that the mutual relationship between bureaucracy and political executive should be neither of collusion nor collision but one of creative cooperation.

The twenty ninth paper deals with public accountability of administration in democracy not only in the negative sense of holding them accountable for lapses but in terms of achieving results in public interest.

The sixth and the last part of the collection deals with public enterprises. In the early years much importance was given to the role of public enterprises in economic development. In the context of the new policy of liberalisation, we are talking of State divesting itself of its commitment of resources to public enterprises. But it is unlikely that they will all wither away. The need for proper management of public enterprises will continue in the years to come. Hence the introductory statement to thirtieth paper and detailed analysis in the thirty first paper on the efficiency and performance of public enterprises in politico social environment in which they function would be found useful even in the new context.

# PART—I

# *GENERAL*

# 1

# Trends in Public Administration in South Asia

The administrative systems of South Asian countries have undergone significant changes during the last three decades. The range and intensity of governmental intervention in social, economic and technological development have increased. As a consequence, the governments of this region have assumed responsibilities of initiating, directing and promoting development through various policies. Important changes have been made in public administration system to respond to the needs of the development. By and large, these countries inherited a particular system of public administration designed for a purpose other than development. The main functions of the system were : maintenance of law and order, collection of revenue and administration of justice. The main-stay of this system was the district and the key official in the district was Collector responsible for law and order and collection of revenue. But now, the primary administrative task is to re-orient administrative machinery to meet the demands of development.

Before describing the trends in the development of public administration in this region it is important to note that this sub-continent comprises of Seven countries : Bangladesh, Bhutan, India, Maldives, Nepal, Pakistan and Sri Lanka. These countries differ in area, population, resource endowments, political ideologies and forms of government. The countries of this region are characterised by severe pressure of population and low standards of living. The developments in administrative systems of these countries are of great importance as they show how the governments of this region are struggling to modernise themselves. The trends in public administration in this region are of great significance as out of every five people in the world, one is a South Asian. The changes in public administration systems of this region have taken place broadly in the following directions :

— planning and its impact on administration.

— re-structuring of civil services.

— decentralisation of administration/peoples participation.

— realationship of civil services with politicians

— administration and citizen relationship.

**Planning and its Impacts on Administration**

All these countries attempted to bring about rapid economic, social and technological development through planned effort. As a consequence of planned effort bodies like Planning Commission were constituted at the national level. Similarly, at the state level in some of these countries Planning Boards were also set-up and in some of the countries notably India, Pakistan, Bangladesh and Nepal, district bodies were also set-up for the planning purposes. This resulted in making planning an important aspect in each Ministry both at the Central and the State levels. It is also important to mention here that in all these countries central government also started a number of centrally sponsored schemes in almost all the spheres of public activity to bring desired changes. In all these countries an important role has been assigned to the public sector. Various forms of public enterprises were established in these countries as regular government departments were found to be inadequate. All the factors mentioned above resulted in expansion of public administration in the field of economic development. At the same time dis-appointment with results of economic planning has given rise to increased importance of the need for major administrative changes consonant with development planning. So much so, Bangladesh, India, Pakistan and Sri Lanka highlighted the importance of administrative aspects of plan implementation in their development plans. Disappointment with results in economic planning also highlighted the importance of proper information system. As a result of this both in the Central planning machinery of these countries as well as in the Central and State Ministries/Departments emphasis is now being laid on monitoring aspect. Recently, in India and Sri Lanka independent Ministries have been constituted for Plan/Programme implementation. Besides, in some of these countries modern scientific methods and tools are being used for gathering information, for processing, storage, retrieval and analysis of data for both planning and operational purposes.

**Re-structuring of Superior Civil Services**

To cope-up with the planned development, the countries of this region re-structured their superior civil services systems. Bangladesh, Pakistan and Sri Lanka unified their civil service systems. In Bangladesh, the civil services was re-structured in 1980 in thirteen functional cadres constituting the Bangladesh Civil Services. These cadres are : administrative, agriculture, economic, engineering, finance, police, foreign affairs, etc. This restructuring was carried out in order to abolish the elitist position of the former civil service, to attract the best talent and to give equal opportunity to all in the higher administrative posts in the secretariat responsible for "policy-making". Other important features are: all the cadres are equal and the entry point in the cadre has been set at the same level. Similarly in Pakistan a Unified Grading System of civil servants was introduced in 1973. According to their areas of specialisation, the civil servants have been divided into fifteen occupational groups like district management, police, foreign affairs, income tax, customs and excise, accounts, information, postal services, commerce and trade, office management, military lands and cantonment, railways, secretariat, tribal areas, economist and planners. These occupational groups have been organised into unified grades: All Pakistan Unified Grades, Federal Unified Grades and Provincial Unified Grades.

The All Pakistan Unified Grades include the secretariat group, the district management group, the police group and the tribal areas group. The Federal Unified Grades include the accounts group, the office management group, income tax group, the commerce and trade group, the customs and excise group, the economist and planners group and the postal group. The Provincial government have not yet evolved the occupational groups for a unified grading structure. This unified graded structure has also provided equality of opportunity for all who enter the service at any stage based on the required professional and specialised competence necessary for each job. This unified structure has enabled promotions to the higher post throughout the range of public service by horizontal movement from one cadre to another. There has also been opening up of the civil bureaucracies at the highest level to non-career civil servants through a lateral entry mechanism. Similarly in Sri Lanka, the Ceylon Civil Services was abolished in 1963. The Public Services are classified between "Staff Officers" and "Non-staff Officers". The staff grades in the "combined services" which have switched over to rank classification are distributed among the administrative, engineering, scientific and professional services, while the rest are among the non-staff supporting grades. While the staff among the combined services are transferable between government departments, there are other departmental services/ posts where the staff are transferable only within the department if they belong to a departmental service or are non-transferable if they are appointed to a particular post. This is significant because as much as 84 per cent of the entire public services fall within the latter category. A very significant trend in case of Sri Lanka is the acceptance of the principle of the political control of the bureaucracy. The appointment, transfer, dismissal and disciplinary control of public officers are vested in the Cabinet of Ministers and all public officers hold office at pleasure. The Cabinet of Ministers also provide for and determine all other matters relating to public officers, including the formulation of the schemes of recruitment and codes of conduct, the procedure for the exercise and delegation of powers over the Public Service. The re-structuring of Public Service in Sri Lanka in recent times provides for greater flexibility which enables Minister to spot talent from outside for appointment as a Secretary to a Ministry. Similarly the administrative system in India underwent farreaching changes with the framing of the Constitution of India, introduction of five year plans and the establishment of democratic institutions at local levels. This transformation from highly stratified formalistic system suitable for routine administration into a development oriented system took place in the division of civil service system into three sub-systems of All India Services, Central Services and State

Services. One basic trend which is discernible in the manning of the top positions in the Central Government is induction of both central service officials and specialists. Radical changes in the structure of civil service in Nepal took place with the transformation from an authoritarian government to a representative government in 1951. The Nepal Civil Service is divided into ten services which include administrative, agriculture, engineering, health, judicial, audit, panchayat etc. Each Service is classified into three classes.

**Decentralisation of Administration**

In order to secure decentralisation both in planning and in the implementation of development programmes, the problem of rationalising the functioning of the civil service systems received considerable attention in this region. The establishment of Panchayati Raj Institutions on a country-wide basis and transfer of some of the traditional functions of civil service systems to these institutions constitute a new policy trend in the civil service system of India. In India a three-tier system of local self government was established; the village at the lowest level, the block at the intermediate level and the district at the top and organic links among these levels were also established. The block agencies were conceived as executing bodies while the district level bodies were to perform coordinating functions with the Collectors as the captain of the team of all the developmental officers. The implementation of this reform was left to the State government as local government is a State subject and it has resulted in a wide variety of patterns. In Pakistan the reluctance of political leadership at the centre to delegate power and resources to the local level has been a characteristic of its government since 1947. The earlier efforts made in this direction were by Ayub Government in the form of basic democracies which came close to altering administration at district level but only for a short time. There is continuity of district level administration in Pakistan in terms of scope and nature of district administration and the power possessed and exercised by Deputy Commissioners. In Bangladesh, a significant development has taken place in the role of civil servants in the process of development. All the senior officers from the secretariat have to spend a few days in the rural areas to acquaint themselves with the problems in the implementation of development programmes. The government is also trying to involve local representatives in the administration at the grassroots level through the formation of "Gram Sarkar" in some villages. Important changes were also made in district administration in Nepal with the introduction of partyless panchayat system. However, in this partyless panchayat system the central administration has not delegated sufficient powers and functions to the local panchayats. In order to have more close corporation with the administration and the people the government of Sri Lanka constituted the district councils and the gramodaya mandals together with the institution of the District Minister. The District Ministers have been given necessary legal powers to coordinate all developmental activities by formulating the district development plan, preparing the district budget, monitoring and evaluating implementation and directly supervising inter-departmental activities.

In these countries new organisational forms to achieve public purposes more effectively have also been created. Departmental tasks that were formerly carried out in the government departments by civil servants are being delegated to these new organisational forms. These organisations have been started for integrated development of command areas, tribal and hill areas and drought prone areas. Special attention has also been given through new agencies to backward regions and scheduled tribes.

**Bureaucrats and Politicians - Relationship**

The contribution that bureaucracy can make to the development process can be effective when the bureaucracy and the political elements cooperate and complement each other. It is of profound interest to know the relationships that obtains between administrators and political leaders. There are two components that are crucial in such a relationship. The first relates to the awareness and understanding of the nature of division of functions on the part of both the inter-acting units. The second relates to the dimensions of inter-action between administration and political leaders in practice and the kinds of demands political leaders bring to administrators, the pressure they apply in support of their demands and the way administrators respond and are seen by political leaders to respond to these pressures.

Below an attempt is made to discuss important aspects of Secretary Minister relationship.

The present pattern of relationship between the Secretary and the Minister is built round certain constitutional provisions. The main elements in this relationship are : the common allegiance of the Minister and the Secretary to uphold the constitution of the country, the overall responsibilities of Ministers to Parliament for policy making, the supremacy of the political executives over the civil servants, the doctrine of anonymity and political neutrality of the civil services and the final determination of policies by the Minister and their implementation by civil servants.

The main difficulty in role perception arises from the different views taken by the Ministers and the Secretaries of what constitutes the Minister's political responsibilities in terms mainly of policy making; and public relations in the matter of mobilising public support and cooperation, informing the public opinion and removal of genuine grievances of the citizens. The Ministers' perception of their political role, on the other hand, includes showing of accommodation to the party interests as well as the interests of supporters. Herein lies the genesis of many a strain in the relations between the two. Matters concerning day-to-day administration, such as appointments and transfers, grant of permits and contracts, etc. may create strain in the Ministers Secretary relationship. The attitude of the senior civil servants towards the political accommodation which the Ministers would like to show, varies. In recent years there has emerged a batch of civil servants who would like curry favour with the Ministers primarily with an eye on advancement in civil service career or lucrative re-employment after retirement. There are also other factors which in varying degrees make for differences in outlook and approach and thereby lead to strains. These include differences in motivations, role perception, intellectual ability, social background, temperament and sense of professional commitment.

The compulsion of the political situation tempts many a minister to intervene in day-to-day administration to accommodate the wishes of his supporters. The big increase in the scope and size of the regulatory powers of the government over the economic activities of the people, particularly in the number and extent of economic controls opens up before the Ministers a wide area for dispensing political patronage. The root cause of political accommodation lies in societal attitudes and values.

**Administration and Citizen Relationship**

Due to planned social and economic development the average citizen comes into contact with administration at an ever increasing number of 'delivery ends'. The citizen's contact with administration arises in the following activities :

— as a beneficiary of the institutional framework and as one entitled to enjoy political, civil and economic rights.

— as a general user of civic amenities and public utilities.

— as a member of a clientele group.

Many times, the complaints of the citizens against the government and those of the administration about the citizens are based on an inadequate appreciation of the other side of the picture. Some of the complaints frequently heard are :

— lack of sense of urgency, slow pace and consequent delays.

— lack of regard for the convenience and comfort of citizen; long and complicated rules and procedures involving repeated visits to administrative agencies; inadequacy of clear and precise information about and guidance for compliance with rule and procedures etc.

— lack of normal courtesy on the part of the government officials.

— disregard of public interest or the rights of certain individual or group under the influence of group, party pressures intrigues and cliques of private individuals with political, economic and social power.

— lack of enthusiasm in work and lack of sense of mission for the achievement of administrative tasks and goals.

— lack of adequate machinery for the redress of grievances and complaints; virtual absence of machinery for guaging public reactions and opinions in respect to particular policies, programmes or activities.

The citizen normally desires from the administration the following :

— an understanding of the objectives of the activities and administrative policies of a particular government department or agency.

— an assurance about and confidence in the major policies followed by an administrative agency for the fulfilment of the objectives, un-influenced by consideration of party, group or private benefits.

— high standard of competence and efficiency in performance.

There are several directions in which considerable efforts have been made to improve the present tone and quality of relationship between the citizen and the administration. More important among these are discussed below :

**Institutional arrangements:** The experiment in democratic decentralisation is based on the philosophy that rural people should directly share the responsibility for managing and directing the development programme in their areas. Similarly, the experiments in the field of urban development by the creation of urban government also help in enlarging and improving the quality of citizens' participation in urban government and administration.

**Methods and procedures :** Though a considerable effort has been made in recent years to rationalise work methods and procedures, much gap remains to be made up in the matter at the level of local administration which touches the citizens every day life at innumerable points.

**Attitudes of public employees :** The common citizen today is very critical about the discourteous attitude of public employees in general. There is a considerable scope for training in public relations of government employees of all types in general and those who come in touch with the public frequently in particular.

The solution of the problem depends, in the last analysis on the quality of political and administrative leadership at the different levels : local, district, State and Centre. If this leadership does not rise to the new demands of the developing economy, administrative reforms by themselves cannot be of much avail.

# 2

# Excellence in Administration

In our planned economy, where the State plays such a prominent role in economic and social reconstruction, excellence in our national life depends a great deal on the excellence in administration. The ubiquitous presence of public administration is felt directly or indirectly every where in agriculture or industry, health or housing, culture or education, journalism or use of mass media, dance, drama or music, sports or entertainment. Administration can do a great deal to help or hinder, to promote or frustrate, the activities of individuals and institutions. Excellence in administration is, therefore, almost a *sine qua non* for national excellence in almost every walk of life of our country.

What do we mean by excellence in administration? It is well conveyed by the motto of the Indian Administrative Service Association which is picked up from the famous words of GITA - YOGAH KARMASU KAUSALAM - administration is a kind of Yoga which aims at excellence in performance.

There are many attributes of excellence in administration or efficiency in performance. The first attribute of excellence in administration is quickness in dealing with public business - whether the disposal of files in offices or correspondence with citizens, redress of citizen's grievances and complaints, sanctioning applications for refund, or loans from public exchequer or banks, or in dealing with queues at public counters. A lot of citizen's precious time and energy can be saved if the public authorities are prompt in dealing with them. It is the absence of promptness which leads to frustration and bitterness and disenchantment among the citizens. Delays also lead to corruption and other serious evils. Promptness is, therefore, the first attribute of efficiency in public administration.

Closely connected with promptness is timeliness and punctuality in operation. The offices and courts must open in time, trains and buses must run on time, meetings must be held on time and appointments must be kept up. India has been fortunate to have Prime Ministers who have all been sticklers for punctuality. Unfortunately, their example has not been always followed by others holding less eminent positions and examples are not wanting of people and officers made to wait for any length of time to await the arrival of the VIP. The behaviour of the VIP sets the tone for the administration and when they themselves upset all norms of punctuality and timeliness, this becomes the rule rather than the exception in day-to-day operations of administration.

The third essential attribute of excellence in administration is the sensitivity and concern for the problems and hardships of citizens in normal times as well as in abnormal times. When the administration becomes callous and indifferent to the problems of the citizens, the very base of mutual trust between the public and the administration disappears. It is not unusual to find electricity failing, water supply discontinued, drainage choked or telephones getting dead without administration taking the slightest notice of these things for days together in spite of repeated complaints.

Actually citizens are not only entitled to get an administration which is concerned for their welfare; they are also entitled to receive courtesy and consideration from those in public authority. But these are rarely to be found. The citizen who comes to a public office for a legitimate claim is sometimes treated as a mendicant and even normal courtesy is not shown to him. I once remember to have gone to a Duty Officer of perhaps the most important airport in India to complain against the dirty bathrooms at early hours which passengers had perforce to use because the scheduled flight was inordinately delayed. The Duty Officer busy with his girl friends had not even the courtesy either to ask what I wanted or to listen to my complaint muchless to take prompt action to set right the defect. When I complained to the headquarters of the Airport Authority, they did acknowledge the letter but nothing followed and apparantly no action was taken. How can such administration inspire the confidence of the citizens ? Every one in administrative authority must recognise that every public servant is required to give the highest courtesy and respect to every citizen which is only his right and not any favour shown to him.

Fifthly, excellence in public administration means not only understanding new projects and schemes but also the proper maintenance of public assets - office buildings, parks and gardens, plant and equipment, buses and trains, bus shelters and stations. Unfortunately, many of these tend to be in disrepair and slovenly in appearance thereby bringing down the whole image of administration.

The sixth attribute of excellence in administration is fairness and objectively. "Show me the man and I will show you the rule" would only make a mockery of administration. Unfortunately, in our administration it sometimes appears that though all are equal some are more equal than others ! Rules are meant for those who are without any power or influence. For those who have, there are always exceptions to the rules. Actually proper administration requires that the persons least powerful and influential receive the greatest consideration and a point is stretched in favour of them than against them. Unfortunately people seem to feel that they must have some influence and pull to get anything done and nothing would be done in the normal course.

Finally, the excellence in administration requires a high degree of competence, knowledge and skill among the administrators, a pride in meticulous performance, a tireless striving towards perfection, a continuous assessment of the shape of things to come and proper perspective, plans and programmes to build up a brave new world of tomorrow.

During the years after Independence, we ought to have built excellence in administration with all the attributes mentioned above. Unfortunately, despite innumerable Commissions and Committees and their reports and recommendations on Administrative Reforms, we still seem to be far away from this ideal and, in fact, we seem to have made administration the scapegoat for every national failure. Day in and day out in newspaper columns and elsewhere, there is a scathing criticism of administration in our country. In his inaugural address President Carter stated that country has no future whose public despise their own Government. Using the same words we can well say that that country has no future which despises its own administration. Let us hope that the IAS officers, the motto of whose Association is excellence in performance, will rededicate themselves to the attainment of this goal and let us hope that their example would inspire all others in the civil service so that administration can command and deserve the trust, confidence and esteem of our people.

3

# Can We Make India Smooth Running ?

Every time one returns to India from any of the Western countries or Japan or Singapore, one is appalled by the wide gap that exists between the ease and convenience of living in those countries and the trials and turbulations one has to undergo here at every step.

It is easy to attribute the ease and convenience of life in those countries to their material affluence and out trials and turbulations to our material scarcities and poverty. But on reflection, one would realise that this is not quite so. There could be ease and convenience even at low material standards of living. Ease and convenience are essentially the function of our individual behaviour as members of a social organisation. The latter is a significant causal factor which not only makes for ease and convenience of social life but also for material advancement.

An article in the Reader's Digest (May 1980) describes Switzerland as the smoothest running country on earth. In that country, a letter posted over-night reaches almost any destination within the country first thing next morning. 4994 kms. long railways linking the most isolated townships run absolutely on time. Maintenance men rush out to scrub traffic signs immediately after rain and storm.

Why is that tiny land so trim ? The answer lies in the qualities of the Swiss people and, in their attitudes to work and towards each other. The Swiss people are deligent, sensible, earnest, responsible and cautious. They believe that work should be well done, no special favours should be granted, everything should be clear and predictable. The Swiss people abhor all forms of politicking and ideological infighting. Swiss management and labour unions enjoy a unique relationship based on partnership instead of confrontation. The last Swiss general strike took place in 1918. In response to the petrol shortage people have started cycling and walking again: anything to cut cost and save fuel.

The attitude in India is just the contrary. We waste disproportionate time on politicking in the name of some irrelevant ideological issues which are only a garb for advancing our private interests. This is so everywhere even in small institutions. We create confrontation, where cooperation is necessary and possible. We are neither sane nor sensible and repeatedly lose our sense of proportion. Above all we have no respect for time and respect for each other as citizens of the same country and members of the same society. As a result, life has become one obstacle race. Nothing will be got done in the normal course and so, we seem to be looking all the time for somebody's influence to get anything done. Our offices, whether in the public sector or in the private sector, have become a source of harassment to the ordinary citizens because everybody at the counter seems to assume that he is doing a great favour to anybody who comes to him though what he is doing is something which he is duty bound to do. Thus, at the bottom of the lack of ease and convenience of life in our country are our attitudes which we have to first change. Some illustrations of my experience in the last few days make clear what I am saying.

*Illustration 1* : My son asked me to pay the school fees at the beginning of the new year. I go to the bank counter in the school. They tell me to go to the accounts office to get the bill. I go to the account office. There are three persons in the office. One is checking some old bills. Two others are gossiping. But none of the three could attend to me because they are not the ones concerned. The man concerned has gone for a cup of tea. In the meanwhile, I must wait and wait indefinitely because none of them knows when exactly the person would turn up. I have another engagement but I must wait since I do not want to come again and I am not certain whether even then I would not have a similar experience, I wait. After half an hour, the man makes his appearance, fills up routine forms, billing for three months fee in advance. Even receiving three months' fees in advance is a favour that the school has apparently done to me. I go to the bank counter. I am asked to fill in various forms myself before the bank clerk obliges me by giving a receipt. The following questions arise :

1. Why should I be made to wait for half an hour in the accounts office ?
2. Why should not the person concerned be present ?
3. If he is away, why should not anyone of the other three attend to the work as is the common experience at any counter in the West ?
4. Why should not there be standardised forms eliminating useless scriptory work ?
5. Why cannot the work be done at one single counter ?

The answer to all these questions is the same; we do not care for the waste of time of an individual. In fact, we do not know that time is money. We have no regard for the individual and we do not think that his ease and convenience is what we should ensure.

*Illustration* 2 : I had to pay electricity and water bill to the municipality. I sent a peon to make the payment through a crossed cheque. The peon goes in the sweltering heat, stands in a queue for a long time and returns without payment on the ground that one paisa for late payment has not been included in the cheque. The following questions arise :

1. Why should one have to wait in a long queue to make payment ?
2. Why could not the payment be accepted and arrears, if any, added to the next month's bill ?
3. Why should it be necessary for the peon to go back all the way, get the addition included in a new cheque to be presented once again ?

The answer is the same — no respect for the time and convenience of the citizen.

*Illustration 3* : My daughter appears for an examination for recruitment to a public sector bank. She is asked to go half an hour in advance. The address of the examination centre is misleading. However, I just managed to reach her on time. I enquired as to when the examination would be over and when I could pick up my daughter. I am told that I should come at 1.00 p.m. or a few minutes thereafter. I reach there in the sweltering heat with the mid-day sun of Delhi burning bright. I find that the entry to the school door is closed and that a number of persons are waiting outside in the terrific heat. There is a sentry at the door with a batton in hand. He does not allow any of the 25 parents to go inside and wait in verandha. I insist that I speak to the authorities. The authorities i.e. the bank official incharge of the supervision of the examination condescends to come only to state brusquely that the examination rules do not allow anyone except the examinees to enter the premises and so he would not let anybody in. I tell him that the premises refer to the examination hall and not to the outside verandah and in any case, in the name of humanity, he should let us stand in the outer verandah. He point blank refuses with rudeness appropriate to the haughty authority. The examination eventually was over only at 2.00 p.m. to the relief of both the hungry examinees who had their morning breakfast at 7.00 o'clock in order to reach on time and the parents waiting outside in the heat for over an hour. The following questions arise :

1. Why should not the time for the examination to be over be correctly indicated in writing ?
2. Why should not there be some waiting hall for the parents who have to pick up their wards ?
3. Why could not the examination be completed at 1.00 p.m. or 1.15 p.m. as indicated ? (They started half an hour late though a candidate was not admitted because he turned up 5 minutes late).

   The answer is that in the exercise of our authority we are so haughty and rude that we forget all standards of decent behaviour and we insist on interpreting the rules in such a literary fashion that we forget their real meaning and the fact that these rules are meant to fulfil certain purposes and for convenience of all concerned. The supervisor pointed out that on same occasion some parent on entry tried to tutor his candidate and because of such an isolated case (real or imaginary) everybody must suffer at all times.

Such examples could be multiplied ad-infinitum. Such experiences are the daily lot of India's ordinary citizen. He has to battle for getting simple things done in public offices and private. He is looking all the times for somebody known to him to help him out or to get the things done even though they are legitimately due to him. Without some acquaintance somewhere nothing gets done. India's citizens are made to spend a disproportionate portion of their daily time and energy on getting over these hindrances to ordinary living and when they cannot get over these hindrances, they fight and abuse each other at the top of their voices in public places creating strain and strife, disturbances and noise which then become the characteristic of our community life. And then we lament that daily life in India has become an ordeal.

A recent report said that India's cities - Delhi,· Bombay and Calcutta — are the noisiest cities in the world. The car drivers keep on hooting like mad men on our streets because the person behind the driving wheel feels that he has the authority to go on hooting no matter how much noise pollution he creates. A pedestrian past whom I was driving gently avoiding him asked me why I was not hooting and whether my car did not have a horn. Horns are for hooting and we must go on creating noise.

Commenting on noise pollution a newspaper laments—"The noise pollution in the capital is fast becoming a despair of environmentalists. All kinds of horns being merrily honked by the owners of big and small vehicles assail in the ear. In flagnant violation of the law many motorists have equipped their cars with musical horns. Some have gone to the extent of installing sirens that are indistinguishable from those used by the police, the firebrigade and ambulance." A recent study in noise pollution points out that loud and indiscriminate honking of horns can increase blood pressure, trigger cardiac disorders, impair digestion, affect hormones secretion, damage hearing, disturb the sleep of children, the sick and the aged and cause irritability, tension, moodiness and insomnia. It can also incite rash driving. Surely something needs to be done about this growing menance. What is needed is some concern for fellow citizens on the part of drivers! Cities like Tokyo and London bigger than the Indian cities are much quieter and in spite of a much larger number of cars, there are much fewer traffic jams because their movement and parking are orderly. One dreads to imagine what life of our Indian cities would be by the end of the century when they would be crossing ten million mark.

One of the surest ways of enriching our lives is to improve our productivity. But how could the productivity of the worker in the office or factory go up when much of his time and energy is dissipated in circumventing entirely unnecessary but self-created obstacles to smooth day-to-day living ? Management experts have noted a tragic downfall of productivity in India. An economist has observed that the Indian economy has developed great expertise in pushing an elephant at one end and producing a mouse at the other. The National Productivity Council has estimated that while fixed capital per worker went up as much as 198 % between 1963-64 and 1975-76 labour productivity in industry rose no more than 20.2 % during the same period. If only in our behaviour as members of society we replace lack of concern and courtesy for each other with mutual respect and helpfulness, extreme attitudes, intolerance and self-centred aggressiveness with sanity, sensibility and sense of proportion, we would not only replace trials and turbulations with ease and convenience but raise our productivity atleast by 20 % saving time and energy that we now spend in sorting out the daily problems of our life.

We need a cultural revolution to change our attitudes which have gone from bad to worse during the years of our independent existence. We should change our attitudes, organisations and procedures with sole aim of making the ordinary business of life smooth and convenient to all our citizens. We would then, inspite of our material poverty, make life bearable and even cheerful to all our citizens.

# 4

# Work Ethic in Government

### Work Ethic in Government, Part of Work Ethic of People

Work Ethic in Government, in the ultimate analysis, is part of the work ethic of the people, their character, traditions and outlook.

### Work Ethic Reflects the Genius of a People

The people of every country have their genius and our concepts of management and teaching in management should be consistent with the ethos and genius of our people. Teaching management expounded in American literature is not consistent with our genius. It is my fundamental premise that management, as anything else, is ultimately connected deep down with the genius of a people. We have to discover the genius of our people. But it is not easy to identify the genius of any people particularly the people of India who are so diverse, and so subtle.

Now is it true that the genius of our people is such that we have no work ethic? Is our attitude such that we somehow want to get a job as a "meal-ticket" for life and that is all there is to a job, and then we do not have what is called 'Work Ethic' ?

### Effort of Strong Leadership to Change the Genius of a People

Where does this word 'Work Ethic' come from? In his call for administrative reforms, the young Prime Minister of India Rajeev Gandhi also talked of inculcation of a Work Ethic in administration. He talked of a new "administrative culture." I have already said that the administrative culture is part of the culture of the people. That does not mean that the culture does not change or that administration cannot change the culture. Administration has a role in changing the culture of the people and this has happened all along in history. A book which has left a great imprint on my mind is the biography of Peter the Great of Russia. It is he who modernised Russia. Russia was a backward state of backward people with feudal traditions. The aristocrats holding high positions in Government used to have long beards reaching right down to the ground and they wore old type of dresses. The whole Russian administration was in that mould. Peter the Great was fascinated by the West. He was moved with a desire to drag Russian people on to the road to modernity. He wanted to change the character and culture of the people of Russia and he succeeded to a very great extent. In fact he started with physical compulsions and coercions of the Russia people to adopt new ways of life. There is also the example of Kamal Ataturk who also used similar methods to drive out traditionalism from Turkey. In China also something like this happened; a rule was introduced that there shall not be a two hour lunch break — a part of the age old Chinese tradition.

There are two types of leaders : leaders who go by compulsion and leaders who go by persuasion. Most effective world leaders have worked through coercion and compulsion dragging people along. India alone has the tradition of great leaders like Mahatma Gandhi and Nehru who were against the use of coercion and compulsion and who believed in a change of heart. The Indian tradition seems to be from the days of Buddha, whose religious teachings conquered China and Japan and the countries of the East merely through persuasion and spiritual force. And we have also the great Sankaracharya who banished Buddhism from the land of its origin merely through persuasion.

**Work to Rule vs Work Ethic**

One point made in the Vellodi Committee Report on Administrative Reorganisation in Kérala was that in Kerala, there is a tendency of 'Work to Rule' that is doing so much, and no more. I do not understand the phrase 'Work to Rule' for if you 'work to rule', you must work a great deal. But Work to Rule seems to be leading to a minimum work being turned out and one would have to ask whether "Work to Rule" is consistent with 'Work Ethic'. It would appear that Kerala people are very conscious of their rights rather than of their duties and therefore, they are more demanding than contributing, though Kerala people elsewhere have a reputation for hard work. Kerala people, have 'Work Ethic' abroad but "Work to Rule" at home. But there is nothing like an inherent work culture and much depends on environment. Sometimes we stamp a people with a label. If anybody is going to tell me that Indians are inherently lazy, and many people say that they are, I am not going to listen to them because I have gone and seen in Malaysia, Tamilians developing rubber plantations when no one else did it. In Mauritius the Dutch wanted to develop sugarcane plantation. The Negroes and Creoles were not able to do it but the Indians did it. They went from Bihar and they developed the sugarcane plantation of Mauritius. Our people went to East Africa and built the railways. This means that Indians working outside India have shown that they have greater "Work ethic" than any other people. And these people of ours have not given up their traditions and culture. Therefore, when Western people say that Indians are lazy, I am not prepared to accept it.

### Backward Sloping Supply Curve of Labour— Indicating Lack of Work Ethic

When I was at the London School of Economics, we were told about the typical law of Backward Sloping Supply Curve which characterised the Indian Labour. The expectation from the Western Labour force is that if more wage is offered, there will be more supply of labour. There is a positive co-relation between wage and supply of labour. But there are some peculiar people in the world to whom this normal law of human beings does not apply. And these people live in countries like India where the climate is very hot, where they do not want to work, do not have ambitions in life, do not want to earn for better life, do not want to improve their standard of living, are satisfied with very little and do not want more. Incentives do not work for them, normal laws of human beings do not apply to them. Their psychology is of being content with what they have, not wanting to have anything more. They have only a fixed kind of demand and a fixed sense of satisfaction. As a result what happens is that instead of putting in more units of work in responses to higher wages, units remain the same, in fact the supply curve goes back because for a given unit of work, workers get more income because of the higher wage. This is called the 'backward sloping supply curve of labour'. This is a typical position where people work less when incentive are offered. Is this a right analysis of our labour force whether in administration or elsewhere in the country?

**Historic Origin of the Term Work Ethic**

The word 'Work Ethic' has a historic origin. Max Weber attributed Work Ethic of the Western people to the typical 'Protestant' religion as it emerged in the West. In the book "Religion and the Rise of Capitalism" RH Tawney, one of the greatest social thinkers of the 20th century, goes into the origin of the rise of capitalism, of modern industrialism and of modern culture of the industrial age which first came to Great Britain during 1760-1820. People attributed it to many things : inventions, the factory system, the profits which came out of commerce, etc. RH Tawney pointed out that the rise of industrialism in England and West was to be associated with the 'Protestant' religion, which gave new ethical values to Western Society and which led to progress, and these values were of "Work Ethic" — this is called Calvinistic Work Ethic. It is believed that the great triumph of the Western civilisation had at its bottom the work ethic which was propagated by Calvin the austere Protestant monk of Geneva. From this came words like "work is workship". Work itself is ethics : This is what Calvin preached and taught and that is what became really the ethical and religious value of the Western people as it took shape at the beginning of the industrial civilisation. The Swedish or the Nordic house wives doing their work on a Sunday cleaning every bit of the house is a symbol of this Western work ethic. It is believed that such a cultural base is absolutely essential for work orientation of any people, not the backward sloping curve of labour.

**Is Work Ethic Alien to Indian Tradition and Religion?**

It is pointed out that in India people do not believe, by tradition and religion, in work ethic. We believe in other values such as fatalism. This is what the Western economists wrote about us as a people. They say that because of the hold of Hindu religion on the Indian mind, people are not concerned with work, they are concerned with other—wordlines, or fatalism. The Indian farmer, they say, is very symbol of this kind of mental inertia. The farmer does not believe in his own entrepreneurship, there is no achievement motivation. That you can shape the destiny of life, that man is the master of his own future, is something which is alien to the traditions of the Indian people. This was what was alleged during years of colonialism. It is also alleged that the religion, Indian tradition and culture are not conducive to work orientation, let alone work ethic. It is further said that the Indian believes in law of 'Karma'. The main point in Gunnar Myrdal's "Asian Drama", one of the notable writings in recent times about India, seems to be that the Hindu religion is at the bottom of India's lack of progress. Even though I have great regard for Gunnar Myrdal as a progressive thinker, I cannot agree with his view, downgrading Hindu religion and Indian traditions. He says that Hindu religion, and generally the Indian tradition, is one which believes in 'Karma', law of Karma, not law of Work. Indians are incapable of fixing a goal and accomplishing that goal with a sense of determination. He called us a "soft state" where people do not want to work hard, do not want to accomplish results, do not follow rules, are not serious as to what they are doing, and not keeping hours of work. Indian people have no motivation in life, no achievement orientation, no work orientation, cannot be relied upon to do a piece of work, are not inspired by specific goals in life, will not do work on time at all and things are never done properly. And, therefore, they say that this lack of work ethic is rooted in the character of the Indian people themselves and Indian administration is held out as the best example of the lack of work ethic of the Indian people. There are typical examples of what happens in our country. We have schools where the teachers do not come, and rural health dispensaries where medicines are not available. Officers do not start work on time and people going to their offices are not properly attended to. Why is it that we have an administration of this sort, where there is no work ethic?

I am not prepared to say that this lack of work ethic is because it is not there deep down in the Indian genius. I have rejected that kind of a formulation, a sweeping generalisation that the Indians are inherently lazy.

**Work-Ethic in Indian Tradition**

One cannot say that there is anything inherently antithetical to work ethic in our country. The 'Bhagavat Gita' says that :

*"KARMANYE VA ADHIKARASTHE*
*MA PHALESHU KADACHANA"*

You must work for the sake of work and not for the sake of the fruit of the work, which means even if there is no return, you should work, this what Bhagavat Gita has said. It is a strong tradition which is oriented towards work. There is a strong sense of duty in the Indian ethos. There is something like "Dharma". — everybody should do his dharma, perform his work, do his duty irrespective of recognition of one's contribution. To say that such people, who are inheritors of such great philosophy, have a religion and culture which is against the work ethic, is simply not correct. And historically I have shown that when Indians have gone abroad they have worked very hard. In fact Indians are accused, both ways, when they do not work they say it is because of the religion. But if they work too hard they say: "these fellows have no dignity". This is what is said about the Indians in Africa. In Africa, the Whites will not open their shops in the bush. They are used to a good life and they do not want to go into the bushes of Africa to serve the tribals of Africa. The only people who have gone there are the Indians who have gone deep down into the remotest areas to open their 'Dukans' and these shops will be open from morning till night. They say, "look at these fellows, they do not keep fixed hours of work". An Indian is prepared to work from morning till night just to promote his business. And if you go to any part of India you will find that the poorest among the Indians are the hardest working people of the world. Now if we work the Westerners do not say that the Indians have a high work ethic. The critics of work motivation of the Indian people do not want to take other things into account viz., low performance may be because standards of health are poor in the country side, due to existence of disease, atmosphere is not good, sometimes people have low nutrition and low health conditions and therefore, they may not be working hard.

## Revival of Work Ethic

Indians are capable of enormous hard work and they can be inspired to work and that is what we should do. The Indians are capable of infinite action. They have deep down in them, very rich reservoirs of initiative and effort. All that is required is to unlock the key to the efflorescence of these deep reserves of hard work and industry and initiative in the Indian people. The Work Ethic has been lost during a long period of dependence and we must bring it back, by inculcating proper values.

Unfortunately, one finds that this is not done and opposite kinds of values like 'work to rule' are being generated. This has happened because over the years after independence we have not nurtured deliberately, a tradition of hard work and a sense of purpose. Much depends on leadership in every organisation. I am not saying that the people at the higher levels are not working hard. 'Long hours of work' is a habit in the higher echelons of Indian Administration. But this has to become universal. It has to be there in every small office, in every part of the country. Is it not possible for us to generate this kind of a 'work ethic' ?

## Role of Communication

Now, what kind of work ethic do we need in offices ? We want a work ethic where everybody is inspired by a feeling of the great mission of administration. In a free country like India which after several years of slavery is trying to re-shape new India, we should deliberately nurture work ethic. Rajiv Gandhi said that India should prepare for the 21st century. My generation of administrators thought that they were working for building free India. Now the administrators have to work for the 21st century. The meaning of administrative goals has to percolate right down to the last worker in every office. And this is the work of communication — communicating the bigness of the work that we in administration have to do in a country like India. This communication is not there, and therefore, work tends to be got done indifferently. The first condition for the generation of work ethic, and this is the task of leadership, is to convey to everybody in administration the greatness of the goals, which the administration has to achieve in this country.

**Management by Objective**

A story comes back to my mind which is recalled by C. Rajagopalachari, who gave the first Sardar Patel Memorial Lecture titled "Good Administrator". It was when the Guindy Raj Bhavan was being built and some workers were working. He asked one worker, "What are you doing" and he said "are you blind ? Don't you see that I am cutting this stone?" "Yes" he agreed "I have seen it, I am sorry for asking this question." Then he went to another worker and asked him, "what are you doing ?" He said "What to do ? I have to do this hard work because I have to look after my family; I have to work otherwise the family will starve." The third person whom he asked, replied, "this is a statue of Buddha that we are constructing, and my work is a part of building up of this great statue of Lord Buddha". He knew the greatness of the purpose, not the other two workers. What we have to do is to orient everyone in the organisation with the greatness of purpose. In management jargon this is called management by objectives. The great objective must be fixed. That objective should be communicated to everybody and everybody's work must have relation to that objective. We should introduce, therefore, the technique of Management by Objectives, in order to generate this kind of a work ethic. Most of the people do not have work ethic in administration because they are not aware of the greatness of objective, of the mission of our administration, of the relationship between what we do from day to day and the achievement of a great goal. These are not explained to our people, they are not inspired to wok with this in mind. And I have no doubt that if they are so inspired, the standard of our work and work ethic will be very high.

## Work Ethic in Times of Crisis

Indian administration is capable of rising to the occasion in the grimmest of tragedies. When there is some kind of a cyclone, the whole administration gets mobilised. When China attacked, the whole of the Indian people got galvanised. In times of crisis, work ethic comes up, but in times of normalcy work ethic sleeps. So what we have to do is to create a feeling of the over-riding common purpose of our people and motivating every office and every functionary to work for that great purpose.

## Morale in Administration

But we are not really caring for the morale of people in administration. We find that the morale of people in administration is very low. In the Indian Institute of Public Administration we made studies of the Delhi Police, and the middle executives in Delhi Administration. Both these studies show a very low morale. People are dissatisfied, even disgruntled, they think their work is routine, boring without interest, of a repetitive sort, conditions of work are not good, etc. So conditions of work, the nature of work, the climate, the environment all these may not be conductive. We have to see that physical comforts are provided. But more than physical environment, is the kind of leadership provided, the mental environment that is available, and the commitment to work, the interest in work, the relationship between work and the great goals. If this happens, there might be a very big change in their attitude to work.

Ability to work depends on knowing techniques and skills and so on. But willingness to work depends on morale and motivation. And we have to create a very very high level of morale and motivation in every functionary in administration. This is neglected, nobody bothers, nobody thinks that there is such a thing as morale. There are no Government Orders to say that you should look after the morale of the people in administration. Though intangible these things are of greatest significance. There is no officer who is appointed to look after the morale and to provide motivation. Government Orders only say that an Officer is on duty for 24 hours. And still we say that there is no work ethic. So it is not a question of ordering people to work : in other words, work ethic cannot be ordered about. It has to be created in administration.

People say that there are two ways to move the human donkey, that is the carrot and the stick. Carrot is incentive, wage and all that is paid. And the stick is disciplinary enforcement. If you do not show ethic, you will be punished. Orders are issued— papers must be disposed of in 24 hours, if anybody keeps papers beyond 24 hours, he will be punished. Such orders have been issued for years, but there has not been any noticeable improvement in the pace of the movement of the files in Indian Offices. What is required is not just saying that an officer must work for 24 hours or that within 24 hours every paper should be disposed of, but to create an inner desire. Work Ethic is an inner thing like morale and motivation, and this inner urge has to be kindled.

I am of the view that in every large organisation where many people work, it should be the specific responsibility of somebody to generate and keep high the morale of that organisation. Morale of the organisation is generated where the organisation and the individual goals are the same. In other words, everyone should find a self-actualisation in his work. How do we see that this happens ? This can only happen through a continuous tradition of working together and a feeling that we are working for an over-riding common purpose, for a great mission. And if there are things of bread and butter which come in the way and which sap morale and motivation they deserve attention. Our study shows that such has been the nature of work and the work environment in our administration that the civil servants are alienated from work. They are alienated from office, from the work place, from their families and from themselves. In the ultimate analysis, if you cannot make your family happy, you cannot make yourself happy. These are intangibles to which we pay no attention whatsoever and I think that in every organisation in Government administration, the subtle intangible things called morale and motivation need a great deal of attention. You cannot order motivation, or a sense of self-actualisation; that has to be done subtly by the leadership in every administration. Who is the leader ? Everybody is a leader in his own place. He is responsible for some people and he is the leader to them. We should have a constant effort of passing on of the urge to work as a goal in itself because it leads to the fulfilment of the larger purpose of the nation.

# 5

# Administrative Challenges in Development

The administrative challenges in development in the coming years are the following :

(i) Stopping the tide of population increase;

(ii) Increasing food production to cope with the rise in population;

(iii) Providing opportunities for gainful employment and income generation, specially to the weaker sections of the community;

(iv) Maintaining national integration, and social cohesion which are *sine qua non* for development.

World population has doubled itself in the last 45 years. and may touch the figure of 7,000 million by 2000 A.D. as against 4000 million now and 275 million 2000 years ago. 15% of world population is in India which is only 2.4% of the world area. In 1951 the Indian population was 361 million and today it is 683. 8 million. (When the paper was first written, now it nears 900 million). The growth during 1971-81 was 24.75% and at present it is over 2.1% per annum, resulting in addition of about 13 million people every year. For every 13 million people each year, 127000 more schools, 3000 more school teachers, 250000 more houses, 4 million more jobs, 14 crore metre more cloth and 13 million quintal more of food are required and this really provides the greatest challenge to administration. As against the world density of population of 22, India's density of population is 221 per Sq. Kilometre. Our population of this magnitude leads to a number of socio-economic problems, like poverty mal-nutrition, illiteracy, high child morta-lity, low life expectancy, unemployment, migration to towns, crowded cities, degradation of environment. These problems throw enormous burden on the administrative system.

To ease the burden, the programmes of family planning should be given the highest priority. A comprehensive family planning programme should be adopted. In this connection, India can draw inspiration from the 37 years old Social worker in Thailand, Mechai Viravaidya. Family planning has to be made an integrated part of economic and social development. Japan has demonstrated that it is possible to reduce the birth rate by half in 10 years. At present there are 130 million couples of reproductive age, but only 25.22 million have adopted family planning. People who have more than two children should be sterilized. The present birth rate of 33 per thousand population could be brought down to about 20 immediately but the compulsory sterlization has to be brought about with the voluntary consent of the people. Our objective was to reduce birth rate from 35 per thousand to 25 in 1984. The current rate in China is 18 per thousand compared to 15 in Japan and USA.

When the population rises to 1 billion by 2000 AD, the number of people below the poverty line will increase enourmously. Population growth affects the calory intake. The Indian calory intake is 1900 per head as against 3000 in richer countries. Population explosion adds to the marginal men with no job and literacy.

Where as illiteracy has been eliminated in the richer countries, the percentage of literacy in India is 48% even nearly fifty years after independence. More than half of the illiterate population of the world is in India. One out of two Indians can neither read nor write any language. While literacy is 48% in the country, amongst the backward classes who constitute 35% of the population it is less than 10%. Providing universal education is a colossal problem.

# 6

# Public Administration for 21st Century

The theme of Public Administration for 21st Century is very much connected with our dream of India of the 21st Century. The 21st Century would make its appearance with the inexorable march of time. We have in view a vision of India as it emerges into the 21st century. We expect the public administration to contribute to the fulfilment of that vision. After all public administration is not an entity by itself. Public administration is not just a group of civil servants working in offices. Rather public administration is the instrument of India as a nation state which has certain challenges to meet and certain promises to fulfil.

## Task of Public Administration after Independence

When India became independent a little before the middle of the century, out leaders who were at the helm of affairs had certain vision of free India. They thought of a democratic India engaged in the task of development for raising the level of living of the mass of people and making their lives richer, fuller and better. It was in that context that thought was given to the refashioning of the administrative system. Paul Appleby, an American expert was invited by Pt. Jawaharlal Nehru and the Planning Commission to have a look at India's administrative system. In this famous report Paul Appleby stated that the task undertaken by free India viz. development through democracy — development for the people as numerous as in India, was an unprecedented task in the annals of human history. In his estimate, India had an administrative system which was one of the twelve best in the world. But that administrative system had to be transformed to meet the new challenges before the free India.The nature of the transformation of the system was explained in our Five Year Plans. One element of transformation was that it was no longer the instrument of colonial rule but was an instrument of democracy. In a system of parliamentary democracy which was established under our Constitution, the administrative executive would be responsible and accountable to the political executive that is the Council of Ministers which would in turn, be accountable to the Parliament and to the people at large. It was the task of the administration to make democracy work as an efficient system. The other aspect of transformation was that the administration would not be an instrument of the police state or the law and order state but would be an instrument of the welfare state or the development state.

As India is marching to the 21st century, we have to ask ourselves to what extent has our administration succeeded in meeting the challenges placed before it by Democracy and Development; it is also necessary to find out what new challenges have emerged. Public administration should fulfil the tasks yet unfinished, taken up after independence; it should also identify and deal with the new challenges.

### Achievements after Independence

Development in India has been attempted through successive Five Year Plans. There have been some notable achievements of five decades of planning. India has been able to have a continuous growth rate of 3.5 % and in recent years 5 % in her gross national product. It has partially modernised agriculture. A country which at one time was living from ship to mouth has now a buffer stock of nearly 25 million tonnes of foodgrains. India has also now a vast range of industries and has built an impressive infrastructure of transport and communication. Health and educational facilities have enormously expanded. A number of scientific institutions have been established. The network of banking has penetrated deep into the interior areas.

### Inadequate Growth Rate

Yet there are notable shortcomings. First the growth rate in GNP has managed just to keep ahead of the population growth rate. It has also been accompanied by creeping inflation. While the growth rate is good as far as it goes; it has not been as spectacular as in some other countries like Japan or South Korea which has had a growth rate of 8 to 10 %. While the rate of savings has gone up from 6 to 7 % to 23 to 24 % the capital output ratio has also increased bringing down the growth rate significantly. One of the elements which can raise the growth rate is increase in the efficiency of our investment which at present leaves much to be desired. Public sector enterprises to-day occupy the commanding heights of the economy but their efficiency specially in the field of basic industries like steel, coal, fertilisers and transport undertakings leaves scope for improvement. The task of improving investment in public sector enterprises is a major challenge before our administrative system. One aspect of the task is the full utilisation of the capacities created which alone can ensure proper return from the investment made. The administration has to identify the causes for under utilisation of capacities created and inefficiency of investment. An aspect of the in efficiency of the investment is the time and cost overruns which characterise most of our public enterprises. As we enter the 21st century we have to address ourselves to the task of evolving a system which will ensure that investment projects are completed on time and within the estimate made for them.

### Change in the Economic System

A more basic reform is associated with the modification of our economic system. We opted for a planned economy and a mixed economy with a large public sector and we instituted a system of controls and licences to ensure that the use of resources would be such as to fulfil the directions of planning. It is now believed that many of these controls have become too complex and too clumsy to allow rapid development. Far from being an engine of development on the right lines, they have become an handicap. We are, therefore, in the midst of the reappraisal of our economic system so as to make it more dynamic. Similar need is felt in countries like China and Russia both of which have now given some limited scope to private enterprises and fostered market oriented functioning of the economy. In China they have distinguished the political system from the administrative system and the administrative system from the economic system. Our political and economic system is very different but we too need some fundamental changes in our system* so as to overcome certain basic constraints that have emerged in our system such as inadequate utilisation of capacity created on the one side and severe constraints in our system including inadequacy of resources both domestic and in terms of foreign exchange for our planning and shortage of power/energy which has become a big handicap for development. These steps taken for modifications in our system to overcome the constraints have often been termed as a policy of liberalisation. We have to give careful thought to see that a system of controls which we have created and our system of administrative procedures and practices become an aid to development rather than a handicap.

### Agriculture Modernisation and Poverty Alleviation in Rural Areas

In a country like India development cannot and does not mean only industrialisation. A more important place has to be given to agriculture and rural development because even after 40 years of planning, 70 % of the people still derive their livelihood from the rural economy as they had at the beginning of our planning. We have to create gainful employment opportunities in rural areas and this would depend on our success in promoting prosperity in agriculture inputs and marketing and processing of agricultural produce. As the end of four decades of development we have seen a certain degree of development in the agricultural economy of our country known by the term Green Revolution. While agriculture in green revolution belt has rapidly advanced, agricultural economy in other parts of India is still backward and stagnant. The challenge before us is therefore, to extend the green revolution to all parts of the country. This is not an impossible task. But it has to be taken in the right earnest so that in the last

* This was written before the introduction of the full scale policy of liberalisation in the nineties.

decade of the century we can see the green revolution spreading in the other parts also. But this would require an "area specific approach" so that the programmes of agricultural and rural development are adapted to the local agro climatic and social conditions. We have to develop a concrete plan which will enable small and marginal and landless labourers to benefit from the green revolution. We cannot have agricultural modernisation which leaves the dry land agriculture and agriculture of the marginal farmers outside the periphery of the development. This would require certain innovative approach including greater attention to minor irrigation and utilisation of ground water resources and measures for soil and moisture conservation in dry land areas of the country. We cannot forget in the euphoria of the green revolution the fact that we have not entirely exorcised the Malthusian ghost of drought and famine stalking large parts of our land. We have to evolve new technology of dryland farming and measures for the production of crops like oil-seeds, pulses and minor millets whose production has been nearly stagnant for many years. We have to create a system of agricultural extension which can take care of the small and marginal farmers and agricultural labourers. Our strategy for poverty alleviation in rural areas must not only consist of employment programmes of rural works but also development of agriculture and ancillary occupations like dairy, fishery, poultry and horticulture which can provide gainful employment opportunities to the marginal farmers and agricultural labourers. In other words, we have to evolve a joint strategy for agricultural development and poverty alleviation in the rural areas.

**Universal Education and Health Facilities**

We have to provide literacy and health for all. It was a shocking revelation of the last population census (1981) that the rate of literacy in India was only 36 % and that amongst women even less. The 1991 cenus no doubt saw the literacy per centage going up to 50. But we cannot allow India to enter into the 21st century with the largest number of illiterate people in the world. Without literacy there cannot be development. One of the causes of development in other countries like South Korea and Japan is near cent per cent literacy. Operation Black Board which forms part of the new educational policy aims at making literacy universal. Our administration has to adopt innovative approaches to bring about cent per cent literacy as India emerges into the 21st century.

## Challenges of Urbanisation

Urbanisation is a concommitant to development. Not only old developed countries like England but also newly developed countries like South Korea, have 75 % of their population now living in the urban areas. In India the process of urbanisation may not appear to be that fast but even here as compared to 10 % of the population living in urban areas at the beginning of the century, the percentage has now gone up to 25 and it is expected that by the end of the century almost half of our entire population may be living in urban areas. It is said that there is one basic difference in the process of urbanisation in India as compared to that in the Western countries. There it has been the result of the 'pull effect' but here it has been the 'push effect'. The migration into cities is specially the result of the spill over of rural poverty. With no more land to be brought freshly under cultivation, there has been tremendous pressure of population on land and the surplus population in the rural areas has grown. It is without any adequate means of livelihood or gainful employment opportunities and it is this situation which pushes the rural people into the cities. The inevitable consequences — the growing number of pavement dwellers, shanties and slums and people without any opportunity for livelihood in the urban areas. The children of such pavement dwellers are often forced into crime including the white collar crimes of our times such as smuggling, black-marketing, illicit distilling and drug trafficking. Some of our major populated cities like Bombay and Calcutta are bursting at the seams without the basic amenities such as transport and sanitation and water supply. The problems in the smaller cities may be less but are not dis-similar in nature. Management of urban development has thus emerged as a serious administrative challenge. There are physical, economic and social aspects to urban development. While physical infrastructure in urban areas has suffered due to paucity of resources, the social and economic aspects have scarcely received any attention. The quality of city life has seriously deteriorated. The individual is atomised and life has become very impersonal. Urban community development programmes is necessary but has not made much headway. We should have clear ideas regarding spatial arrangements of our economic and social life so that we do not have a apoplexy of unmanageble cities and the anaemia of non viable village habitations without basic amenities of life.

## Harnessing Science and Technology

From the very beginning of our planning, we have laid emphasis on science and technology as the means through which development would be brought about. As a result of this a number of scientific departments and institutions have come into existence. At the Centre, in addition to the Deptt. of Science and Technology there are specialised science departments such as Deptt. of Atomic Energy, Space, Electronics, Science Research, Agriculture Research, Defence Research, Ocean Development, Non-conventional Energy etc. What is more important is that not only should we have a big R&D effort to promote science and technology, it is equally important to see that the results on research are quickly transmitted to the process of production. We should have agencies which can carry forward the results of research and of science and technology to the field. A lot more perhaps needs to be done to strengthen the science administration at the State and local levels.

In recent times, special scientific missions have been established with such purpose in view. These missions are in the field of rural drinking water, oil seeds production, immunisation, rural literacy and communication. However, much would depend on the manner in which administration can be oriented to adopt the "mission approach" in applying the result of research to the task of development.

There are many items of activities which are not covered by the mission programme but lend themselves to a similar approach: for example the Deptt. of Non-conventional Energy is engaged in the promotion of installation and use of bio-gas plants and harnessing solar and wind energy. We are thinking in terms of setting up only a lakh and half bio-gas plants in a year whereas a country like India with vast bovine and human population, the scope of individual and community bio-gas plants is simply great. In China this activity has been taken up on a mass scale with millions of such plants being set up. In India too we need to have similar mass programmes.

**Democratic System—Panchayati Raj**

But while in China this has been done in a totalitarian system in India development has to take place through a democratic system. In a system of parliamentary democracy which we have adopted, the political executive and administrative executive should be able to work in unison and also should be able to elicit participation of the people in the process of development and economic and social change. We have decided that the system of democratic administration should not be confined to the two levels of our federal polity viz. Centre and the States but should also be expanded to the local level through Panchayati Raj system. The system was started with great enthusiasm in the 60s following Balwant Rai Mehta Committee's recommendation but soon the enthusiasm diminished and Panchayati Raj system fell into disarray for various reasons. It is necessary that these institutions are revived and become instruments of decentralised planning and development with a high level of popular participation. Administrative support should be available not only to the Central and State Governments but also to local government institutions. It is said that there has been in recent years, a great deal of proliferation of schemes, programmes and agencies at the local level and they should all be brought together under a comprehensive system of Panchayati Raj. The State of Karnataka has gone ahead recently with such a comprehensive system of Panchayati Raj. We should watch with great expectations the outcome of the system. There is no doubt that the administration of a vast country like India cannot be carried out without the active and efficient system of Panchayati Raj all over the country.

**Refashioning Administrative System**

We in India have to evolve an integrated system of administration based on collaboration and cooperation between the Centre, State and local administrations. This is essential because without the support of national policies, programmes of State and local governments cannot succeed. At the same time, without the input of local resources, identification of local needs and cooperation of the local people, centralised schemes, plans and programmes would not only be inappropriate to the specific requirements but would also fail in their implementation. For a successful functioning of such a three tier system of democracy, we need to have an efficient administrative mechanism for policy making at the Centre and the State and project, plan and programme implementation at the field level. We must have a system of administration which is action oriented rather than paper oriented, field oriented rather than HQ oriented, people oriented rather than authority oriented, result oriented rather than target oiiented. We must rid the administration of the old evils of delay, red tape, circumlocution, nepotism and corruption. And we have to modernise it with the introduction of the new Information & Communication Technology (ICT).

**Environment Preservation**

While administration should meet some of the continuing challenges of development in democracy, it must also face new challenges that have emerged. Firstly, we have come to realise that development has been at the cost of environment. Nature's life supporting system has eroded threatening not only the process of development but even the survival of our civilization. Some people have conjured up the nightmare of "treeless India"—which would be nothing less than a disaster. Development therefore, has to be consistent with the preservation of environment. A new Deptt. of Environment has been created at the Centre but similar activities should take place at the Central and local levels to stop denudation of our forests and grazing lands. Fortunately several local activist groups have emerged and have aroused the consciousness of the people to need for environmental presentation. But while they have secceeded opposing development which threatens environment they have not been sufficiently effective in promoting positive effort in promotion of programmes like social forestry, wasteland development and preservation of grazing lands. These positive tasks should also receive attention.

**Materialism and Consumerism**

Development has given rise to the revolution of rising expectations. While the poor have every right to desire the level of living which is consistent with human dignity, for the more affluent materialism has tended to become the "be all and end all" of life. Excessive consumerism has eroded our characteristic outlook of life and the cherished human values which constitute the eternal verities of our culture and heritage. We have to see that these values are not sacrificed at the altar of development.

India has been the only civilisation which has existed without break for the last five thousand years. India was at the acme of human civilisation. Prof. A.L. Basham has written about the 'Wonder that was India'. The challenge before Indian administration is to bring India to that level of achievement. India of the 21st century should be politically strong and stable, economically prosperous, scientifically advanced, socially cohesive and just and culturally rich. And it is the task of administration to dedicate itself to this goal.

# 7

# Importance of Field Administration

Administration in India, as everywhere else, could be divided in two parts—the staff administration and the line administration; the secretariat administration and the field administration. This applies as much to the organisation of the Central government administration as to the State government administration, though the former sometimes tends to consider the State administration as a whole as field administration. If the secretariat constitutes the apex of the administrative pyramid, the administration at the village, block, tehsil, district and divisional levels described in totality as the 'field administration', constitutes the base of the administrative pyramid. Between the apex and the base at the intermediate level, is the administrative organisation of the various Heads of Departments.

The apex administration is considered as the 'higher administration' and the field administration is considered to be the 'lower administration'. The term 'lower administration' is analogous to the term 'lower economics' employed by Myron E Sharpe in his book 'John Kenneth Galbraith and the Lower Economics'. This term 'lower economics' was suggested by Galbraith himself. "He pictured the structure of economics as a hollow pyramid. At the base, the sides are transparent and have many openings to the outside. As one approaches the apex the sides become increasingly opaque and impermeable. Economists dealing with practical matters dwell at the base and they have easy communication with the outside world. The practitioner at this level merits little esteem; in contrast economists dealing with pure theory can be found near the top of the pyramid. They are protected from outside influence. Their work is formal and has little or nothing to do with reality and is very highly regarded by the profession".*

If we replace the terms 'economics' and 'economist' in this passage with the terms 'administration' and 'administrator', the passage will read as follows "the structure of administration is a hollow pyramid. At the base, the sides are transparent and have many openings to the outside. As one approaches the apex the sides become increasingly opaque and impermeable. Administrators dealing with the practical matters dwell at the base and they have easy communication with the outside world. The practitioner at this level merits little esteem; in contrast administrators dealing with the secretariat administration can be found near the top of the pyramid. They are protected from outside influence. Their work is formal, and has little or nothing to do with reality and is very highly regarded by the profession".

It is true that periodically those who are at the helm of administration pay lip service to the importance of the "field administration" or the "lower administration". The latter is often described as the cutting edge of administration. It is stated that the real administrative work is done at the field level. Recently a leading publicist even suggested that more prestige and importance should be attached to the field administration. Senior officials should work at the field level. Special allowances must be given to the field administrators rather than to the secretariat administrators. The Collector or the Deputy Commissioner should be considered equal in rank to the Secretary to the Government. These ideas however have still remained aberrations. It is the secretariat positions of administrations which are considered prestigious while the field positions have increasingly lost their influence and importance in the eyes of everybody including those working at the field level!

The reasons for this state of affairs are not difficult to understand. The real administrative power and authority is concentrated in the secretariat. It is the administrators at the secretariat level who are close to the powers that be. It is

* "John Kenneth Galbraith & the Lower Economics" by Myron E Sharpe, Macmillan International Arts & Science Press, Inc 1973.' p. 1.

## THE ADMINISTRATIVE PYRAMID

*Apex — Secretariat Administration*

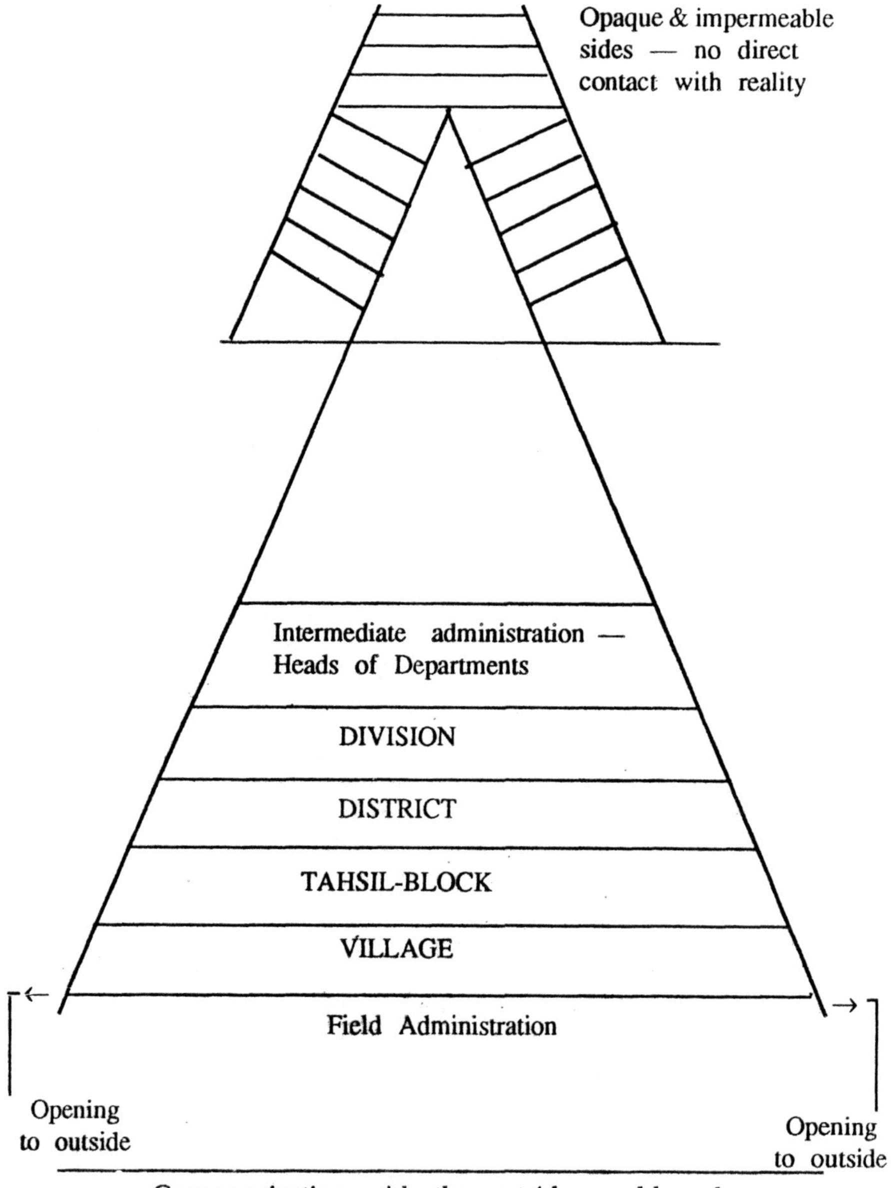


Communication with the outside world and direct contact with reality

they who are in constant touch with those who wield power and patronage. It is they who are prominently seen on all occasions when the power of the State authority is displayed. On the other hand, those working in the field administration are in the back-waters. Being out of sight, they are also out of mind of those who matter!

Being thus counted out of the core of administration, those working in 'lower administration' are considered nothing more than hewers of wood and drawers of water. They are supposed implicitly to obey orders and carry out programmes and policies of Government in the shaping of which they have no share. They are at the receiving end of the orders and communications from the secretariat. They have to give all priority to the communications from the State Government which must have precedence over every other aspect of field administration. The field officers have to be at the beck and call of the secretariat. Even at short notice they have to leave their field administration to attend the meetings convened in the secretariat which may even at the last moment be cancelled! If the demigods of 'higher administration' choose to descend to the field on occasional visits, lower administrators at the field level must receive them, make all arrangements for them and accompany them on their tours. The vice-versa is not true even in respect of those who hold the highest positions in the field administration! The field officers visiting the State capital must fend for themselves. At the meetings held at the State level, it is expected that the officers at the field level have mainly to listen to the authoritative pronouncements of those who serve in the 'higher administration'. What they (the former) have to say is of little or no significance since it does not emanate from the seat of authority. Authority is attached to the position in the apex of administration and not to the authority of experience born out of close association with people and practical problems in the field. Thus the high prestige attached to the higher administration and low prestige attached to the lower administration is a typical example of "apoplexy at the centre and anaemia at the periphery"!

Administration careerists, therefore, tend to consider an escape from the field administration as the highest recognition of merit! Jumping the lower levels of the administrative ladder, they secure direct entry into the sanctum sanctorum of administration, viz., the secretariat. Once securely perched there, they start indulging with gay abandon in the "exercises of higher administration" in the rarified atmosphere away from the reality of the field. Many examples could be cited of those distinguished administrators who have made a name in the 'higher administration' but who have never held even once the basic positions of field administration like the Deputy Commissioner (Collector) and the Divisional Commissioner. A division is as though developing between those who are sentenced to long spells in field administration and others who are privileged to spend the entire administrative career in the higher administration of the secretariat.

Is this division of labour desirable? Is it conducive to healthy administration and to the realisation of the goals of administration? The answer must be in the negative.

Those *cloistered* for long in the cocoon of the secretariat tend to get more and more out of touch with reality. Inspite of that, they tend to develop pretentions to omniscient knowledge. They tend to feel that they are all knowing administrative demigods. They start passing facetious or cavalier comments on the failures of field administration forgetting that the policies and programmes for which they were responsible might themselves be unrealistic and impractical and hence incapable of successful implementation! They formulate stereo-type schemes and impose them on all areas indiscriminately, irrespective of varying conditions in the field. They push aside all objections emanating from the field as mere excuses to hide the inabilities of the field administrators. A persistent objector from amongst the field administrators could easily be condemned as incompetent and a malingerer. Huge expenditure is incurred on such stereo-type schemes, cooked or hatched in the higher organisations of administration, without getting commensurate results! A change in authority might lead to a sudden scrapping of the stereo-type scheme and its replacing by new one. The former may be forgotten as if they never existed! The field administrators are not expected to know why the old scheme is abandoned and a new scheme is introduced, why policy shifts and why priorities alter. "Theirs is not to question why, theirs is only to do and die".

This picture must change if administration is to deliver the goods because if it persists, policies will be shaped with the advice of those who are out of touch with reality, and programmes will be implemented by those demoralized administrators who consider that the field administration is a thankless and unrewarding task! The field administrator is constantly exposed to the reality of the field problems. He is exposed to stresses and strain, to the various pressures emanating from the pressure groups amongst the public. He is held responsible for any untoward incident, his explanation may also be called for and displeasure of government communicated to him. The chances of such exposures may increase if the field officer is more active. If he keeps his activity to the minimum, no field problems may arise though the public may not benefit. On the other hand if he tends to be positive and dynamic, he may sometime raise a hornest's nest and get himself in trouble. One mistake, one lapse, may have serious consequences, but great achievements may go unnoticed! Successful disposal of cases or papers, quick redress of public grievances or a resolute persuit of development activities in local areas may not receive any notice because in the vast totality of administration and particularly in terms of the priorities of the higher administration all this may not mean much!

Successful formulation of policies and their implementation would, therefore, call for a root and branch change in the outlook of administration. Field administration must gain greater prestige, administrative achievements in the field must gain higher recognition, field jobs must assume higher importance. Level jumping in the administrative ladder must be discouraged; positions in the higher administration must not be assumed by those who have not delivered the goods in the field administration. Only those that are successful in the field administration must be selected for positions in the higher administration so that their advice in shaping policies bears the imprint of reality. Those who have had a very long spell in higher administration must be sent to field and given a long spell in the field administration.

At the same time the relationship between lower administration and higher administration must undergo a change. The lower administration must not always be at the receiving end.

The higher administration must seek opportunities to learn from the experience of those working in the lower administration. Policies must be shaped after consultation with those working at the field level. The evaluation of policies must also be done with the help of the feed back from the field. There must be studied attempts to identify sustained practical achievements in the field which must receive recognition and reward. Only then "lower administration" will receive the prestige that is due to it; and only the field administration clothed with prestige, recognition and high morale can ultimately deliver the goods which the administration and Government are expected to deliver.

# 8

# Promoting Efficiency in the Civil Service

The welfare of the people in a modern State depends to a great extent on the efficiency of the civil service. The ordinary citizen is now-a-days concerned with the civil service literally from womb to tomb and can derive satisfaction to the extent to which it is efficient in dealing with his problems and fulfilling his needs. How can this efficiency be promoted? An answer to this question requires a clear understanding of: (i) the concept of efficiency; (ii) its criteria and measurement; and (iii) the practical steps that can be taken to introduce efficiency.

According to Herbert Simon, author of "Administrative Behaviour", one of the standard books on scientific management, "Efficiency involves on the one hand the maximisation of income if costs are considered as fixed and on the other hand, the minimisation of costs if income is considered to be fixed. In practice the maximisation of income and the minimisation of cost must be considered simultaneously, that is, what is really to be maximised is the difference between these two." This concept is derived from economics, where the central concern is with the calculation of cost and benefit.

However, the transplantation of this concept to the field of public administration is not quite easy. In economics, benefits and costs are measured in monetary terms. But the input and output of administration do not easily lend themselves to monetary measurements. What monetary value can be attached to the maintenance of law and order, or the maintenance of the record of rights of farmers? The difficulty exists even in the social service departments like education and health which do not produce marketable goods and services.

The difficulty is not confined to the measurement of output; it also exists in relation to the cost of input. In most of the Government departments the cost, in the main is related to the salaries and allowances of personnel. While these figures may be readily available, it is not easy to relate a specific work to a specific expenditure, since the employees are responsible for a multiplicity of services.

### Joint Investment

The output of a government department depends not only on the effort of the functionary at the lowest level but also the supervision by the higher functionaries. Thus the increase in agricultural production may be the result of the services rendered by the village level worker, the extension officer at the block level, the district agriculture officer, the director of agriculture and even the Union department of agriculture, all of whom play their part in the formulation, supervision and execution of various schemes. It may be impossible to measure separately the contribution of a department or an office, much less of an individual functionary. The output and input of Government offices are an example of what economists call 'joint investment and joint product.'

The administrative organisation of Government is not necessarily based on relating the specific output of work to a specific input of personnel. An ongoing organisation may be called upon to undertake new and diverse activities, sometimes without any additional staff whatsoever. An example of this is the 20-point programme, most of which is implemented through the existing district organisation. No additional staff is appointed to deal with the work of abolition of bonded labour, enforcement of minimum agricultural wages, abolition of agricultural indebtedness, distribution of house sites to the siteless or construction of Janata houses, though each one of these programmes involves substantial additional work.

**Parkinson's Law in Reverse**

This is an example of Parkinson's Law in reverse, though few commentators on public administration have cared to take notice of this. Indeed, some of the basic administrative organisations functioning at the field level appear to have an infinite elasticity in their capacity to work. In a situation such as this where the existing administrative organisations undertake new and additional responsibilities, the measurement of input and output and their co-relationship necessary to measure the efficiency of civil service seem to be an impossible task.

Do we then give up the attempt to apply the criteria of efficiency to administrative services? There are some areas where the maximisation of return and minimisation of cost can be applied for instance commercial projects like the construction of a hydroelectric scheme or an irrigation work. These lend themselves to cost-benefit analysis. It is desirable that their operation is strictly governed by the criteria of efficiency, replacing market cost and return if need be by social cost and benefit, so that the common phenomenon of cost escalation and schedule slippage can be avoided.

Even though neither the output nor the input of the functionaries in a Government office is divisible, it may be worthwhile to attempt to apply the cost-benefit concept and criteria of efficiency through performance budgeting. The work of a whole department could be evaluated on a macro basis and compared with the calculation of cost also on a macro basis. This is what performance budgeting does.

But the fact remains that the cost-benefit criterion is more or less theoretical in its application to the bulk of work of the civil service. Therefore it becomes necessary to adopt other tests. Normally this is attempted through the criterion relating to the speedy disposal of business. The Government work turns round papers and files and therefore if these are disposed of quickly, the office must be considered to be efficient. In fact the whole administrative effort seems to be mainly concerned with the application of this criterion.

A distinction has to be made between disposal of paper

or a communication and disposal of a case. While a paper may be disposed of by, say calling for a report from the lower authority or sending a communication to a higher authority, the disposal of a case depends on the final decision in the matter. It is often found that while the rigid time limits for disposal of a paper are observed, the ultimate disposal of cases is not necessarily accelerated. What matters is not merely disposal of a paper within a time; it is the quality of disposal.

For the citizen, the important point is the final disposal of a case and not the movement of papers from one desk to another or from one office to another. Unfortunately, this is what happens in most Government offices and departments. Papers move from one table to another, from one office to another, from one department to another, from one level to another, in an interminable misery-go-round. The administrative effort involved must be considered to be yielding no return whatsoever.

This, therefore, brings us to the conclusion that the criteria relating to the disposal of business in a Government office, must be applied qualitatively rather than quantitatively. Since this is not always done, statements regarding the disposal of work by Government offices and their review by the inspecting authorities tend to be of a routine nature and do not contribute materially to the acceleration of work or improvement of efficiency.

The quality of work can improve only if the present emphasis on disposal of a paper within a time limit is replaced by emphasis on an in-depth analysis of a case by the very first authority concerned with it. This person must collect all relevant facts and examine the alternatives available so as to enable a firm and final disposal of the matter, avoiding interminable back references from the higher to the lower offices.

Such analysis requires a thorough knowledge of the relevant law, a deep understanding of policies and programmes and competent satistical service through a data bank.

Sometimes demand is made on lower offices to furnish statistical information which is not readily available and which requires a full-scale survey that cannot be undertaken by a routine administrative authority. For example, to frame policies regarding finance for farmers who are unable to get bank loans on the normal criteria, information was recently sought about the number of such farmers. Innumerable reminders have not helped to get this information quickly because the normal administrative machinery is not geared to do such work.

Thus efficiency in the sense of disposal of work in Government offices, requires a greater intellectual effort on the part of all the civil servants who must be concerned, with the realisation of objectives than mere adherence to the letter of the law, the rule or the circular. The absence of adequate knowledge of the subject-matter is a real gap in administrative organisations, more especially the summit organisation, namely the secretariat, whose orientation is clerical in nature putting a premium on procedure and precedent rather than purpose and object.

Nothing short of an internal revolution in the administrative organisation of Government can lead to a breakthrough in the disposal of business. So long as this qualitative change is not brought about, no amount of campaigns or drives or observance of 'disposal week' will serve to improve the efficiency in the civil service.

The need for a qualitative change applies not only to the office, but also to the field organisations. These are concerned with the fulfilment of programmes like small savings, tree planting, agricultural demonstrations, etc. Here again the target orientation does not necessarily result in the achievement of the objectives. In order to show that small savings targets are achieved, funds are collected at the end of the year, only to be refunded at the beginning of the next year. Similarly to fulfil tree planting targets, the trees are planted but are not looked after later.

## Morale and Motivation

A qualitative change in the administration or what I may call an "internal administrative revolution" can only take place by a radical change in the morale and motivation of the civil servants, in addition to the strengthening of organisation and improvement of procedures. A more positive system of reward and punishment is necessary to bring about this change in morale and motivation. While for even technical mistakes there could be a prolonged departmental enquiry, real case of corruption may go scot-free. At the same time outstanding performance may not even be taken note of.

Training, a proper system of reward and punishment, and other improvements in personnel management should aim at a qualitative change in the civil service which alone can bring about an improvement in efficiency in the real sense of the term.

# 9

# India's Political Administrators

The term 'Political Administrators' refers to the officers of the Indian Civil Service and its successor, the Indian Administrative Service. The term is so used because, it correctly connotes the work that was done and is being done by the members of these Services. They have been and are administrators in the larger sense of the term. Dr. Potter has approvingly quoted my definition of what constitutes administration in this larger sense viz: "the total effort to translate the aspirations, ambitions, ideologies and ideals into policies, plan programmes and building up organisations and institutions to take charge of these plans and programmes manning them with personnel-both competent and motivated and continuously leading, directing and coordinating their efforts so as to realise the objective in view". Further more, there officers are termed as *'Political Administrators'* because of administration in its larger sense is a part of politics.

What was the tradition of the ICS and to what extent has the IAS continued the ICS tradition? What was the 'administrative legacy' of the ICS and how far it was carried over after independence?

The ICS had a definite tradition. First, the pre-occupation of the ICS officers most of whom were recruited year after year, through competitive examinations was to serve the State as "trusted servants of the State" for the fulfilment of its purpose. During the colonial days, the purpose was to perpetuate the colonial rule which necessarily implied putting down the freedom movement. But when the situation changed, first with the introduction of dyarchy in 1919 following the Montague Chemsford Reforms, 1919 and later under the 1935 Act, set up, under which Ministries consisting of Indian leaders of the freedom movement came into power in the provinces, the ICS officers adapted themselves to the change. Here is an example of how they did so. The Government of Bombay raised the question with the Govt. of India whether the papers concerned with the freedom movement should not be handed over to the Governor so that they do not fall in the hands of the members of the popular Government that was to come in existence. The Indian Civil Service officers at the Centre and in several other States who were consulted had no hesitation in pointing out that the ICS officers will have to serve with loyalty under the popular Ministries and it would not be consistent with this loyalty and trust to hold back papers from them, even though they may betray the action taken by the Civil Service Officers against some of the members of the popular Governments.

The members of the Indian Civil Service came from the higher middle class. However, the officers of the Indian Civil Service did not consider it a part of their duty to subserve the interests of any class whether the capitalists or the feudal landlords or the middle-class. The district officers considered that the people of the District were their charge and they considered it their bounden duty to subserve the interests of the people entrusted to their care. This role of the Civil Service as embodied in the ICS tradition was more in tune with the Max Webor's concept of bureaucracy as the rational institution of the 20th Century rather than the Marxian interpretation of the civil service as a class institution subserving the vested interests of the dominant class. Serving the State with loyalty, trust and devotion to duty was considered by the members of the Service as a matter of honour.

The second aspect of the ICS tradition was its leadership role. The members in the Indian Civil Service were at the top of the Service. They held all the higher positions as Secretaries or Deputy Secretaries to Government at the Centre and in the States and as Commissioners of Divisions and Collectors of Districts in the field. As compared with the number of posts in the entire apparatus of administration, they constituted a very small number, but they held the key positions and had decisive influence on the working of the administrative system. They constituted the "Steel Frame" of India. The third aspect of the ICS tradition was that it was a generalist Civil Service, Officers of the ICS were not narrow specialists. They were expected to take a broad view of the administrative problems and arrive at a common sense solution - a solution that would be effective and would work. The norms and values of the ICS were cast in a gentlemanly mode of the Western Society.

Soon after the attainment of the independence, there set a large exodus of European ICS officers. In fact, there was a decline of the European elements in the Civil Service and the ascendancy of the Indian elements after the World War I itself. Though entrance examination to the ICS continued to be held in England, unlike before the World War I, fewer and fewer European officers found it attractive to join the Indian Civil Service rather than the Home Civil Service. From 1922 onwards, the examination started being held in India and opened a second route for the Indians to join the Indian Civil Service. During World War II, the entrance examinations were not held and an attempt made to re-start the recruitment to ICS after the World War II proved abortive. Even though the selections were made out of the Army officers to the ICS, they could not actually be posted. Though some European ICS officers continued to serve in India after the Independence, they soon realised that they were unlikely to be given any positions of real trust and responsibility. They saw the writing on the wall and preferred to go back taking advantage of the terminal benefits offered.

As for the Indian ICS officers, though they had served the British rule, some of them at least had their sympathies with the Indian political leaders and in any case were quick to take advantage of opportunities to hold higher posts created for them by the exit of the European officers.

In Sardar Vallabhbhai Patel, the Service found a tower of strength, who on the floor of the Constituent Assembly, eulogised the role played by the officers of the Indian Civil Service in the critical post-independence conditions and saw to it that the Constitution provided for the due protection of the terms and conditions of the Service. He also got the agreement of the Chief Ministers of the States for the constitution of an All India Service called the Indian Administrative Service as a successor to the Indian Civil Service.

The Officers of the Indian Administrative Service had to work for the new set up that came into existence after the Independence. There were three special aspects of this set up. First, with the advent of democracy, the members of the Civil Service were accountable to the elected Government at all levels; Central, State and even local levels. Second, the administration was not for the perpetuation of the colonial rule, but for putting into effect the wide-ranging programmes of development, for raising the standard of living of masses of people. Third, the Central and State Governments were constituents of the federal set up in which the Constitution itself earmarked the role for each constituent. Did this change mean any break in the ICS tradition?

In giving an answer to this the following matters deserve consideration. First the continuity of recruitment to the Indian Administrative Service. The competitive examination started in 1948 and every year on the basis of All India Examination, the best amongst the candidates who appeared for the examination are recruited and allotted to various States. They are put through an initial programme of training at the Mussorrie Academy. The training programme consists of General Administration, Law, Economics and Management. It also helped indirectly in inculcating 'gentlemanly norms' of behavior and instilling a measure of self confidence. This is followed by a field placement as per the new sandwitched pattern after which there is again the concluding part of training at the academy. Thereafter, the probationers go to their respective States and follow the same career pattern as the officers of the ICS viz: District posting, State Secretariat, Central Secretariat, back to the States and again to the Centre. On the basis of the analysis of facts and figures regarding the postings of the IAS officers, it may be said that the ICS tradition of job rotation continues. Then, there is the question of the relationship between the Civil Service and the Ministers which has become important in the democratic context. Inspite of some tension and uneasy relationships, the general position has crystalised that while the Civil Service officers have some amount of autonomy within the sphere of delegated powers, they have to be ultimately accountable to the Government consisting of the political leaders of the party in power. Also, in the federal set up, the officers of the Indian Administrative Service have provided the administrative links between the Centre and the States, since they hold higher level positions in both. The IAS officers continue to hold per-eminent positions in the administrative set up and the attempts such as the report of the Administrative Reforms Commission of personnel administration to limit the scope of the IAS to a particular functional area viz. the Revenue Administration have not succeeded. With continuous job rotation, the IAS has also retained its generalist character.

Thus the IAS continues the ICS tradition. The essential features of the ICS traditions have persisted without fundamental change into 1980s. The ICS traditions survived in the form of IAS because of continuing political support of the Congress Government. Persistence of ICS tradition has given strength of the bureaucratic structure in the areas of maintaining unity and order while making it less successful in encouraging innovation, specialist expertise and responsiveness to local demands all important ingredients of development administration.

# 10

# The ICS and the IAS

The Indian Civil Service has won laurels as one of the best Civil Service ever established in the administrative history of any country. Lloyd George, the British Prime Minister described it as the steel frame of India. It was often called the "Heaven born service". Sir Henry Maine declared ICS "as a remarkable group of public servants any country has produced". The ICS earned a reputation for efficiency, integrity and devotion to duty. To be sure some of the Indian leaders did denounce the Indian Civil Service as "neither Indian nor Civil nor Service" but perhaps it was done more as a denouncement of the imperial rule than as a true assessment of its performance.

As could only be expected all the Indian members of the ICS found real fulfilment of their careers only after independence. No doubt there were some good features of administration during the British days but there was a clear realization on the part of the ICS officers, that the administration during the British days was extremely limited. As Vishnu Sahay, the doyen amongst the ICS officers put it "There is no comparison whatsoever between what government did in the British days and what it is intended to do now; everything is about fifty times more than what it was during those days". Those ICS officers who had bulk of their career ahead of them after independence were indeed very fortunate because vast vistas of creative work and opportunities opened out before them in varied and challenging fields like external affairs, national integration, economic and financial management, international trade, and planning ambitious public sector enterprises.

At the time of independence, there was an idea that all the members of the ICS should be sent home after giving them some compensation. However the idea was given up and not only were the services of the ICS officers retained but even the constitutional protection was accorded to them, thanks to Sardar Vallabhbhai Patel who won the respect and loyalty of all the members of the Indian Civil Service. L.K. Jha recalls how just before the national government of Independent India was formed he invited all the Indian members of the ICS residing in Delhi and told them that "free India would rely on the dedicated service of all of you", the all being the Indians serving in the ICS cadre at that time. He called upon them to "help us in the task ahead". This, indeed, was the finest hour for the ICS.

The British members of the ICS who formed the majority naturally left though some of them had no doubt served the Indian masters when provincial government was formed in 1937. Some of the English ICS Officers even donned Khadi dress in order to join the spirit of the times. But, on the other hand, the other British ICS officers were clearly out of sorts and even demoralised with the advent of independence. However, even after the British members of ICS left they continued to recall their days in India and some felt so nostalgic that they revisited India with their wives to go to the remote district places where they once served as young District Officers.

It becomes clear from the narrations that though British and Indian officers belonged to the same Indian Civil Service, the two elements were not really fully blended. They did not always mix freely at social level and sometimes Indian members joined separate clubs as they were not welcome in the clubs which were exclusively for the British.

Though serving the British to the extent required by service conditions the officers of the ICS want us to believe that all of them were in favour of independence rather than the perpetuation of the British Rule. Some of them tried in their own way to soften the repression of the freedom movement and did what they could, in their own way, to be of service to the national leaders even though they had to put them behind the bar. However, after Independence the ICS Officers had to serve the same national leaders when they came to be at the helm of affairs after independence.

These national leaders were real stalwarts. They were towering personalities and the ICS officers had no hesitation in acknowledging their greatness. One of them has described that these leaders were "Everest group personalities"- Pt. Jawaharlal Nehru, Sardar Patel, Dr. Rajendra Prasad, Rajaji, Pt. Govind Vallab Pant and Lal Bahadur Shastri, to mention only a few amongst them. Talking about Pandit Nehru, the first Prime Minister of free India, Dharma Vira says, "He was a person who was always prepared to listen to the other person's point of view. He encouraged officers to speak out freely in his presence." Govind Narain recalls that Nehru's manner of conversation was so endearing that it invoked a high sense of loyalty and devotion to duty. M.K. Kriplani says that Nehru was born leader of men who shed graciousness all around. Satish Chandra recalls how at 1.30 a.m. at night Pandit Nehru himself gave a ring to find out about late information regarding ravages caused by Delhi flood. Satish Chandra felt that 'while we were all asleep, here was one who in all his preoccupations cared even about little things." Of Sardar Patel, Dharma Vira says those who knew the strong man of India, realised that he was a very considerate and kind individual. Khub Chand calls him an unrivalled administrative genius. Sohoni has recollection of the extremely phenomenal memory of Dr. Rajendra Prasad. Satish Chandra recalled how when he started explaining to Pandit Pant, Chief Minister of U.P. about steps taken by him to maintain law and order in the District, Pantji told him- "If I misbehave in your district you can arrest me". In his desire to cleanse New Delhi Satish Chandra could give notice to Pantji himself; one quality of these great leaders was that they were prepared to listen to the views of the Civil Servants, even though they were contrary to their own. In fact they positively encouraged the Civil Servants to be free and frank in tendering their advice. Moreover, they had the magnanimity to accept the responsibility for a wrong decision rather than make a scape-goat of the civil servant. Officers working under them never felt politically influenced, embarrassed or over-powered or asked to do things which they would not have otherwise done. It is this that enabled the ICS officers to work with full confidence and without inhibitions. No wonder, the ICS Officers were able to give their best in the first 10 or 15 years of independence.

However, things started deteriorating after the first generation of leaders, one by one, left the scene.

The next generation of leaders did not have the same spirit of compassion and broadmindedness. Some of them not only did not want frank and free advice but wanted the civil servants to toe their line. No wonder the confidence of the bureaucracy started weakening and they could not give their best. While the honest and the independent-minded officers were sidetracked, yesmen started flourishing. One point which all the veteran ICS officers stress is the need to restore the atmosphere of confidence among the civil servants. This alone can reverse the trend of deterioration that has set in our administrative system.

Among the many manifestations of deterioration in administration is the tendency to concentrate everything on the top in the absence of delegation. Even in the exercise of delegated powers, there is constant *interference.* Promotion and postings unrelated to merit and based on the factor of personal loyalty have destroyed the morale and motivation of the civil service. Political patronage has taken a heavy toll of administrative objectivity, which was a good feature of administration during the British days. One ICS Officer who fined his own wife for driving without licence. Such example of objectivity in maintaining the rule of law would be unheard of in today's administration.

In the judgement of the retired ICS Officers, the falling administrative standards are not due to the low calibre of the IAS, which is successor to the ICS but due to the changes in the environment in which civil service has to function. One of the distinguished ICS officers recently observed to me that he would have ended as a dismissed Government Servant if he were to work in the changed environment. The persons in the IAS today-atleast those holding high ranks in the entrance examination are all of as high a calibre as the members of the ICS but they have to be provided the atmosphere in which they can give their best.

Another factor which has affected the performance of the IAS is the low salaries in real terms. The relentless inflation has eaten into the real value of the rupee but the salaries are practically stand-still. If inspite of this, quite a large number of IAS Officers still continue to remain honest it is because of their immense attachment to profession.

There were some features of the British administration which were conducive to good administration and which we seem to have given up but which we perhaps need to bring back. One of them was the personal interest in the training of civil servants which their seniors took. A young officer joining his first posting was personally received at station by the Collector and was his personal guest for several months. There was free and friendly association an esprit de corps among the officers. Today, formal institutional training is long but the informal personal training no longer exists. The other features of the British administration were the appreciation of good work done by the junior officers. Thirdly the importance of the man on-the-spot was recognised and he was supported. Fourthly, the district officers spent a good deal of time touring in the countryside, living under tents which gave opportunities for directly knowing and remedying the problems of the people. Today these officers have no time for this because they are engaged in attending innumerable meetings, going to Head-quarters of the State or responding to the urgent calls of the VIPs. Fifthly, close and frequent inspections and surprise checks by supervisory officers kept administration alert. Sixthly, there was no hesitation in upholding the Rule of Law. These are good features of the British administrative practice which need to be reestablished. The Civil services today has to continue play an important role in contributing to the progress of the nation and preparing it for the twenty-first century. There is stress today on administrative reform. Ideas given by the veterans of yester-years can show us the way for harnessing the capacities of the civil service for the progress of the nation.

# 11

# Civil Service Yesterday and Today

When I was interviewed for the IAS way back in 1952, the Chairman of the UPSC, and ICS officer presiding over the Board which interviewed me suddenly asked the question. "Why are you thinking of joining the IAS"? Without hesitation, I replied, "Because I want to serve the country". He did not ask further question on this point but I felt that he was somewhat disappointed, probably thinking that I was either trying to be idealistic or hypocritical, and a more candid reply would have been that I wanted a comfortable living. Looking back over my career in the civil service spanning over 35 years, I feel that the reply I gave was correct. The IAS may not have given me a comfortable living, but it has certainly provided numerous opportunities for public service.

**Process**

When I joined the service in 1953, the nation had just embarked on a process of planned development. In my early years of service as a Sub-Divisional Officer, what I was called upon to do was to initiate this process for the people falling within my administrative jurisdiction consisting of more than 500 villages. It is in these villages that I began work of setting up community development blocks, establishing cooperatives for the supply of institutional credit to farmers who had long been in the clutches of money-lenders, providing basic facilities to villages, organizing shramdan or voluntary work-all this through people's organisations such as farmers' associations, youth clubs and mahila mandals.

Later, as Deputy Commissioner of a district, the area and the content of development work widened. For before me was the challenge of rapidly developing 560,000 acres of famine-stricken area irrigated for the first time under the Tungabhadra project. The water was taken to the field but the farmer would not take to irrigation because he was not used to it. Our job was to motivate the farmers for irrigated farming and for the use of chemical fertilizers and other agricultural inputs.

After my assignment as Sub-Divisional and District Officer I went to the State and Central Secretariats and headed national institutions of training but returned to the field after 14 years, first as Administrator in charge of Command Area Development under the Malaprabha and Ghataprabha Irrigation Project and thereafter as Divisional Commissioner in charge of the Bombay-Karnataka region with more than 5,000 villages in my jurisdiction. Returning to the field, I realized that the work we had done in the early years had not been wasted.

Agricultural production and productivity had increased. The farmers were no longer strangers to the use of agricultural inputs like hybrid seeds or chemical fertilizers. They used institutional credit through their membership of cooperatives which had now been strengthened by the commercial banks and regional rural banks. Regulated markets had been established. High schools and colleges were providing education to the rural people. Electricity had brought light to the villages.

But village people, more conscious than in the past, had still higher expectations and these had to be fulfilled. More specifically, special attention had to be paid to backward areas and the weaker sections. As Divisional Commissioner, I presided over organisation dealing with small and marginal farmers, agricultural labourers and drought-prone areas. I experimented with a Village Planning Commission to set up "growth centres" in rural areas.

These references to my field assignments are mere illustrations of what I and my generation of post-Independence administrators were called upon to do in the course of their careers.

Now, the question I would like to ask is this: Does the performance of the IAS in particular, and the civil service in general, deserve a condescending attitude? Does it warrant unsavoury comparisons between the IAS and the ICS? Nari Rustomji recalls his own days in the ICS to show that today's young IAS officers lack the vital spur of enjoyment and zest that inspired him and his colleagues. But what did his zest stem from? It arose out of the "joy of relaxing by moonlight at the end of the march amidst the peace and stillness of the mountains towering around us".

Such joys may not be readily available today but does it mean that there is no zest today? The enjoyment from implementing numerous projects for bettering the lot of the poor is incomparably greater than that from relaxation amid mountains. What can stimulate more zest and provide greater incentive to effort than the urge to see darkness dispelled in remote villages, to convert land stricken with famine for ages into a rich source of food and fibre, to provide drinking water through quick working rigs to village communities who had never known safe drinking water, to provide houses to the landless? These, today, are the compensations to the not-so-comfortable life of the IAS officers. These programmes have brought them nearer to the people than ever before. The farmer today goes to the administrator as a matter of right for inputs, services and various amenities.

The ICS officers of Mr. Rustomji's generation were happy that they were being paid for "this unforgettable excursion into wonderland". Officers of the IAS are happy because they are being paid for the wonderful experience of being participants in a great endeavour—the endeavour to build up a new India. Everywhere young administrators are making their silent contribution. The distant Lahul Valley, where only 10 years ago the farmers were eking out a livelihood in bitter cold by growing kuth - a medicinal herb, which was exported to Tibet-has today become one of the biggest producers of seed potato which the Lahul farmers are supplying to West Bengal, Tamil Nadu and Maharashtra. How has this come about? It was the work of an IAS Deputy Commissioner who, 10 years ago, introduced the Lahul Valley tribals to potato cultivation.

In the distant Car Nicobar Island, many years ago, I met a young IAS officer who had picked up the Nicobari dialect and had set up a consumer cooperative organization. And only a few months ago, I had the heartwarming experience of meeting a lady IAS district officer bravely planning and organizing rescue and relief operations for people inundated by the surging waters of the Ganga.

These and numerous other achievements go unrecorded though they are the ones through which the nation makes progress, the ones from which the IAS administrator of today derives professional satisfaction. While in the field, he is directly involved in these programmes; in the Secretariat, he is making his contribution to the making and shaping of these programmes. New projects have made necessary new institutions and organizations in whose creation and management the administrator today has his part to play. These institutions and organizations were unknown to the ICS officers of yester year who worked in the traditional hierarchical structure for rather limited programmes, mainly in the fields of revenue and law and order administration.

Indeed, looking at the range and content of the development programmes today, one would consider the opportunity to participate in public administration as a practical expression of one's sense of patriotism. This is all the more praiseworthy because it is unconnected with selfish or partisan considerations. It is the administrator alone who is called upon to work for the betterment of the people as a whole.

This may appear to be an idealistic picture. It is said that the administrator of today is a victim of political pressure. He is bullied or harassed for doing his duty and, if he does not yield, is transferred to a remote area. Under such pressures, the administrator may succumb or even make common cause with those who put pressure on him in order to feather his own nest. There may be many such instances but there may yet be people who neither succumb nor compromise, who follow the straight and narrow path of public service with a sense of dedication.

**Plight**

Such an administrator may be an unknown person. His may be a thankless task and his plight may be worsened by the ruinous erosion of the real value of his salary which has made bare existence a struggle. In England, the current annual salary for a Second Permanent Secretary is about Rs. 6 lakhs.

In India it is Rs. 42,000. Even allowing for the difference in the price levels in two countries and what India can afford, this must be considered a niggardly salary.

For years together, the process of economic development and social change in India will require dedicated public service. The importance of the role of the IAS and of other civil services as participants in the task of nation-building is bound to continue, calling for ceaseless endeavour, abundant compassion and a sense of fairness and balance. The services deserve the appreciation and support of the nation.

# 12

# Role of Administrator in the Changing Environment

Before independence the role of the administrator in India was that of the servant of the imperial masters or the agent of the colonial rule. The goal of colonial administration was the perpetuation of India's status as a dependent country and administrator was to help make this possible. The general attitude of the colonial rule was that of laissez-faire vis-a-vis economic development and social change. The State was described as law and order State or police State or night watchman State. Its functions were that of revenue collection and maintenance of law and order. The police and revenue administration was established through out the country but matters like industrial and rural development were neglected. Despite this, the colonial rule did have some outstanding achievements to its credit such as establishment of universities; a network of railway and postal services; establishment of agricultural research institution like the Pusa Institute and several agricultural and engineering colleges; construction of irrigation dams and projects. Despite this there was stagnation in agricultural and industrial development. The country repeatedly suffered from droughts. There was not even one per cent growth in India's agricultural production during the first fifty years of the century. However, despite the laissez-faire approach of the State the local officers like the district collector could take initiatives on their own. This was because of the considerable freedom available to the collector as the representative of the State and as "a man on the spot" who was always supported by the administration. Developmentally inclined civil servants could, therefore, launch projects in which they were interested. Sir Malcolm Daring took initiative in the spread of cooperative movement in Punjab. Another civil servant in Gurgaon F.L. Brayne took to village development schemes in the field of health and sanitation. Lord Curzon established the Archaeology Department and many civil servants produced excellent district gazetteers and studies on tribals.

After independence the nature of the State and the scope of administration completely changed. The State came to be known as the "Welfare State" rather than the Police State and the scope of administration was emphasized as that of development rather than regulation. Economic development and social change were considered necessary from raising the level of a living of millions of people. From 1951 onwards the country embarked on series of Five Year Plans. The Directive Principles of the Constitution provided the basic parameters of economic development and social change based on liberty, equality and social justice. In the new set up the role of the civil servant was described as that of "an agent of change". Change was sought everywhere through a wide spectrum of activities such as agricultural extension, community development, promotion of cottage and small industries, construction of huge irrigation and power projects, establishment of basic industries in the public sector, abolition of uctouchability, universal primary education etc. Development was to be achieved in the framework of parliamentary democracy. Secondly, people became sovereign and the civil servant was not only accountable to a democratically elected government; he had also to be responsible and responsive to the people whom he served. He was the servant and not the ruler; and also an agent of change. He was to be "friend, philosopher and guide". This is how the village level worker was described. But that role had also to be played by other officials including the District Collector or District Magistrate who also became the District Development Officer. The number of development departments in all sectors grew both at the State and at the Central level and the civil servant had to make his contributions to the formulation of plans, policies, programmes and projects for economic development and social change. He had also to play the role in implementing the same. Thus vast opportunities were available to the civil servant in the new context.

To what extent have the civil servants been able to play the role as "agents of change?" According to some observers of the administrative scene they have not been able to play this role in a satisfactory manner. For example they were not able to elicit or enlist the participation of the people in programmes of development. This led to the establishment of Panchayati Raj institutions in the hope that they would be able to kindle the spark of the popular participation in programmes of development. It has also been pointed out that civil servants are somewhat lukewarm in implementing radical programmes like land reforms. Civil servants on their part sometime concede that they have not been able to play the role of an agent of change because of the constrains in which they have to function. Another formulation is that the change is big a process which goes far beyond what could be expected from the work of civil servants. It can be brought about by economic and social leaders rather than by civil servants. The third and probably the most important charge is that the civil servents are concerned with the promotion of their own interest and there is hardly any service motive. Let alone acting as agents of change, civil servants even do not carry out their normal duties and responsibilities and are often given to corruption. All these must be considered to be a far cry from the image of the agent of change which was conceived of at the dawn of India's freedom. Many training programmes have been launched in order to impart knowledge, develop skills and bring about attitudinal change or with a view to making the civil servants "an agent of change". Have the training programmes failed to bring about the change in attitude?

In more recent years, the emphasis has been on the role of the civil servant as a manager rather than a bureaucrat. It is said that the role of bureaucracy ill-suits the civil servant in to-day's conditions. Some academic writers have stated that the Max Weberian model of bureaucracy has to be rejected. Is this correct? Weber mentioned some characteristics of bureaucracy such as impersonal holding of office, a hierarchical system based on command, control and compliance, discharge of duties and responsibilities according to rules and procedures and prescriptions and compensation to the civil servants according to definite salary scales and not on a commission basis. In Weber's view, bureaucracy was the rational institution of the 20th century. Weber's bureaucratic model brings out the objective role of bureaucrats. It also brings out the functioning of the bureaucracy as a disciplined force. These characteristics are important for administration including development administration working within the framework of parliamentary democracy.

But it is true that these characteristics of objectivity and discipline are not enough. The civil servant requires other qualities such as empathy with the people, imaginativeness and responsiveness and modern skills and techniques of managements. But in asking for these additional qualities will it be right to throw away the baby with the bath water, that is to give up the essential attributes of objectivity and discipline?

A sharp distinction is made between the manager and bureaucrat. A bureaucrat is rule bound; he is the slave of rules. On the other hand, the manager is concerned with management techniques to achieve results rather than conform to the rules and regulations. The relevance of management techniques to public administration cannot be ignored and indeed their importance has to be recognized and administrators systematically trained as managers. But public administration is more than management. Public administration is accountable to Parliament. Public interest has to be served and has also to be seen to be served. Goals of socio economic development rather than mere commercial profitability are often the objectives of public administration projects and public enterprises. Thus public enterprises though established as public companies and supposed to be governed by purely commercial considerations cannot afford to overlook certain policies and directions of Government. Precedents have to be observed and awkward precedents cannot be created. Public administration has to be open to examination and public scrutiny. A manager in public administration has to bear all this in mind and has therefore to combine his role as manager with that of the civil servant or bureaucrat.

Indeed the model of a manager is not adequate for describing the role of an administrator. He has to have the empathy of a social worker otherwise he would not be able to win the confidence of the people to give satisfaction. He has to be a "social scientist in action" in order to understand the environment, its past, present and future, the problems arising out of that environment; the alternative solutions that are available for dealing with these problems; translation of those solutions into strategies, plans, policies and programmes, understanding of the problems of implementation, monitoring and evaluation. All this is not possible for a civil servant who merely adheres to rules nor even for a manager who concentrates wholly on profitability on commercial considerations. Thus to play a proper and an effective role; a civil servant has to be a combination of a bureaucrat, a manager, a social worker and a social scientist in action.

# 13

# Transplanting British Administrative Institutions

There was a saying that "the sun never set on the British Empire". This statement was true till almost the end of the first half of the 20th century. However, after the World War II, the countries of Asia and Africa emerged to freedom. They looked upon political freedom as an opportunity for economic development and social change, for translating the aspirations of the masses of people for a higher level of living, into a reality.

The emerging countries, however, needed suitable administration to organise the task needed for the purpose. The British had already created administrative structures in these countries. These were mainly meant for maintenance of law and order and the collection of revenue. It became necessary for these countries to refashion their administrative organisation for the realisation of the new goals.

Apart from these colonial countries, the British empire also included the self-governing territories like Australia and Canada inhabitated by migrants from the mother country. These self-governing territories evolved their own pattern of administrative organisation.

It is interesting to have a comparative picture of the administrative institutions of the mother country, those transplanted to the British colonies and those evolved by the self-governing territories. Comparisons can also be made with the French Administrative Institutions as they evolved both in France and her erstwhile empire in Africa.

The British administrative institutions were the result of "the two stage evolution" of British democracy. In the first stage the power passed from monarchy to aristocracy or landed oligarchy after Charles I was beheaded in 1658. Then over a period of time, the democracy broadened gradually through extension of franchise so as to provide a mass base needed for a modern democracy. The landed aristocrats who took over power in 1688 evolved the ethic of gentleman-amateur and created in their own image the "administrative class" to which were recruit the cream of graduates from Oxford and Cambridge. Secondly, they also allowed decentralization of administration with the local squires providing the voluntary local leaders for a British Local Government which as Prof. Wheare described was "Government by Committees". The third special feature was the administrative dominance of the Treasury which combined the functions of control over expenditure and staff management.

These British institutions were *not* transplanted into self-governing territories of Australia, and Canada. In Australia, from the very beginning there was no question of the gentleman amateur ethic which was conducive to the creation of the "administrative class". The migrants to Australia were precisely those whose background was the opposite of that of the aristocratic class. Recruitment to administration was, therefore, of young men at school leaving stage. On the other hand, the State had to undertake the task of the development of natural resources to bring about rapid economic development - a task which in Britain was left to the private entrepreneurs. The assumption of these responsibilities by the State led to the recruitment from the beginning of a large number of professionals in the Government services of Australia who dominated the administrative services; the specialists were not only drawing higher salaries; they were at the top as well as being on tap.

In Canada there was recruitment of the more qualified persons from the universities to the administrative set up. But the development of the administrative class was more on the lines of the developments of the management class in the U.S.A.

In India, the institution of the Indian Civil Service was created which in fact provided a model to the Home Civil Service in Britain. It consisted of educated elite from Cambridge and Oxford. It was based on Macaulay's dictum that those young men who showed greater capacity, talent and promise in the university would continue to show their superiority over their contemporaries in their later careers. Also excellence in examinations in subjects like literature and mathematics, subjects which are not of any relevance to administration whatsoever, would nevertheless provide the best method of testing the quality of mind which is far more important for administrative competence than feats in some narrow specialization. The I.C.S. therefore provided par excellence, example of administration by the educated elite.

However, the British did not follow the decentralization model in India. Instead, they vested considerable authority in the man on the spot i.e. District Collector. However, this was an example *not* of decentralization but of administrative deconcentration The District Officers were essentially a part and parcel of the centralized imperial administration.

On the other hand, in Africa the British introduced a different administrative model under the leadership of Lord Lugard- the model of "indirect rule". By their experience in India the British became so hostile to the educated middle class in India that they decided to rule Africa through local chiefs wherever they existed or by creating them where they did not.

Thus the different administrative structures arose in the different countries because of different historical circumstances.

After the attainment of independence, India did not give up the concept of the administrative class. The administration continued to be politically neutral. But it came more and more under the control of democratic institutions including the political executive and the parliamentary committee. In African countries, on the other hand, like Tanzania and Zambia, because of the very narrow class of educated people, the existing talent was used by them simultaneously for political and administrative management. The State appointed the political commissioners at the State and District levels. Secondly, they created "one party State". Thirdly, they removed the distinction between political management required for the mobilization of the people and administrative management required for the execution of the tasks. As a result, the Civil Services were politicized — though after experience these countries realised that there is a limit to politicization of services and indiscriminate mixing up of the task of political management and administrative management.

The differing patterns of administrative institutions in Britain, self-governing territories and the erst-while colonial countries which recently emerged to freedom cannot be explained except through historical analysis in a meaningful manner. The administrative pattern at any time is a result of historical traditions on the one hand and the challenges and demands on the newly emerging situations, on the other.

# 14

# Whither Indian Bureaucracy?

When India became independent, it decided to set up a democratic State and not a bureaucratic State. Bureaucracy was to be the instrument of democracy for the fulfilment of the national purpose viz rapid economic development and abolition of poverty. Nehru believed that a reformed bureaucracy could be the agent of socio-economic change and an instrument of transformation of the Police State into a Welfare State.

To be sure, it was a conscious departure from the role of the bureaucracy in the colonial era - the role of maintenance of law and order and collection of revenue. But it was felt that there was no other organised force except that of bureaucracy to undertake the myriad tasks of development - rural and agricultural development, industrial promotion and building up social and economic infrastructure. Whether it was designing of new schemes and programmes, setting up new organisations or even mobilizing the people to participate in the programmes, it was bureaucracy that came into the picture. This opened vastly new fields of action to the bureaucracy and gave its members a heightened and much nobler role which could give them a sense of fulfilment. The glow of this euphoria lasted for several years after independence under the leadership of the stalwarts who were at the helm of affairs.

Soon, however, this new atmosphere of the post-independence era started losing its elan. The idealistic glow of the administration of the early years began to fade. And the limits of bureaucratic action started becoming apparent.

For example rural development and poverty alleviation turned out to be tasks far too complex to be fully tackled in the bureaucratic mould or through stereotype schemes. As Gandhiji noted long back sustained and dedicated work over years was needed to bring about a transformation even in a single village community. It was unrealistic for a transferrable official to accomplish this task. The administrative effort was too dilute to make an indepth impact or to bring about a lasting change.

Bureaucratic limitation was also seen in the management of public enterprises - another new task for bureaucracy. The management of economic enterprises needed flexibility and fast decision making which was not possible within the framework of financial rules and regulations of government. The imperatives of public audit which insisted on strict conformity to these rules further tightened the straight jacket on these enterprises making them too rigid to respond to changing economic environment. Moreover, as a result of the ethos of the socialist pattern of society and the burden of social responsibility and welfare imposed on these enterprises on one hand and a multiplicity of objectives placed before them amongst which profit making appeared to assume a position of low priority. It was no wonder that their survival started depending in an increasing measure on the support of the public exchequer.

Planning and control mechanism also brought out the shortcomings of bureaucracy. Centralized planning led to centralized administrative attitudes which inhibited impulses and initiatives at state and local levels. Centralised mechanisms made private enterprise concentrate on manipulating levers of administration rather than on promoting economic efficiency and productivity which are components of real economic performance. With big public spending and powers of control, the lobbies of big business and contractors increasingly attracted the bureaucracy even at higher levels to the lures of easy money.

Degeneration set in another way also. One of the essential attributes of bureaucracy is political neutrality. As Dr. Rajendra Prasad, the first President of free India observed, "it is the business of democracy to *represent* all interests and it is the business of bureaucracy to *eliminate* all interests". The doctrine of political neutrality was intended to enable bureaucracy to work under governments of different political parties with a sense of neutrality, objectivity and impartiality. But with the same party in power for several years after independence both at the Centre and in the States, this was forgotten and bureaucratic autonomy in its own sphere was increasingly eroded-autonomy to give frank and free advice rather than a convenient advice on policy matters and to apply law and implement policies and programmes without fear or favour. I remember even Jawaharlal Nehru presiding over an annual general meeting of the IIPA taking objection to the concept of neutrality which was the title of the lead article in the Indian journal of Public Administration released on the occasion. His contention was that bureaucratic neutrality was all right during the colonial era but was not appropriate in free India where bureaucracy cannot be neutral to the welfare of the people. From this it was logical to proceed to the next step - the concept of neutral bureaucracy giving way to the new concept of "committed bureaucracy". And this is what Indira Gandhi did - and with disastrous consequences to the objective and impartial working of the bureaucracy. When politicians used to long enjoyment of seats of power started confusing public assets with private property, and public purpose with party and partisan interests, the doctrine of "committed bureaucracy" came handy to unscrupulous politicians to twist the bureaucrats at will to achieve their objectives. The essential vulnerability of bureaucracy ensured that a large majority of its members would crawl when asked to bend. Those who appeared to be reluctant to compromise could easily be marginalised if not actually penalized. Rightful claimants could be reduced to abject suppliants and thus made pliable. No wonder objectivity and impartiality became a casuality. Also *clever* politicians, in such situations, could find easy scape goats in bureaucracy for actions for which they themselves were responsible. It is notable that in post-independence India while a few members of bureaucracy have been penalized, not a single politician has met the fate of some venal politicians in a state like Singapore!

Bureaucracy lacking in objectivity and impartiality and expertise and indepth knowledge (which frequent transfers at will without any career planning cannot allow to develop) increasingly lost its capabilities to do the tasks which it was expected to discharge viz. at higher levels contributing to policy making and at the field level, competent policy and programme implementation. Bureaucracy's role was squeezed out between experts of various sorts giving convenient advice to politicians on policy matters and politicians themselves deciding who would be the beneficiaries - witness loan melas and now public funds being allotted to Members of Parliament and Members of state legisatures for distribution at will. No wonder a young IAS officer working as private secretary to a Union Minister told me sometime back that in Delhi there is a feeling that IAS is no longer needed! In the states, the officers of the State Civil Services have started questioning the supremacy of the IAS and attacking it with increasing ferocity. In this they gave the ready support of some State politicians who find the "independence" of the IAS an inconvenient obstruction in rendering "public service".

A question arises whether in the wake of privatization and politicisation, bureaucracy - neutral and development oriented-has any role to play. True privatization would mean vacation by the State of the "commanding heights" of the economy and increasing reduction of its role in direct management of the economy. But even the 'vacation' has to be an orderly process as seen in UK, whose Prime Minister, Mr. Major has offered to our government his country's expertise in divesting the State of its involvement in public enterprises. Even for orderly arrangement of disinvestment, efficient bureaucratic action is necessary. Furthermore, the need for the State setting up a proper legal, financial, social framework and a strong infrastructure for the operation of the private enterprise would continue. Years ago, Gunnar Myrdal characterised India as a "soft state", a State where laws, rules and regulations are not properly enforced. A system cannot work if the rules of the game for the working of the system are not observed by all concerned. It is for the State to see that the rules are observed. A soft state with a weak bureaucracy cannot do so.

While politicisation has gone apace in the country with the broadening of democracy, the era of monopoly of power by a single political party has come to an end. Bureaucracy need not be bonded servants of a single political party or a political personality. Civil servants can now act as servants of the nation and the government - no matter of what political party or headed by what political personalities. The political arrogance emerging out of a continuous enjoyment of political power need not any longer frighten them so long as they act according to rules, their prescribed duties and code of conduct and in public interest.

In the wake of politicisation, elective institutions and non-governmental organisations may have a greater role to play. With the 73rd amendment to the Constitution, Panchayati Raj institutions have become the third tier of the Indian polity and as many as 29 items - most of them related to local development have found a place in the local list. The NGOs have grown in number and variety and could undertake the responsibility for implementing an increasing number of programme of local development. Yet neither Panchayati Raj nor the rise of NGOs would spell the euthanasia of bureaucracy at the district level. Panchayati Raj institutions cannot function without administrative support and a good high level bureaucracy would still be needed at the local level.

The role of bureaucracy as envisaged at the dawn of freedom might have to undergo a change. But the need for a good bureaucracy at all levels continues in the interest of objective administration necessary for an orderly development of the country and its stability.

# PART II

# POLICY MAKING

# 15

# The Concept and Importance of Policy Formulation in Government

## Importance of Policy-Making

The function of policy formulation is of such critical significance in government work that it is sometimes considered to be the proper measure of the capacity to govern. Without policy, government and administration are rudderless. Successful policies make for successful government and administration. On the other hand, when the policy fails, the government fails.

## Policy Making and Other Functions of Administration

Though the function of policy-making is thus described as one of the most important functions of government and administration, it is not the only function and has to be distinguished from other functions before its own distinct character is properly understood.

## Policy Forming and Decision-Making

It is often said that administration consists of decision-making. What is the relationship between policy formulation and decision-making? Every decision is not a policy decision. Most day-to-day decisions are in respect of individual cases and are taken within the existing framework of policy. Policy decisions are also decisions but are to be distinguished from other day-to-day decisions in that the policy decisions are of general application. They have wider implications and longer time frame. They provide framework in which decisions are taken by administrators in their day-to-day work. Thus policy decisions do not lead to just a single act of administration or government but rather they support a course of action, perhaps over a long period of time. They point to a chain of causation between initial conditions and future consequences. They have a broad spectrum of consequences. They provide a sense of direction to administrative action and often affect the destinies of community at large.

**Policy Making and Planning**

Another important function of government is planning, specially in countries like India where the system of planning has been accepted for promoting economic development and growth. Like policy, planning also provides a sense of direction. Indeed, that planning should be adopted as a method of economic management is itself a policy decision. However, the plan is exhibited in the shape of various targets in different sectors of the economy and different quanta of public and private investment required to reach those targets. Allocation of resources for the investments in various sectors of the economy is considered to be at the core of planning. However, it is very rightly said that a plan needs a proper policy framework. Targets could not be reached just because investments are made. They have to be backed up by a proper policy framework. The policy framework itself would consist of an amalgam of policies in various fields - fiscal and monetary policy, taxation and banking policy, wage and price policy etc. It has been rightly stated that plans cannot succeed without a proper policy framework. Policy formulation is a phase of planning function. The basic decisions in regard to approaches, premises and strategies of the plan are policy decisions. It has been further observed that while there is a great deal of enthusiasm for greater and greater investment, there is no commensurate concern with analysis in depth to lead to proper policy formulation. In recent years, attention has been drawn sharply to this disparity between ambitious planning but careless policy formulation. If a choice has to be made between ambitious planning and careful policy formulation, it has been suggested that a choice has to be made in favour of the latter.

### Policy Formulation and Project and Programme Formulation

Policy formulation has also to be distinguished from project and programme formulation. A project represents an investment for a particular purpose - whether it be the establishment of an industrial enterprise or construction of an irrigation dam, or a power house, or the setting-up of an educational institution. Programmes are to be distinguished from projects, in that, they are not necessarily characterised by one single investment but may consist of a number of items of activity of one or several agencies. Thus, we talk of a 20 - Point Programme or a programme of distribution of hybrid and high-yielding varieties of seeds or of chemical fertilizers. The programme may contain a schedule of activities to be taken up by various institutions or individual functionaries. Projects and programmes may be the consequence of policy but neither programme nor projects in themselves constitute policies.

**Policy and goals**— Fred Riggs has noted the distinction between goals and policies. Goals are what policies aim at but do not by themselves constitute policies.

### Policy — The Function of the Highest Echelons of Government

Thus, distinguished from plans, programmes and projects, the function of policy formulation may be defined as of determining the course of action in a particular field or providing a frame of general reference for individual decisions. While the projects and programmes lie in the domain of field administration and planning could be the function of a technical organisation, policy-making has to be the function of the government proper i.e. of the highest echelons of administration.

### Who Formulates Policy ? What are the Major Sources of Governmental Policy-Making ?

It is often stated that it is for the political executive to lay down policy and for the administrative executive to carry it out. This distinction between formulation and execution of policy as well as the role of the politician and the civil servant is not always very clear-cut. The civil servants at the higher level (and this includes the technocrat and the scientist as well as administrators) do contribute to policy formulation and the politicians do take interest in the implementation of policy. However the nature of their contribution may differ. The politician in authority may be expected to be mainly concerned with the political aspects of public policy such as those related to the manifesto of the ruling party and the impact of the policy on various sections of the population or the interest groups, the civil servants may be expected to concentrate on the feasibility of the policy and its effective implementation and the organisation and management required for the purpose.

What is the role of the Parliament/Legislative Assembly vis-a-vis policy-making? The political executive is accountable to Parliament and as such Parliamentary endorsement of major policies of government may be considered to be essential. However empirical studies have shown that while Parliament/ Legislative Assembly discusses policy at even influences it, it does not initiate let alone formulate policies. One of the reasons is the lack of organisation at its disposal required for technical work involved in the formulation of policy. Even bills which are passed by the Parliament/Legislative Assembly and become law are first framed by the bureaucracy and approved by the Cabinet. Private members bills seldom become laws.

**Types of Policies - Ideological Policy**

Policies are of various types. They could be classified as ideological policies, macro-policies and sectoral policies. The ideological policies flow from the very basic character of the government itself or from the fundamental constitution of the country. Thus, the policy of laissez faire was characteristic of the early phase of the capitalism in countries like Britain. The policy emanated from the basic theories prevalent in those days such as that of Adam Smith, the author of the "Wealth of Nations" acknowledged as the first systematic treatise on economics. Adam Smith postulated that "the invisible hand" in the free market would ensure that the effort of private entrepreneurs or other economic agents in pursuit of self interest would automatically result in the common good. It followed, therefore, that the government should only provide the general framework of law and order and perform sovereign functions like those of currency and coinage and leave the economic field free for private capitalism. Hence the basic policy of laissez faire and the maxim that "that government is the best which governs the least".

On the other hand, many countries, specially the developing countries, have given up the laissez faire approach in favour of planning which arises from the concept that the State should take a major role in directing economic activity for accelerating the pace of development and for ensuring equitable distribution. Equally basic is also the policy of State ownership of the means of production. This policy is justified on many grounds including that the private ownership of all the means of production may lead to the concentration of the resources in few hands and may not lead to the use of resources for the common good. Thus, both the policies related to planning and social ownership of the means of production are highly ideological in nature.

## Macro-Economic and Development Policies

There are other general policies which may be more technological than ideological in nature. The main examples of general policy are the macro-economic policy and the development policy. The macro-economic policies and development policies have necessarily many dimensions. Thus, the macro-economic policies cover such important items as price and income policy, fiscal policy, banking policy, wage policy, and policies to regulate and promote production. The development policy may cover the entire gamut of policies to promote savings and investment, generate entrepreneurial ability, build up public sector enterprises, develop human resources and create a sense of motivation and achievement in the people.

## Sectoral Policies

Then there are the sectoral policies - the defence policy, the foreign policy, the agricultural policy and the food policy, the industrial policy, and the science and technology policy. Besides there are inter-sectoral policies like the personnel policy. Sectoral policies have often inter-sectoral implications. Thus, the defence policy is not just a question of policy for Army, Navy and Air Force; the defence policy is linked up with the domestic economic and industrial policy and with the foreign policy. If the domestic economy is strong, it can support a big defence effort. On the other hand, with a brittle economy, a strong defence has to be ruled out. Similarly, where the foreign policy creates friends rather than enemies beyond the frontiers of the country, the defence policy itself would assume a different dimension.

Within the framework of the macro-economic and sectoral policies, are policies within an organisation or an institution.

**Policies Related to Various Social Sciences**

There is another way of looking at the policy, namely, from the point of view of various social sciences. Thus, among policies with political science emphasis are the foreign policy, military policy, the electoral policy, policy regarding legislative change and reform and free speech and civil liberties policies. Policies with economic emphasis are those of economic regulation, labour policy, communication policy, taxing and spending policy and agriculture policy. Policies with sociology or psychology emphasis are the anti-poverty policy, policies regarding scheduled castes and tribes and backward sections of the society, criminal justice policy, education policy and population policy. Policies related to urban and regional planning are the land use policy, the transport policy and the environment protection policy. Policies with natural science or engineering emphasis are: technological innovation policy, health policy, energy policy and biochemical policy. With the enlargement of the sphere of State activity, the various kinds of policies are also increasing in number.

**Process of Policy Making**

How do policies originate ? There are two kinds of origins of policy. First, the policy is initiated by governments and administrations themselves on their own initiative and second, policies are initiated in response to the challenge and problems faced by government. The policies of the first type are an attempt to fulfil the promises made to the people in the manifesto on the basis of which a political party comes into power. In order to justify its very existence, the Government and administration are called upon to analyze the economic and social conditions, formulate, identify problems and issues and formulate policies. They are, in a way, a fulfillment of the inherent responsibility of Government. On the other hand, the latter type of policies arise in response to emerging problems and situations. Thus in response to rising prices, Government has come out with anti-inflationary policies. In response to increasing crime, the Government has to come up with a policy to bring down crime. Examples of adulteration which develop into a public scandal make it necessary for government to work out a tighter anti-adulteration policy. The widespread eruption of cases of bride burning compels the government to look into problems of women in the society. The crimes against the untouchables make it necessary for government to come up with a tighter anti-untouchable policy. In a way, these two processes often overlap. For example, if the government were to be aware of the problems of various sections of the society, or various aspects of the government, they themselves would come forward with the requisite policy measures by anticipating problems or being sensitive to them. It is only a government whose ethos is that of laissez faire that will wait for problems to come up. In a developing country, the government cannot afford to adopt such an attitude, and must anticipate problems. But this does not always happen. Government is not always in close touch with all sections of the society and problems do arise when not anticipated by government. Often, these problems of some sections of the society are picked up by the interest groups who articulate them through representations or even demonstrations. Many problems, though perceived and pursued in a general way, may suddenly erupt in a specific manner. Thus, while the general policy of government may be one of supporting the prices of agricultural commodities, there may be sudden fall in respect of certain commodities like onion or ginger or potatoes or minor millets like bajra which might not have come within the purview of the general policy. In such cases extension of general policies to specific cases becomes necessary.

Policies may be distinguished between long term policies and short term policies. Here again, the distinction is not clear. Long-term policies may themselves consist of a series of short-term policies.

In a large country like India, some are Central policies, some are State policies, while others are joint policies. Their relationships are mutual. The Central policies cannot succeed without the cooperation of the State and the State cannot formulate policies except within the framework of the Central policies.

Policy-making is a complex process. Policies often emerge in strikingly different ways. Policy issues and options are often not clear. Data relative to these are not always available.

### Analysis, the Basis of Policy

Policies are ad hoc or perfunctory if there is no detailed machinery to comprehensively examine facts, bring out their implications and the relationship between cause and effect, between measures and their impact. In the absence of these studies, the policies may not be based on appreciation or awareness of facts and therefore may fail. Thought and investigation must precede policy formulation if policies are to succeed. Often policies are the result of comprehensive examination by authoritative commissions and committees like the National Agriculture Commission and the Rural Credit Survey/Review Committee. However, sometimes decisions, right or wrong, may have to be taken long before analysis is even partially complete; also by the time analysis is complete, situation might have changed materially. As a result, policies may be the outcome of opportunities, sposmadic pressure or sheer chance rather than purposive analysis. In any case, analysis of various factors relating to a policy problem or situation has to be an unending process. The process of analysis and decision-making should go hand in hand. Hence, often elements of ad hocism irrationally enter into decision-making. Often policy may be the outcome of political compromise. As pointed out by Sharda Prasad, Information Adviser to Prime Minister of India in his address to Public Relations Society of India-"Policy-making is a product of ideology, attitude, national interest, class interest, national and class prejudice, and the interest of self-preservation."

### Policies and Their Implementation

Just as plans cannot fructify without the policy formulation, policies would not achieve the results without their implementation. Policies which do not take into account the capacity for implementation and enforcement are doomed to fail. The surest mark of a weak government is its failure to enforce its policies. Policies may fail because the instruments for the enforcement of that policy have not been built up. For example, it is futile to talk of nationalisation of wholesale trade in food-grains without the government building up the whole structure and machinery of procurement, storage, transport and retail distribution of foodgrains. The formulation of policy, therefore, includes the formulation of detailed steps for the implementation of these policies. These detailed steps may include providing the legal framework, devising suitable machinery of organisation and management, recruitment and training of personnel and the communication of that policy to the people or the client group and securing their cooperation.

In the analysis of public policy, the importance of policy implementation is often not taken seriously. There is an implicit assumption that once a policy has been formulated, it will automatically be implemented. The assumption may not be true particularly in the Third World countries for the following reasons. *First,* policies in the Third World countries are conceived with the basic process of nation-building. Hence while policies in the Western countries tend to be incremental in nature, in the Third World countries they tend to be ambitious, even sweeping designed to bring about development and social reform—specially in the years immediately following independence. *Secondly,* a number of factors may act as constraints in the implementation of government policy like insufficient or even wrong direction and control by political leaders, opposition to policy itself, lack of qualified personnel, incompetent bureaucracy and corruption. As a result of these constraints, implementation of policy is often half-hearted and not implemented with vigour. *Thirdly,* policies are often initiated by governments *without* consulting affected individuals and groups including political parties whose role may emerge at the implementation stage of the policy process.

In understanding the policy process, it is essential that the implementation process is also explored and evaluated. Policy makers (especially in the Third World nations) should devote more time and effort to understanding and mastering the *implementation* strategies. This will enable to minimise discrepancies in the implementation process and would also enable formulation of more effective policies. Thomas Smith has identified *four* components in the policy implementation process viz. (1) idealised policy, (2) implementing organisation,

(3) target group and (4) environmental factors.

**Monitoring Policies**

Once policies are formulated their implementation has to be effectively monitored. Often in course of implementation new facts and problems are disclosed and policies have to be reformulated.

We, in India, have evolved several policies over the last 35 years. Not all policies have been successful. For example, the industrial policy envisaged a large public sector but the public sector has not fulfilled all the expectations. The policy of regulation of industry has not succeeded but, on the other hand, led to black economy and misuse of industrial licensing. The policy for the increase in agricultural production has only partially succeeded. The policy of land reform and cooperative farming has failed because of lack of capacity to implement the policy. The policies of panchayati raj or democratic decentralization have not been successful because of lack of steady and long term political commitment. The science and technology policy, though based on the concept of self-reliance, has led to a technological gap. The educational policy has not succeeded either in elimination of illiteracy or improvement of the quality of education. There are so many areas where policy re-examination is called for.

Policy formulation and implementation is a *continuous* process. It may not have a final definite end.

**What is Policy ?**

The theory of policy-making may well begin with the definition of the term 'policy'. The term 'policy' refers to *overall programmes of action* towards a given goal as distinguished from specific government actions. The Oxford English dictionary defines policy as a *course of action* adopted or pursued, which is considered advantageous or expedient. A third definition says, "any set of recommendations about what ought to be done or what will be done when power changes hands, constitutes a policy." Policy making involves a *long series of related activities* rather than a single discrete decision. Decision-making may be a single action while a policy connotes *continuous activity and adjustment.* It is a *process* rather than a single once and for all act. While government policies often require legislation, increasingly, whether in economic planning or foreign affairs, ministries also enunciate policies and programmes which do not have sanctions of legislation to carry them out.

**Model of Policy-Making - Incrementalism**

The descriptive model of policy-making process found in the writing of Lindblom, Wildavsky and Sharkansky is widely known as *incrementalism*. It stipulates that public policy develops *incrementally*. In other words public policies this year are related to public policies last year. The best single predictor of next year's policy is this year's policy. For example, the current State government expenditures are closely tied to previous State government expenditures rather than to any socio-economic and political variables. But this does not contradict the statement that public policies this year and last year are a product of economic forces. Thus, incremental explanations do not necessarily contrast with other explanations which attribute policies to economic, social and political factors. Policy -making is both sequential and incremental. Policy-making in a large measure is a process of remedying past errors in policy. Policies may be one which seek to achieve acceptable levels of goal accomplishment rather than maximisation of results. Policy may be based on feed back information so as to make a better choice. Policy-making typically is a never ending process of successive steps. It is typically serial or sequential. A politically feasible policy may often be incremental or marginal - i.e may often be incrementally or marginally different from existing policies. This reduces the complexity of factors as well as the number of alternatives in the policy-making process. However as Peter Self points out, "Marginal incrementalism cannot cover the sudden increase in public expenditure or switches of public policy".

**Policy Innovation and Environment**

In contrast to policy incrementalism is the concept of *policy innovation*. Such policy innovations are linked to environmental conditions. Factors like urbanisation, education, wealth provide socio-economic environment conductive to policy innovation. Another factor is professionalism amongst legislators and bureaucrats. They attend national conferences, read journals, wish to build up professional reputation and thus are motivated to *translate new ideas into innovations*. Thus professionalism is related to policy innovation.

Some times it is contended that the political system and the extent of democracy are not as important as environmental resources in shaping public policies. In particular social security and welfare programmes are closely related to the levels of economic development. Public consumption expenditures are similarly related to levels of economic development though nations may differ in economic systems. It is believed that nations with representative and participative political systems are more responsive to policy decisions relating to the social and economic conditions affecting their citizens. However, this is not quite correct because it is found that in Communist nations public policies are even more responsive to the socio-economic characteristics of their populations.

### Symbolic Policy

Some policy may be described as of symbolic value. For example, Government policy towards poverty may not have any significant impact on the poor, but it will show that government cares about poverty. What governments say is as important as what governments do. Often, the chief goal of public policy is to provide catharsis for discontents rather than bring about significant changes in the prevailing patterns.

### Factors Determining Policy

There is a full range of complex forces shaping public policy. The factors which are determinants of public policy include economic, social, political, technological, cultural and historical. Amongst them are pluralistic *political variables* like voter participation and party competition, but there are *environmental variables* also reflecting the level of economic development which are sometimes more influential than the political variables. Federal grant-in-aid is a very important determinant of the State policies because it frees the States from the constraint over their resources. Economic constraints are the most important forces shaping public policy. Government institutions, administrative arrangements and political processes also determine the content of public policy.

### How do Social, Economic and Political Factors Shape the Policy?

There are two aspects of policy study. First, how are policies made and, second, what happens after the policies are made. What are the consequences of policy?

Policy analysis involves the systematic identification of the causes and consequences of public policies. Public policy *causes* may be attributed to independent variables — social, economic, technological or political. While dealing with *consequences* of public policy we deal with the policy impact. Here the policies are independent variables while social, economic and political conditions are dependent variables.

Path analysis is a technique of analysing the *causes* and *consequences* of public policy. In the path analysis relating to causes the policy is placed at the far right of the diagram and the direct and indirect *causal paths* are traced back through intermediate and independent variables in the environment conditions. In the study of *policy impact*, the impacts are placed at the far right of the diagram and policy variables are placed as intermediate variables. Policy impact are the consequence of government activity. Here policies are independent variables and society conditions are determinant variables. Path analysis thus enables to understand better both policy *determination and policy impact*. The policy impact or consequences may be intended or unintended. Planning, programming and budgeting system inaugurated during Johnson Administration is an example of extensive multi-dimensional policy impact analysis. Also, economic analysis has to find out whether policy implementation was consistent with economic policy declarations and to what extent the real goals of the policy makers have been realised. Impact may be direct or indirect, latent or manifest, intended or unintended. The policy impact analysis may proceed as follows: (1) Enactment: authoritative statement of new policy in the form of statue, ordinance, resolution, order, or judicial decisions. (2) Administrative reaction: Some bureaucratic reorganisation may have to be undertaken. This is the phase of policy implementation. (3) Primary contact between government and target population. (4) Primary impact felt by the target population. (5) Secondary impact: Groups not initially regarded as target group may be affected i.e."spillover" effect of public policy. (6) Systemic impacts. (7) Feedback. (8) Altered policy output : The cycle is completed, and a new phase begins as impacts of previous policy are feed back into the system and are converted into new outputs.

The policy has macro effects on the economic, social and political system. For example, a new foreign policy may increase the prosperity of farmers, or may have a serious inflationary effect on the economy in general.

There can be two approaches to the study of policy impact. One is to discover the various impacts of policy and the other is to find out the impact on environment of various components of policy.

All policies must be analysed together, not in isolation, because policies are interacting. Fixing on a single policy is not likely to provide a sufficient basis for appraising the total impact of governmental action on a particular environment. Impact analysis is complementary to decision-making studies.

### Policy-Making Process

The policy making process has two broad components — the rational, scientific, analytical process and the process of interaction between contending forces of political power. Wildavsky has labelled these two components as "intellectual cogitation" and "social interaction" respectively. Thus the following types of questions arise in the policy making process: To what extent do information and analysis count in the making of policy? What are the major sources of power in policy making ? In assigning policy making, what is the comparative role of constitutional and other legal rules as against the informal rules? Do ordinary citizens influence policy choices ? As a result of technical complexity of government, is the job of policy-making moving away from politician to technician ?

### Policy-Making as an Analytical Process

In the words of Wildavsky policy analysis is about the realm of rationality and responsibility where resources are related to objectives. It is about calculation and culture.

A sequence of steps or a set of inter-locking moves mentioned below may be thought to indicate the policy making process :

1. preliminary appraisal or enquiry into the problem;
2. identification of roles or objectives;
3. canvassing of possible policies to achieve the goal; and

4. choice of decision on the basis of comparison of consequences that flow from each of the alternative policies by choosing that policy with consequences most closely matching the goals.

Lasswell indicates the policy-making process as consisting of (1) intelligence and planning, (2) recommending, (3) prescribing, (4) invoking, (5) applying, (6) appraising, and (7) terminating.

According to one common formula a perfectly rational policy-maker would : (1) identify his problem; (2) clarify the goals and rank them according to the importance; (3) list all possible means or policies for achieving each goal; (4) assess all the costs and benefits that would seem to follow from each policy; and (5) select the package of goals and associated policies that would bring greatest relative benefits and the least relative disadvantages.

According to McNichols, the processes of policy formulation are as follows :

1. Analysing the situation
2. Determining basic objectives and developing plan of action
3. Organising the plans into action and setting up control measures to appraise results, and
4. Reappraising the situation — objectives, plans and controls — to reach out courses of action.

**1. Analysing the situation :** This is the fundamental process of examining of the facts and data available in a given situation. Each situation represents a complex of events at a particular point of time. Before public policy is formulated, facts, figures and data have to be collected to complete the picture. It has to be seen whether the information is sufficient to analyze the situation. If it is not, additional information has to be gathered.

**2. Selection of major problem areas and their focal point of action :** Basic objectives have to be set. Programmes of action have to be planned. Personnel and resources have to be organised, and efforts have to be directed towards the attainment of predetermined goals. Basic objectives provide a continuing guiding force for all activities.

**3. Formulating plans and strategies** : A course of action has to be chalked out to reach pre-determined goals through optimum utilization of skills and resources. The master plan has to be worked out to provide the overall blueprints or the co-ordinating factors. The plans may have to be frequently shifted or adjusted. This is according to strategy of action. Arrangement for alternative plans have to be considered. Time schedule has to be worked out and departmental plans have to be coordinated.

**4. Implementing through organisation and control** : The transition from policy making and operation to planning to executive action is accomplished through the essential step of structuring the organisation. For controlling policies and plans into action, a smoothly functioning team has to be developed out of the people within the organisation. Their activities have to be coordinated towards predetermined goals. There has to be a continuous flow of pertinent information. Efficient controls are dependent on good planning, sound administrative policies and clearly defined organisational structures. When the control system indicates significant weaknesses in the areas of objectives —political or organisational, the whole cycle of the administrative process has to be repeated and new courses of action charted to confirm the shifts and objectives and changes in plans.

The rational policy formulation process is often described as a policy cycle consisting of the following stages: (1) intelligence, including gathering, processing and assimilation of *information* by the participants in the decision-making process; (2) promotion: i.e. mobilisation of support for action, and brief prescription; (3) formulation of general goals and instrument norms; (4) invocation of the provision and characterisation with concrete situations in terms of norms; (5) application and final a characterisation; (6) termination; (7) ending of prescriptions; (8) appraisal of the task to which the policy objectives have been achieved.

Prof. Simon has explained the decision-making process as follows :

"The first phase of decision-making process is searching the environment for conditions in which the decision has been taken." This he calls the 'intelligence activity'. The second phase is the 'designed activity' consisting of inventing, developing and analysing possible courses of action. The third phase is the 'choice activity in which there is a selection of a particular course of action from those available. This involves investigation of several alternative plans offering different combinations of benefits and costs between which a choice is made. The choice aims at "maximising" or "Satisficing".

Wildavsky has summarised the attributes of policy analysis as follows : Policy analysis is *descriptive* in that it is designed to explain how a situation has come about. It is *prescriptive* in that it aims to give advice on what should be done. It is *selective* in that it is oriented to particular people. It is *objective* in that it gets people to agree on the consequences of a variety of alternatives. It is *subjective* in that it is worked out by particular people with individual interests. It is *argumentative* in that it leans towards one view rejecting another. It is *inventive*, because it represents creative juxtaposition between resources and objectives. It is *retrospective* because it involves establishing a view of the past that will justify a desired future. It is *prospective* seeking rewards of the future.

This way of stating the process, however, does not bring out the political aspects of policy-making and the strikingly different ways in which policies emerge as an outcome of political compromise amongst policy makers who do not necessarily have the problems in view but who react to occasions and opportunities.

Thus, policy-making is an extremely complex process — both analytically and politically — without any clear-cut boundaries between two elements and for which there is no beginning or end.

## Skills Required for Policy Analysis

Policy analysis requires different skills like those of administrators, economists, engineers, lawyers and persons with technical knowledge in specialised fields. A number of agencies are also involved. For example, the irrigation policy may be determined out of interaction between Ministry of Irrigation, the Ministry of Food & Agriculture, Planning Commission, the World Bank, the aid-giving countries, etc.

The policies would also be influenced by recommendations of Commissions appointed by government which systematically appraise the policy choices.

Planning involves analysis of the inter-relation of policies. Policy framework is an integral part of planning. Hence policy analysis is a part of the process of planning.

**Limits to Policy Analysis as the Basis of Policy Formulation**

There is limit to policy analysis because to make an inventory of all possible policy alternatives, to track down all possible consequences of these policy alternatives and to match the multiple consequences of each with the statement of goals is beyond the time and energy that the policy makers can afford to devote to problem solving. The policy maker will become exhausted long before the analysis is exhausted and hence analysis can never be complete for complex policy problems. The policy maker will have to take a decision long before the analysis is completed. Analysis remain forever unfinished.

Most of the society's problems are shaped by so many variables that a simple remedy for them or governmental programmes which solve the *problem* is really impossible. Often alternatives available to the policy-maker cannot be reduced to quantitative terms. Policy analysis techniques like cost-benefit analysis depend on too many arbitrary assumptions to provide an acceptable answer to policy problems. Even when policy is based on exhaustive analysis, it may run into numerous detours, delays and blind alleys. The dynamics of the policy process is such that policy is always a compromise which may be irrational. There is also the absence of *reliable scientific knowledge* about social problems. However, *reason, knowledge and analysis* are appropriate tools in consideration of policy question despite the obstacles in gathering reliable scientific knowledge. It is much better than relying on the rules of the thumb or muddling through.

The second limit to policy analysis is that policies involve elements of both facts and value. An analysis cannot verify values. Different values are in conflict with one another. It may be said that public interest would provide a criterion for the choice of values. However, even if public interest is referred to as common good, different people may have different concepts of public interest. Thirdly, not all policy makers want rational decision. They want to cling to their own beliefs.

Inspite of these limitations of policy analysis, many new tools and techniques of policy analysis have been developed. These include input-output analysis, use of computers, operational research, etc.

**Political Process of Policy Formulation**

A whole complex of factors combines and interacts in the formation of policy process. Policy is made through a complex process by which persons in power exert power or influence over each other. There is something like a policy-making ladder with the chief executive like the Prime Minister at the top and the apathetic non-voting citizen at the bottom; in-between are Prime-Minister's cabinet colleagues, legislative leaders, policy-making judges, high level administrators, interested group leaders, public opinion leaders, politically active citizens and ordinary voters. Proximate policy makers, interested group leaders, skilled practitioners of policy analysis, managerial elite, elite of wealth are all policy makers. Most citizens influence policy very little but energetic citizens can influence policy to an extent.

The *proximate policy makers* are the members of the cabinet, or government, members of parliament, and administrative officials of various kinds. In the process of policy-making, the policy makers have to cooperate with each other. All the proximate policy makers have to abide by the rules either laid down in the Constitution or otherwise. However, there could be extra legal authorities participating in policy formulation. The chief executive has often sources of administrative help outside the Cabinet, often called the "kitchen Cabinet". Money plays a big role in policy-making.

*Citizen participation* in policy making is rather thin and is confine mostly to citizens choosing their top policy makers through elections. But direct participation in policy decisions through voting is almost impossible but for a few decisions. The layman citizen has to choose amongst vague alternatives in so far as he can affect policy at all. According to Lindblom mostly the citizen vote for a good man without respect to policies. Furthermore he opines that in many traditional societies like India leadership is not sufficiently motivated to attack problems and for using public policy for positive purposes. Sometimes civil disobedience is a method of citizen participation in the play of power in policy-making.

*Parties* make competitive offers of attractive policies or policy disposalships. Because of marginal swings, voters can have a powerful influence on some specific policies. Citizens shift their vote more because of the effects of policies than because of the policies themselves. *Opposition parties* formulate coherent criticism of government policies and provide possible alternative policies for citizens. Parties provide a framework of public thinking about policy. *Interest groups* also persuade ministers and officials. It is only by reaching them that they can realise their ends. *Interest groups* are sometimes represented in Committees. Policy-making is often on group basis where organised interest groups seek a political accommodation. Only certain groups of high social and economic standing count in the policy process. Politicians assume the role of brokers among conflicting interests. Parties often act in support of particular interests or attempt to synthesise or aggregate a variety of interests into some version of the general interest. Public policy may be described broadly as a process of bargaining among leaders of public institutions and private groups. The political process has input of numerous demands frequently contradictory and inconsistent while political attitudes are often vague and ambivalent.

Policy-makers are pressurised by political groups and interested parties. Often organised interests play a defensive role. These interests have to modify their tactics if their demands appear to be inconsistent with the predominant cultural norms. Hence most of the lobbying is often done silently and not in the glare of publicity.

In government there is often a day-to-day cooperation between civil servants and the interest groups which provides a great deal of information on which policy decisions are made. The interest groups also provide a transmission belt for information.

There is a legal-institutional approach to policy formulation — the group theory approach and the elite bodies approach.

Politics is often dirty politics where politicians place their personal interests and those of the party above the so-called public interest. Parties are often boss-dominated machines and thrive upon graft and corruption. Parties are also seen as fragmented ineffective structures unable to solve public problems.

The most important policy maker in a system of Parliamentary Democracy is the *Prime Minister* while that position is held by the President in American Government. The chief executive whether the Prime Minister or the President participates at all stages in legislative and administrative policy-making through the broad formal or informal authority of that position.

It is sometimes said that in the parliamentary system of government as in Britain or India, the crucial policy decisions are taken not in the Cabinet but in the inter-departmental committees, the Cabinet Committees or in conversation between the Prime Minister and the individual Minister. Thus, it is said that the Prime Minister and not the Cabinet is the crucial element in the decision-making process. On the other hand, it is pointed out that the Prime Minister's influence on policy formulation may be exaggerated. Government business has so increased and involves so many technical and complex factors that no one man is able to survey the whole field. Policy initiatives come from many sources, not just from the Prime Minister but also from the party policy, from the recommendations of civil servants who work out schemes to suit various interest groups before the Prime Minister knows about them, from administrative necessity, from sheer pressure of events at home and abroad, and from the demands of public opinion channelled in various ways. Thus, the Prime Minister is not necessarily able to initiate the policy he or she wants, nor shape the policy as he or she desires.

Prime Minister is not often involved in the germinating stage of policy. That is why Harold Wilson expressed the view that Prime Minister should come on policy discussions at an early stage. He also attached to the Cabinet Office certain academics and civil servants, economists, scientists and technologists in order to provide him with new sources and advice. In any case, Prime Minister has to gain the support of his Cabinet to carry out his policies.

The great bulk of policy-makers are members of the staff of the individual departments with operating responsibilities. The Cabinet Secretariat is not a policy-making unit but is the centre of communication and secretarial organisation on which the smooth working of the policy-making and execution depends. In the department, the Minister receives his final advice through the permanent Secretary, who alone has an overall view of the organisation.

No policy decision is taken without consultations with the department concerned which has to be put in the picture. There has to be horizontal and vertical movement of the policy paper which is also considered by innumerable inter-departmental committees including Cabinet Committees.

In Britain, there is no strong Parliamentary committee structure comparable to the French or American and hence parliamentary influence on policy is rather limited. Certain academic and expert institutions bring to bear a disinterested approach on policies. However, in the main stream of day-to-day government the time available for thought and action in policy making of a long-term sort is rather limited. The atmosphere in which the civil servants work is hardly conductive to reflection. The civil servants have no time to think. Policy-makers are rather persons amongst a mass of persuasive and persistent influences.

The President in America has enough policy-making powers. His image is that of the great engine of democracy. He has the legal authority and extensive staff assistance which bears on his energy, and as Alexander Hamilton has stated, "energy of the executive is the leading character in the definition of the problem". President's role has expanded far beyond that described in the Constitution. The chief executive is sometimes wondering whether he ought to support policies that he thinks best or the policies that the voters want.

Most policies have to be set by legislative enactment. In American Government, Congress is the major institution for initiating and creating policy issues, second only to the President. Members of the Congress contribute actively to policy formulation through their membership of relevant functional Committees and appropriate Subcommittees. The position is not quite the same in a system of Parliamentary Democracy where the policy initiatives, legislative or otherwise, are almost always taken by the executive. Every time the legislature passes a law it legalises a statement of policy. In the American Senate policies are often talked to death.

Policy makers pursue their own versions of *wiaespread and*

*common interest* as well as *segmental or group interests.* In a parliamentary system of government, the policy-making leadership of the Cabinet is often delegated to one of the *Cabinet Committees.* All legislation in Parliament come from the Cabinet. Members of Parliament surrender policy-making authority to the Cabinet and specially to the Prime Minister, while in the American Government legislators think it essential to keep their function within their own hands.

*Administrators* play a major proximate policy-making role. Administrators can bring to bear a fair and objective outlook and nonpartisan and equitable approach on the processing of policy making, steering clear of illegitimate political pressure and in pursuit of "public interest", though the latter is often a complex and elusive notion. The elected officials often delegate policy-making to appointed officials. However the respective contribution of politicians and administrators is related to the whole system of high level government. The technical expert also in various ways is the policy maker. The complex policy-making in the modern State requires batallion of experts to carry out the work of policy formulation and execution in each specialised area of government. Rational policy-making depends on specialised expertise in multitudes of areas far above the capabilities of any one man. Administrators, therefore, increasingly depend upon various forms of expert advice. Number of policy posts are being filled up by specialists who have often direct access to Ministers.

*Judges* too make policy through their judicial pronouncement.

Independent Commissions outside the executive influence of government policy, participate in the policy-making process. Public corporations also supplement the traditional organs of government. This leads to fragmentation of the policy-making function. There are many centres of power - the chief executive, the executive administrators, the commissions, the corporations, and the parliamentary committees, private groups — who all participate in the policy-making.

There has been in recent years increased inter-dependence of the national and State Government with the massive expansion of various programmes. The Federal Government gives grant in aid to States for promotion of its policies and programmes.

Fragmentation of power scatters the policy delivery system amongst executives, administrative and judicial institutions, and further amongst the national, State and local governments. Diverse influences are brought to bear on policy-making from the social origin of men who make decisions to the ability of government officials to keep track of what is happening in their society. Policy making is often composite.

There is a need for coordination of all these. It is the chief executive who has the authority to provide central leadership required for policy coordination.

There is an organized cooperation amongst proximate policy makers. There is also an informal cooperation amongst proximate policy makers. Amongst the factors behind informal cooperation are reciprocity, bargaining and mutual adjustments.

The proximate policy makers make their policy decisions within the constraints of existing preferences but they re-construct interests in order to give a new scope for policy-making. Policy-making may involve compromise, but it is a moving compromise. Policy-making is a process of conflict and compromise which may make effective action difficult.

Policy-making is a product of the inter-actions of various participants. Many a times it emerges out of a confused inter-play so that no one can be specifically identified as an author of a policy choice. Policies may arise inspite of insufficient deliberations because of pressures. They may be inconsistent and they may reflect the irrationalities of the policy-makers themselves. Policies are often affected by indecisiveness, inconclusiveness, procrastination as well as narrowness of rules. Policy-making system, therefore, is not always thoughtful and informed. Policy-making has to cope quickly with problems and find solutions even before all facts are known. Study and thinking are expensive and time consuming. Policy makers learn through trial and error.

The sources of public policy are both popular demands and the preference of government officials. Sometimes the government responds to the public, at other times it runs contrary to public sentiments, and at still other times it governs in the midst of public apathy.

It is necessary to understand government's structures and

procedures to understand how politics shapes public policy. Robert Salisbury has hypothesized that the degree of fragmentation or integration of the decisional system has a great deal to do with the types of policy output produced by the system.

**A Balance View of Policy Formulation**

It is because of the importance of the political process and interaction in policy making that it is sometimes said that all important policy decisions are ultimately taken on political grounds and hence analysis and calculation are harmless but ineffectual pursuit. However, this is not quite correct. Policies have to be politically feasible, economically viable, administratively possible and technically sound. Hence the importance of objective analysis. Objective analysis is often influential in decision-making at the highest level. The policy makers themselves identify and formulate problems in the context of environment or opportunities and demand policy analysis, though some participants in the policy-making process may be hostile to analysis.

The play of power is not a substitute for policy analysis. Policy analysis is incorporated as an instrument of the play of power. In the process policy analysis may change its character.

Policies have to be both rational and acceptable. Political and administrative action makes them acceptable while policy analysis makes them rational. Also policies have to be capable of being operational. Thus, acceptability, rationality and feasibility are the three essential criteria of a policy.

**Policy and Ideology**

Ideology is often the basis of public policy. Marxist Leninist principles was a guidance of policy in the USSR. Democracy, liberty, pluralism and private enterprise influence American thinking about public policy.

**Uniqueness of Policy**

Each example of policy-making is unique. Every policy-making situation is likely to differ in some important respect from every other. One can never fully understand how a specific policy output has been achieved without taking into account some unique elements in the pattern of mutual adjustments through which the policy is decided.

## Policy and Administration

Policy process involves a totality of governmental institutions and levels. The policy-administration dichotomy cannot be taken seriously. The theorist who makes an orderly distinction between policy and administration,with politicians settling the broad issues and officials filling in the details is at odds with the reality. Rather policy making is conducted by a mixed group of politicians and career officials. The top professional administrators wield considerable influence on policy formulation. Indeed policy making is the chief aspect of the administrator's job. Policy and administration, though separate entities, are two inter-related parts of the same governmental process. Policy may be motivated by influence derived from values and conditioned by choices of values. Values may be the ultimate determinants of policy in that they condition the perspective of the need. But policies must be executed and here administration comes into play. Policy is set forth in broad outline by the law-makers leaving detailed execution to administrators within the limit of the discretion delegated to them.

In the modern government bureaucracy has come to be equated with administration. The function of administration is assumed to be the implementation of public policy, the making of policy being the prerogative of the sovereign representative of the people. However, bureaucracy participates in the policy-making process in many ways. Bureaucracy is the only conceivable instrument capable of formulating and implementing the policies modern government is called upon to undertake. Bureaucracy is divided in specialised departments which can develop a greater appreciation of the needs of various interests and the most appropriate means of satisfying those needs. The bureaucracy has a fair share in the implementation of public policy in public interest. One is the exercise of the rule-making authority granted by the legislature. Innumerable directives, orders and commands are issued daily from public offices each of which in some way makes or states policies. However, bureaucratic expertise is required by the political executive in reaching policy decisions. Even the legislature depends on administration for information and advice. In policy-making administrators tend to be more effective and less conscious of wielding power. The administrator also draws from time to time from his clientele group. Bureaucracy is sometimes grilled for too much policy initiative or for too much inertia, or too spirited an action or too stubborn a delay.

**Public Policy and Public Interest**

Public policy has to pursue public interests. However, there are few interests which could be assumed to be also of all the public in common. Where there is no identity of interests, public interest reduces to the majority interest. There is also the question of ethical criterion of policy. Walter Lippmann defines the public interest to be "what men would choose if they saw clearly, thought rationally, acted disinterestedly and benevolently. Public interest is an undefinable concept. It is difficult to reach the consensus on the absolutely appropriate moral principles to be applied in making policy. Even though public interest cannot be defined with precision, there is the belief that ethical norm such as public interest does exist.

**Policy and Information**

Amount of information available to policy makers is crucial to the efficiency of the policy-making process. However, policy makers of necessity have to take decisions based on the conflicting or inadequate information.

**A Model of Policy Delivery System**

Policy-making is fragmented and diverse. Policies must be delivered as well as formulated. Citizens, legislators, administrators, judges, officials at the national, state and local levels, all participate in the policy formulation and delivery.

The components of the policy delivery system are following :

1. Environment
2. Demands and resources : They carry information and materials from environment to public officials.
3. Conversion Processes : They transform demand and resources into public policies. This covers both formal structures and procedures.
4. Policies that represent the formal goals, intentions or statements of government officials.

5. The performance of policies sets actual delivery to the client. The policies and performance have an impact on the environment. It is then transmitted back to conversion process as the demands and resources at a later point of time.

**Policy Environment and Internal Characteristics**

The policy environment has three elements : ideology and values, ethical standards and institutional arrangements. The internal characteristics of public policy include : (a) power arrangements, (b) historical context, (c) individuals and their roles and impacts, (d) organisational structures, and (e) formal and informal norms of conduct and behaviour.

Goals attainment is the primary function of policy. Ecology sets forth the goals or ends which public policy must attain. Public policy is to be seen in the milieu in which it is set. Programme blend into policies and policies merge into a co-ordinated pattern that might be termed as the 'plan'. The range of *public interest as a value* has undergone expansion with corresponding increase in functions undertaken by public authorities. Ethical standards refer to actions and individuals and groups within a valuation field. *Institutional mechanism* is important because public policy has to function within the range of constitutional latitude and that of the legal system. Any public policy involves a cluster of interaction of institutional influences.

Public policies are both the products and instruments of change. Public policy is an overall social field. It has a historical dimension and follows a meandering course through time. Values and ethical system, institutional arrangements, and social dynamism are cardinal elements in the totality of public policy. Internal aspects viz., power arrangements, pattern and process of leadership and interest groups provide apparatus of policy formulation.

Individual personality factors also explain the policy like the imaginative skill of an administrator or the obstruction of a clientele group. Human action and interaction is the beginning and end of policy field.

**Institutional and Organisational Instruments**

The relation of formal structure to policy is significant. Policies are products of organisation. They involve totality of government institution. Formulation of most public policies requires professional guidance, and the dividing line between the professional guidance and policy preference may be thin.

**Relationship Between Policy-Making and Policy Analysis**

There has to be an *effective communication* between the policy analyst and the policy maker. While the policy maker is decision-oriented, the policy analyst is theory-oriented.

The policy maker places greater value on partial information available at the time of action rather than *complete scientific* knowledge acquired after the time for action is past. He is interested in the right guide to public action. On the other hand, the policy analyst seeks scientific rigour and methodological analysis. While the policy analyst is concerned with explaining the causes and consequences of public policy, the policy maker is interested in intervention. If the policy analysts explain the societal problems but do not distinguish between the causes which can be affected by the public policy and those which cannot, they fail to give the policy maker any handle for action. If policy research is to be used in policy formulation, then there should be a method of translating the results of research into the realm of reality and policy.

**Need for Holistic Perspective in Policy Formulation**

Public policies often suffer from lack of a clear holistic perspective or a systemic view. Policy formulation in a complex field is hardly possible without a comprehensive perspective. Only a cohesive systemic perspective can take care of apparently unrelatedness of policies. The absence of this may lead to the lopsided policies.

# 16

# Policy Making in India

Of the many functions of governance of any country, that of policy-making is certainly the most important. A Government is known by its policies. If the policies succeed government succeeds and if the policies fail, government fails. Policies give a sense of direction and purpose to the day today functions of government and administration.

Soon after independence, Jawaharlal Nehru was able to evolve a comprehensive framework policy in almost all the important areas of governance — political, economic, social and technological. He had given deep thought to them even before independence. He had articulated his ideology of democratic socialism which was a blending of democratic values of freedom and socialist concern for equity. This was reflected in the resolutions — many of them drafted by him—adopted at successive sessions of the Indian National Congress. Though Dr. B. R. Ambedkar was the Chairman of the Drafting Committee of the Constitution, it was Nehru who provided the ideological underpinning of the Constitution. If his concern for freedom was embodied in the chapter on fundamental rights, his commitment to equality and welfare was enshrined in the chapter on Directive Principles of the Constitution. As a Prime Minister, he had to address himself to the task of translating these ideas, concerns and commitments into policies of government.

Though Jawaharlal Nehru was an ideologue, as Prime Minister and hence the first administrator of the country, he had to temper ideology with pragmatism and adopt a cautious and balanced approach to the tasks to government. All ideologies have to be tested in the crucible of experience and those which fail this acid test undergo agonising reappraisal as is currently happening in China and the USSR.*

The task of policy making has to begin with meta-policy — the policy for identifying and prioritising policy goals and issues.

**Political Policy**

Nehru's most important policy goal was the preservation and consolidation of national unity and integrity. The deep rooted fissiparous tendencies in India in the form of communalism constituted a challenge to the attainment of this goal. Policy is a response to challenge. Nehru's response to the challenge of communalism was the policy of secularism. The policy implied that all citizens of India irrespective of their communal denomination would have equal claims on the services of the State. By the same token, all communities will have equal allegiance and loyalty to the State and the nation. Indeed in the precarious situation obtaining after partition, it went beyond this and stood for protection of minorities with a view to giving them a sense of security. In post-partition communal riots in nation's capital, Nehru personally intervened to protect the members of the minority community from the crowd fury.

However neither the concept of secularism nor the policy to promote it, was fully spelt out. No wonder severe problems cropped up in the year that followed and which have persisted in an aggravated form till today. Policy is not merely a statement of objectives, it also requires series of measures to reach the objectives. Secularism means separation of religion from politics. This concept of secularism was continuously sacrificed at the altar of communal politics. Candidates were set up having in view the communal composition of the electorate. Appointments to Cabinets and other posts in government and administration were made keeping in mind communal considerations. Dignitaries holding exalted positions in Government confused secularism with Sarva Dharma Samabhav and attended functions at religions institutions. The policy of reservation of posts not only for SC & ST (beyond the period of ten years) but also for backward classes accentuated non-secular casteist tendencies.

* USSR has since disintegrated.

Secularism in the ultimate analysis, is an attitude of mind and an attribute of social climate. The policy to promote secularism should, therefore, aim at fostering and promoting rational thinking and liberal outlook through a sustained programme of citizenship education. Unfortunately this was not attempted. To this day, we do not even have a commonly accepted statement of the content and implications of secularism. And in the meanwhile those in authority are seen using public positions, funds and authority to participate in all kinds of religious ceremonies and functions under the auspices of a burgeoning crop of religious institutions. And these are prominently displayed on State controlled TV giving wrong signals regarding State policy. True to our genius, we seem to be going back to our particularistic tendencies to identify ourselves with jati culture when secularism requires us to absorb universalistic outlook of a rational order.

**Law and Order**

With the advent of Independence, it was a stated goal of policy that the police State of colonial days would be replaced by the welfare State. The need for the police state in colonial days arose out of the alienation of the people from the foreign rule. Police was the coercive instrument of the State for keeping down the people. Since after independence Government represented the people, the need for frequent use of the police as a coercive instrument of the State, it was felt, would not arise. Nehru was opposed, in principle to give additional power to the police since he feared that they would be used to harass the people. People themselves could be organised for self protection. There would be greater use of voluntary force or home guards. However, these expectations have not borne out. Crime took new forms like smuggling, black marketing, foreign exchange, racketing and drug trafficking. A new phenomenon of criminalisation of politics emerged. Social discontent erupted out in the form of collective violence in different parts of the country. Terrorism struck in Punjab. The security of VIPs was threatened requiring special police protection. In response to new forms of crimes new types of central armed police forces came into existence. Their number increased by leaps and bounds and so also expenditure on the diversified police apparatus.

The Union Home Ministery partaking more and more the

character of a police deploying organisation has now mooted a proposal to divide the country into separate security zones, each being in charge of a central force to assist law and order authorities. The policy of converting law and order State into a welfare State has vanished into thin air and police State has come back with a vengeance. Despite proliferation of the police forces, military has often been invited to deal with civil strife. Frequent use of force has come to be described as "State violence" — a complete negation of law and order policy which Gandhi and Nehru would have liked to evolve in independent India. They laid stress on dealing with people's grievances to remove discontent, and reducing the distance between people and administration. The roots of breakdown in law and order go deep down into socio-economic situation which gives rise to simmering discontent; a chance happening provides the spark and soon it blows up into a widespread conflagration. A crisis requires massive force to tackle it but the very emergence of crisis is a product of accumulated neglect which lies at the bottom of social discontent. Under the stress of recurring crisis, rather than perhaps as a result of a well thought out policy, Government have been compelled to go on strengthening the police forces in complete reversal of policy which Nehru envisaged as the appropriate set up in a democratic State.

### Defence and Foreign Policy

What happened in respect of the internal coercive force viz., the police has also happened in respect of the external coercive force viz., the military. Mahatma Gandhi said that since independent India will be at peace with the rest of the world, she would have the smallest army imaginable.

Following the foot-steps of his master Nehru evolved the policy of peace and non-alignment so as to not involve India in the cold wars of super-powers. His defence policy was in consonance with his foreign policy. Indian army would be purely for defence purposes and would not be engaged in distant theatres of war. Nehru believed in reducing defence expenditure so as to maximise resources available for development.

Unfortunately, his policy of peace received a shattering blow with the Chinese aggression in 1962. Thereafter, India steadily built up her defence forces at great cost inevitably eroding resources available for development. With military might has grown the military mentality which thinks of India's role as the super-power and the gendarme of South Asia Region a role flatteringly suggested in US journals. And this at a time when Gorbachov had given the lead for a new detente between the super-powers. Surely India is finding herself in a false position which neither Gandhi nor Nehru would have approved and would have shown the courage to correct. But again the position seems to have been reached not so much as the product of a conscious policy design but as a result of adhoc responses to emerging situations. Time has come for a reappraisal of defence and foreign policies in steadfast pursuit of our long term goals and ideals and of course our interests.

**Economic Policy**

Both Gandhi and Nehru looked upon political freedom as an instrument of economic freedom to be gained by raising the levels of living of the masses.

While Gandhiji believed in production by masses, Nehru went in for mass production through modern industry based on modern technology. Nehru readily accepted for the Second Plan, Mahalanobian model emphasising heavy industry. But he wanted development based on equity. He believed that such development cannot be brought about through the vicissitudes of market forces; it had to be planned. Hence in the face of the opposition of his Finance Minister, John Mathai, he set up the Planning Commission. Steering clear of unbridled capitalism on one side and totalitarian socialism on the other, he preferred the third way where private, public and cooperative sectors would co-exist to pursue the goals of national planning viz., rise in standard of living of the masses of people, full employment and self reliance. However Nehru's well thought out policy approach, developed several snags in the process of implementation. First, planning brought in its wake a control mechanism which throttled the economy; second, through its losses public sector became a drag on the economy; third the pursuit of self-reliance led to preoccupation with import substitution, with attendant sheltered high cost economy and out-of-date technology; fourth and as a result of all the three, the economy could achieve a comparatively lower growth rate.

Under the pressure of circumstances and the World Bank and Aid Consortium, India was compelled to modify the past economic policies in recent years. Many industries have been delicensed and brought outside the scope of MRTP Act. The economy has been opened to investment by multi-nationals. But political compulsions seem to have prevented government from boldly coming out with a full fledged formulation of policy in all its implications. The liberalization policy has been halting, hesitant and ad hoc. Government have been reluctant to come out with a clear statement of its policy of liberalization.* Government have not shown the courage of denationalising even those losing textile mills, which no matter what investment is made to modernise them, will never be able to break even, lest it should be construed as retreat from Socialism. Nor have they been able to come out with the promised white paper on public sector enterprises lest the Government should be seen to be less than committed to the holy cow of the "public sector". Government have continued to proclaim its ideological commitment to Socialism though in UK, the home of Fabian Socialism, even the labour party has been forced to retreat from its doctrinaire position and even USSR, Eastern European Countries and China have moved in the direction of marketisation and privatisation.

In the absence of a clear cut policy based on full assessment of the consequences flowing from it, Government have often taken measures which are like leaps in the dark. Thus liberation of imports was expected to boost exports and solve the problem of balance of payments. That did not happen. The gap in the balance of payments only widened. Export led growth *a la* South Korea is possible when exports are competitive. That requires drastic increase in productivity. Sustained increase in productivity requires a series of policy measures which have not received the kind of sustained attention which they deserve.

Another area which has suffered from weak policy is that of population control. The policy of population control suffered a severe set back because of excesses during the days of emergency from which it has not recovered so far. And yet no notable increase in per capita income or improvement in quality of life is possible without attaining zero rate of population growth.

Agriculture is an area where the policy is said to have succeeded in attaining the goal of food self sufficiency. In the early years when the Grow More Food Campaign failed to

* This was written before the liberalisation policy introducing from 1991 onwards; however several statement in this paragraph are valid even today.

reach the goal partly due to recurrence of drought, short term compulsions of feeding the nation, made it inevitable to resort to food imports of the order of 17 million metric tonnes under the PL 480 Programme. However, by depressing agricultural prices it had the effect of providing a set back to the long term objective of increase in food production. It was only in the late sixties that price support operations under the auspices of the FCI combined with sizeable increase in agricultural productivity through the hybrid seed technology specially in respect of wheat that a break through was achieved. And yet the limitations of the Green Revolution became apparent in a few years. It was confined to the North West belt and has yet to spread to areas in the East; it has to cover pulses, oil seeds and lesser millets; and supposed to be neutral to scale, the Green Revolution technology is found not neutral to resources and hence as between the small and marginal farmer on one side and large farmer on the other. Further-more, droughts could provide set back to the achievements of the Green Revolution through vulnerability of agriculture to vagaries of nature, though it has apparently diminished. Yet the policy of crisis management in dealing with drought has to give way to a long term policy of draught-proof development. It has to be a part and parcel of a policy of ecology preservation and sustainable development.

The broader policy issue of balancing productive with distributive aspects of development is yet to be satisfactorily resolved. Nehru was appalled that the gains of planning have accrued to the haves rather than the have-nots. Dr. D. R. Gadgil spoke harshly against the growth of ostentatious consumption. Yet the Five Star culture has only prospered with years while stark poverty still stares in the face both in rural and urban areas. Cities have been unable to cope up with their rapidly increasing population. Indeed they have, to a large extent, become slums with abominable conditions of sanitation, water supply and housing. A comprehensive policy regarding urbanisation and spatial aspects of development has yet to be worked out. In the meanwhile black economy and related crime seem to have cast their dark shadow over national life distorting not only the economy but also debasing social values. Expert groups have brought out at least in broad outline the dimensions of the black economy but there is no comprehensive policy to curb and ultimately eliminate the black economy.

In the meanwhile, human development sector—health, education and housing and infrastructure sector specially public transport and roads continue to suffer from inadequacy of resources. The new education policy was ushered in with great fanfare but its implementation was thwarted by insufficient budgetary allocations. The housing policy has the laudable objective of shelter for all by the end of the century but does not indicate precisely the resources and materials needed and how these could be provided. Same is true of the goal of "health for all". While we bemoan the rapid increase in private vehicles like two wheelers, public transport for mass transit is woefully inadequate while roads and highways are much below mark. We seem to be unable to provide adequate resources for these essentials.

Policies are not just wishes or declarations of objectives. They have to be "implementable" and should indicate the availability of resources, organisation and personnel, allocation of responsibility and time table for implementation.

For resolving competing claims for mounting expenditure on defence and different sectors of development like agriculture, industry, social services and infrastructure, a clear cut long term fiscal policy is required for raising of resources and regulation of expenditure. A policy document was issued but hardly followed up, resulting in whopping deficit and an extraordinary situation where capital resources had to be drawn upon to meet revenue deficits.

A basic policy issue extending over the entire gamut of political, economic and social problems is that relating to centralisation and decentralisation. Nehru stood for cooperative federalism, panchayati raj, cooperation and planning at local levels. Though he stood for a strong Centre in the interest of unity and stability of Indian polity, he also wanted States to be autonomous and Governors to function not as agents of the Centre but constitutional authorities above the arena of partisan politics. Though he understood that planning necessarily implies Centralisation, he wanted participative, democratic planning. This was in strong contrast to the system in China with a strong centralised State. However, frequent imposition of President's rule on the basis of less than impartial recommendations of Governors, proliferation of central agencies and centrally sponsored schemes, reduction of panchayati raj institutions to a state of suspended animation, and district planning proving a non-starter – all put paid to progress towards decentralisation.

Thus, policy making in India has suffered from many deficiencies—lack of clarity of goals and precise definition of objectives, inability to resolve the antinomy between the short-term and the long term, resort to ad hoc measures under the pressure of circumstances and lobbies of pressure groups, failure to think through policy, taking into account direct as well as indirect consequences, lack of implementability because of failure to provide the underpinning of resources, organisation and personnel, absence of coordination of policies in one area with another and sub-policies with over-all overriding policies and sheer absence of policies or policy gaps in respect of major problems and challenges crying for attention. Policies inevitably are a political process and a product of interaction between contending forces. But sound policies can only be a product of rational, analytical, cogitational process if they have to deal satisfactorily with problems and challenge of today and tomorrow and become an effective instrument of transforming the given environment into the preferred environment. Then alone will policies be objective not subjective or populist, integrated not fragmented, long term not short-term or ad hoc.

Is there any place in the machinery of government where this latter process is carried on? Any place where there is requisite competence and sustained concentration? The policies are supported to be approved by the cabinet. The policy papers are submitted to the Cabinet by individual-ministries and departments. Though Cabinet is a place where policies are approved, it is hardly a place for their in-depth consideration. The latter may be expected to be provided by the individual ministries and departments which submit policy papers for consideration. Looking at the working of the White Hall, the Fulton Committee in UK felt that the permanent secretaries of the departments and their deputies and assistants were so much preoccupied with day to day administration that they had hardly the time or the inclination to address to policy matters. The position in India is no different. Fulton recommended that every department should have a technocrat secretary (apart from the administrative secretary) who should be solely concerned with long term policy aspects. This particular recommendation was never given effect to may be because of the opposition of bureaucracy but also may be because in the very nature of the case, policy formulation can never be divorced from the day to day issues and indeed often arises out of them. Here is, therefore, a first rate dilemma in policy making—policy making cannot be divorced from day to day considerations but cannot be done effectively if allowed to be submerged by them.

An alternative to Fulton proposal is the appointment of a special officer to assist the Secretary and Ministry in policy making. This has been attempted in India by creation of a special post of Joint Secretary on an experimental basis in the Departments of Home and Agriculture. However, it is doubtful whether this has served the purpose. Policy making in these major departments is too complex a process to be tackled by a single officer of limited experience. No wonder the Joint Secretary has become a senior assistant to the Minister who could assign specific tasks to him—may be some related to policy making. A better alternative would be the constitution of a small policy group in every department comprising of top administrators who should keep a close watch on emerging policy issues, the on-going impact of existing policies and the new policy formulation that becomes necessary. But members of this group should not be bogged down in daily chores but must have enough time and freshness of mind to bring to bear on policy issues.

There is another limitation to the departmental formulation of policy. In the very nature of the case the department would be formulating policy from its own perspective rather than from the perspective of Government as a whole. No doubt the rules of business require that the policy paper should incorporate the comments of all the departments concerned. But this hardly satisfies the requirement of a holistic perspective on policy issues. Only the Cabinet can have such a holistic perspective. But the Cabinet does not often have the time or the inclination to work on policies in depth. Often the agenda of the Cabinet is over loaded and on the top of it current happenings needing urgent attention take away the time and attention of the Cabinet. To take the load of the Cabinet, Cabinet

Committees are constituted such as CCPA (Cabinet Committee on Political Affairs) and CCEA (Cabinet Committee on Economic Affairs). For specific purposes, GOMs (Groups of Ministers) are constituted when policy matters of complex character are for consideration. But like Cabinet, Cabinet Committee & GOMs need expert assistance. In the present set up, this is provided by Committees of Secretaries (COS) though we do not have a systematic tie up between Cabinet/Cabinet Committee and COS as in Tanzania. But the COS suffers from the same handicap as the Cabinet itself. The Secretaries participating in meetings of COS have neither the time nor the expertise for indepth examination of policy issues.

General Sundarji in his Leslie Sawhnay lecture stated that the "core group" of secretaries (a special COS) without adequate secretariat support is unable to deal with policy problems. This lacuna in defence policy making to which General Sundarji has drawn attention is after all a special case of the general lack of satisfactory policy making mechanism in our governmental and administrative set up.

The one device which we have extensively used is the appointment of expert committee/committees. But often for political or other reasons, the reports of the Committee gather dust in the shelves of secretariat. Often secretaries find it difficult to find time to go through these fat tomes and must depend on summaries prepared by the subordinates which while formally correct may miss the essence of the rationale and spirit behind the recommendations. However the Committees are occasional while the work of policy-making is continuous.

A recent phenomenon especially in the USA, is the emergence of "think tanks" in various areas of administration which can offer expert policy analysis and suggest fresh policy formulations. Apart from the fact that such "think tanks" are available only to a limited extent in India, a major handicap is that we have not as yet established a tradition of government agencies drawing on the analysis and recommendations of the "think tanks" since the former tend to think policy making as their exclusive preserve in which outsiders cannot be allowed to intrude and more so because most of these matters are labelled as "confidential" and "top secret". For a think tank or for that matter for even a governmental agency to make any contribution to policy- making, it should have an access to what Yehzhel Dror has called the CMG — Central Mind of Government. In every governmental set up the CMG has to be identified. In our set up, it is easily identified with the PM himself and with those to whom 'policy window' is open for the exercise of their "policy entrepreneurship".

We have an expert agency in the Planning Commission which at least in the economic sphere of governmental activity can provide sustained attention to policy issues. But as has been noticed, the Planning Commission's pre-occupation with allocation of plan resources and the routine exercise of annual plan making tend to get the better of the function of policy making. The connection between plan and non-plan activities like the Defence and Police is, of course, beyond the ken of the Planning Commission.

The inadequacies of the Planning Commission in the field of policy-making can be made up by another agency viz. PM's Group of Economic Advisers. But while it has offered some policy recommendations, it does not seem to have been brought into the policy-making process on a regular basis.

An agency which can assist the Cabinet in policy making is the Cabinet Secretariat. But as at present constituted, the Secretariat is not designed to provide substantive assistance in policy making. In the main it is designed to service the meetings of the Cabinet and its committees and the COS. In the U.K., Edward Heath, identifying the need of policy assistance in an expert manner, constituted the Central Policy Review Staff (CPRS). But Margaret Thatcher who supplanted him, finding little use for such agency, gave short shrift to it.

Another summit agency is the Prime Minister's Office (PMO). Though it has grown in size and contains some officers with considerable expertise, it can hardly provide sustained attention to all that is involved in policy making, though it has the unique advantage of access to CMG.

Thus, it is that the most important function of Government viz. policy making often gets most neglected. Perhaps some thing like Heath's CPRS located in the Cabinet Secretariat could provide the right mechanism for policy analysis and appraisal and fresh policy initiatives. But its utility, in the ultimate analysis, depends on the CMG — its willingness, inclination and ability to absorb policy advice.

# 17

# Policy Making in India—Three Case Studies

Policy making is the most important function of Government and yet in India, especially in recent years, it has been most shoddily performed. No wonder the desired results are not attained, problems are not properly tackled and the nation suffers.

Policy is an instrument of transformation of a given environment into a preferred environment. Problems arise out of the environment—political, social, economic and technological but it also the resources needed to provide solutions. It is the function of a policy to precisely identify the problems, prioritise them, formulate alternative approaches and solutions, to make a choice among these alternatives on the basis of comprehensive analysis of benefits and costs, to articulate the choice in terms of goals expressed in quantitative terms, clear out, to provide organisation, personnel and resources to ensure an effective implementation of the policy, and to lay down a mechanism for a continuous monitoring of the policy and finally for its evaluation so that after a period of time the policy could be reformulated. This is the proper 'policy path'. But some steps in this path are missed and the policy stumbles.

A policy in a sector is a part of the framework of a main policy applicable to the entire system—economic, social and political. The policy statement should bring out the relations between the sectoral policy and the main-policy. At the same time, a sectoral policy has to broken down into a number of sub-sectors and the relations between the sub-sectors and the sector as a whole have also to be brought out. The main policy, the sectoral policy and the sub-sectoral policy have to be a consistent whole.

Recently, the Government has issued drafts of three policies-agricultural policy, technological policy and the national policy on education—1986 with modifications undertaken in 1992. How far do they satisfy the criteria of a policy identified above?

## Agricultural Policy

The agriculture policy resolution is indiscriminate in the use of the terms, "objective", "challenges" and "problems". It mentions as objective of policy allround (wrongly spelt as 'alround') "development and economic viability including horticulture, livestock, fisheries and sericulture", "(increasing agricultural production and productivity to ensure food security for the rising population" as one of the major *challenges,* and "under employment, unemployment and malnutrition" as *problems.* No quantification of development production, productivity, unemployment, underemployment and malnutrition has been attempted or even broadly indicated. Nor is the inherent relationship between these brought one.

For realising the stated *goals,* for meeting the *challenges* and for solving *problems,* the policy has to indicate a series of inter-connected *measures.* Developing untapped potential, upgrading land and efficient management of water resources, supply of improved seeds, implements, machinery, credit and other critical inputs and promotion of scientific research and technology transfer through training and extension are all included in the "shopping list" of *challenges* though these are all *means* for facing the challenges. These measures for augmenting suppliers of critical *inputs* and building of basic infrastructure have to be supplemented by measures on the *output* side viz. development of post-harvest technology, increasing processing, marketing and storage and improving terms of trade in favour of agriculture. Policy in relation to each one of these measure has also to be clearly worked in relation to some precisely qualified objectives. This has not been done.

Agricultural diversification and promotion of horticulture, fisheries, dairy, live stock, poultry, bee-keeping, sericulture have all been mentioned but no detailed policy statement in respect of each of these sectors is forthcoming.

For operationalising various measures, the policy document expects the effort of governmental agencies to be supplemented by cooperatives, local institutions of farmers and non-governmental organisations but their roles are not precisely defined.

As a result of all these shortcomings, the policy statement appears vogue and lacking in focus precision and cohesion. It does not indicate how precise goals can be accomplished through precise measures. Nor does it indicate how the policy is a departure from the past. No wonder, it looks like old wine in old bottle".

Almost as an after thought the document states that "sustainable agricultural economy" requires a *new* policy *re*-orientation. But not enough thinking seems to have gone into this new reorientation and is not reflected in the policy document.

Agriculture is a multi-dimensional subject and a policy statement on such a subject should appropriately take the form of one basic statement containing an *integrated framework* supplemented by sub-policy statements relating to each *sub-sector* and each of the major set of measures.

**Technology Policy**

The same lack of conceptual precision as to the objectives and vagueness about measures to reach the objectives characterizes the draft Technology Policy.

In the absence of clear-cut goals, the policy refers to various concepts of technology which it simultaneously seeks to promote viz. (1) state of art technology, critical technology, technology of upgraded traditional skills, domestic technology and foreign technology. It is not clear wether all these technologies are supposed to coexist. The reference to various kinds of technologies without a meaningful statement of their respective role reflects confusion in the minds of the policy makers. The concept of 'appropriate technology" no where figures in the draft policy statement though it was sheet -anchor of the policy of technological self-reliance followed by the country, so far. But we are giving a go-by to the policy of technological self-reliance, consequent to the new economic policy of globalisation.

Various institutions are responsible for various dimensions

of technology development, absorption and dissemination. The role of these institutions in relation to the various dimensions has not been clearly brought out in the draft policy. The policy is right in laying emphasis on the links between R and D institutions, national laboratories, universities and other academic institutions, technology ministries and industries. But it is necessary to go beyond a general statement to bring out more concretely the needed inter-linking. In particular the policy does not bring out the present status and the future role of the universities in the field of science and technology.

**The Education Policy**

The policy runs into fifty pages but hardly leaves any impact on the reader nor does it give any confidence that it will rectify the accumulated ills of our educational system. It begins with a pompous statement that "education in India stands at the cross roads today" but does not explain what these cross roads are and how we have reached them. It does not begin with a critical analysis of the present educational environment and the problems it is riddled with but simply makes a pronouncement regarding the need for a radical reconstruction of the educational system for national integration and national progress, all-round development-material are spiritual cultivation of moral values, closer relation to life and improving quality of education at all stages, with greater attention to science and technology. These ideas, with some variations (left unexplained) are strewn throughout the policy document but hardly even concretised or operationalised and therefore remain vague and mere pious sentiments.

The policy deals with all the stages of the educational system in the pre-primary, primary, the secondary, the higher secondary, the undergraduate and the post-graduate—besides adult literacy, non-formal education, vocational education and distance education but is weak on the inter-linkages between these various stages and components of education. Thus the policy document remains a loose and amorphous statement.

It talks of education as a means of development of manpower for different levels of the economy and yet talks of delinking degrees from jobs. It should rather have talked of degrees which are a terminal recognition of knowledge and skills imparted through suitable educational courses.

The policy statement inspite of its prolixity skirts the major issues of our educational system. One of them is that while the educational system has undergone phenomenal quantitative expansion, it has been accompanied by rapid qualitative deterioration. Some reputed educationists have said that today the teachers do not teach and the students do not study. Secondly, there is the pervading problem of lack of discipline which is probably the major reason for deterioration in quality. The educational scene has become a free for all with power sections and profit managers entering the educational system driving out all those who stand for idealism and high standard of education. Strikes, demonstrations, mass copying, intimidation of invigilators, false mark-sheets and degree have all become rampant. Thirdly, the educational system, more especially the system of higher education has become the victim of resources crunch. We have set-up an education system which we are unable to maintain in a good shape. The irrelevancies of a policy document which evades such major issues is all too apparent.

# 18

# Jawaharlal Nehru and Public Administration

Jawaharlal Nehru was a multifaceted personality with many splendoured life. He was a foremost freedom fighter - the right hand of Mahatma Gandhi and his chosen heir. He was a politician and a statesman of the highest order. He was a scholar and a renowned author. He was a thinker and an intellectual; but he was also a superb administrator. While a lot has been written about the other aspects of Jawaharlal Nehru, not much has been written about Jawaharlal Nehru as administrator. It is his own letters to the Chief Ministers which bring out clearly the portrait of Jawaharlal Nehru the administrator.

## Nehru's Letters to Chief Ministers

After he assumed the office of the Prime Minister of India, Nehru became the first administrator of the country and continued to remain so for a long period of 17 years. The letters to the Chief Ministers clearly bring out Nehrus' general direction and approach to administration, the objective at which it was aimed, the basic considerations which governed it, its philosophy and principles, the major policies both internal and external that he laid down—political, economic, social and technological and the manner in which he tried to build new institutions and tradition of public administration.

## Nehru's Dedication to India's Progress : Two Basic Objectives

Nehru's sole concern was India's progress. He was dedicated

"to the great tasks that had fallen to the lot of our generation" and allowed himself no rest till the tasks were accomplished. These tasks centred round two basic objectives. First, the stabilization of the India polity and second, economic progress. Immediately after independence, the first objective was all important. After the political integration of India was accomplished under the firm leadership of Sardar Patel, Nehru could breathe a sigh of relief and feel free to concentrate on the long-term objective of economic progress.

**Mahatma's Ideals**

He wanted his administration to uphold the ideals and principles which Mahatma Gandhi placed before the nation, and follow his "moral and ethical approach to problems". "The essentials of Gandhi's teaching" he wrote are "clear enough and appear to me to be clearer day by day". One of them was the idea of self reliance. "It is well to remember that the lesson the father of the nation taught us was to rely on ourselves and not to look too much to others for help. The strength of a nation comes from within not from without. It is relying on ourselves that we achieve success". Another lesson learnt from Mahatma Gandhi was adherence to truth and non-violence.

**Right Policies and Right Means**

As a follower of Mahatma Gandhi, Jawaharlal Nehru was as much concerned with means as with ends. "We must follow the right path and not imagine that a narrow opportunism of the moment can possibly benefit us. In the end, a nation gains both prestige and success by adhering to the right policy even though it may not bring immediate result. India has built up a reputation for right and impartial conduct chiefly because of Mahatma Gandhi's magnificent personality and the emphasis he always laid on right means; that was not merely a moral precept, but a wise and expedient policy. In the days of difficulty ahead of us, we should try to remember the teaching of the master and not allow ourselves to be led astray by momentary passion."

**High Standards**

Following Gandhiji's ideals Nehru desired that both in

national and international conduct, India should live upto high standards. Nehru was keen that in public affairs only the highest standards must be maintained and even bonafide errors could not be tolerated. That is why Nehru accepted the resignation of his first Finance Minister Shri Shanmukham Chetty as a sequel to the strong exception taken in Parliament to the Government's withdrawal of the Income Tax cases against some industrialists. Later, when another of his Finance Minister Shri T.T. Krishnammachari was indicted by Justice M.C. Chagla in Mundhra case he had also to leave. These examples show that though he regretted the departure of able colleagues, he trusted that these incidents would indicate to all concerned our desire to maintain high standards in public life. "In public interest it is better not to slacken or gloss over error even if individuals occasionally suffered."

In the same spirit of maintaining high standards in public life Nehru suggested to Chief Ministers that financial patronage at their disposal in regard to licences and contracts should not go to any individual whose record in regard to payment of Income Tax had been bad.

Nehru regretted a general weakening of the moral fibre. He thought that corruption and nepotism are but manifestations of a general phenomenon. He regretted "that a great urge that carried us forward during the past quarter of the century based on a sense of duty and willingness to sacrifice for a cause is not visible except in few individuals". That was in his letter of 4th June 1949 less than two years after the attainment of independence.

### Broad Outlook : No Single Pattern

Nehru stood for a wider vision and a broad outlook. In dealing with India's problems he wanted vision, broad mindedness, large hearted tolerance and human understanding keeping in view the various customs, habits, cultures and ways of living in India. "This wonderful country of ours has infinite variety and there is absolutely no reason why we should try to regiment it after a single pattern. We should recognize fully and encourage the rich variety of India's life and culture." He wanted people to remember that India was a composite country-composite in many ways in religion, in custom, in languages, in ways of life etc. "India can hold together and make progress if we practice wide tolerance and understanding of the vast number of people who inhabit of our great country." But he saw basic unity in India's rich variety and diversity. Through constant tours he kept himself in touch with different parts of India from Kashmir to Kerala and North East to Maharashtra and emotionally identified himself with people living in these areas.

### Eagle Eye on the Administrative Scene

As the topmost administrator of the country Jawaharlal Nehru kept an eagle eye on the national and international situation, analysed the changing environment, identified emerging problems and challenges both external and internal, worked out appropriate responses and solutions, initiated appropriate policies, programmes, institutions and procedures and evaluated their effectiveness.

### Balance Between Idealism and Realism

Though, Jawaharlal Nehru was considered to be an idealist, his approach to problems was always cautious, realistic, balanced and practical. He would not decide without verifying all the consequences. He tried to find a middle way between "too much caution and too much risk." He balanced idealism with realism. "A narrowly realistic approach trying to avoid all possible risks is probably in the final analysis the least realistic of all. On the other hand, the idealistic approach by itself leads nowhere or rather frustration in the end. Risks have to be taken but they have to measured risks - Great things can never be achieved by methods of counting house and the cautious approach of men who lack daring." His was a practical approach concerned with results. In the ultimate analysis, "the world was not be governed by theories but by actual results achieved." While a country is influenced by its ideological approach, ultimately it is the practical consideration of consequences that will prevail. "The problems of today in India or elsewhere cannot be solved by some purely academic approach or by a dogmatic creed of yesterday." For example, though land reforms were part of his leftist ideology and he wanted States to take speedy steps to introduce land reforms, he cautioned them that the resources needed for compensation should be taken into account in determining the pace of land reforms. Similarly, while he was aware that prohibition was a part of Gandhi's constructive programme, he cautioned the States about loss of revenue. In choosing the national anthem, while he was fully aware of the sentimental attachment to 'Vande Mataram' as a song of freedom, he went for 'Jana Gana Mana' because it could be set to tune better and would receive greater appreciation on ceremonial occasions in India and abroad. Though he was convinced about the special role that India could play in world affairs, he was aware of the limitations imposed by India's military and economic strength as compared with that of the world powers. "We refrain from condemning much that we dislike." He showed great patience in dealing with the problem of liberation of Pondicherry and Goa.

**Adaptation to Changing World**

He was aware that in changing world, policies would have to be adapted to the changing situations and environment. "We have to be wide awake all the time and responsive to new trends, new forces, new ideas, new developments. Blind doctrinaire approach would not serve the purpose. In a rapidly changing world, nothing is more dangerous than the static state of mind and complacency." Nehru tried to balance the compulsion of short term situation with the requirement of long termview. While laying down long term policies, he adapted them to changing situations. While choosing the alternative approaches, he balanced the short term with the longterm consideration.

**Open Windows**

Like Mahatma Gandhi, he believed in keeping the windows of his mind open and letting in the breeze of fresh ideas. It was he, who initiated the practice of consulting the economists and other interests before formulating the budgets. He always welcomed meeting foreign visitors and getting their assessment, though he would not always accept their recommendations. Thus, he invited Dr. Trone and Dr. Bettleheim on Planning and Economic Coordination, Dr. Boyd Orr on increasing food production and Paul Appleby on administrative reforms. He was prepared to learn from the experience of other countries. He personally visited a number of countries and recorded detailed notes on what India could learn from different countries. "Nearly all of them are far more developed than India - working hard, building and constructing their country." He was greatly impressed by the manner in which West Germany and Japan rose like Phoenix bird out of the ashes of destruction left by the Second World War. He attributed their economic progress as well as of other European countries like Sweden and Switzerland to hard work, discipline, use of scientific methods and higher industrial and agricultural techniques. He was impressed by the manner in which manpower was harnessed in China for great production schemes. He took keen interest on the Soviet techniques of planning as also of countries like Yugoslavia which till recently were industrially backward and mainly agricultural countries. In understanding the situation in different countries he was objective in his assessment; he tried to avoid extreme likes and dislikes since these, "coloured our visions."

### Importance of Communication

Nehru's letters to Chief Ministers showed how much importance he attached to communication in administration. Despite his heavy responsibilities as Prime Minister, he maintained the flow of his fortnightly letters and shared his thoughts and experiences with the Chief Ministers. He expected the Chief Ministers, in turn to keep him informed of development within their States and did not hesitate to remonstrate to those who failed to do so. He considered that this two way communication was essential for keeping in "personal touch" with each other and developing a "union of minds".

### Centre-State Cooperation

Behind this system of communication was Nehru's concept that the success of the Indian Federal system depends on close cooperation between the Centre and the State. Nehru was personally responsible for providing basic thinking to India's constitution when it was framed and one of the basic ideas was that of cooperative federalism which implied that Centre-State cooperation was *sine qua non* for fulfillment of the national purpose. "If we are to go ahead with our planning in a big way, a certain measure of coordination is necessary." This was particularly important in areas like food and agriculture where States had to play a major role in increasing food production and procurement of surplus food.

Nehru wanted each State to realise that the Government of India was not partial to any State and thought of India as a whole. "India has to pull together and advance as a whole and not in bits and patches." Though each State naturally would think of itself, it has to appreciate problems and difficulties of other States. His was a cooperative approach between the Centre and the State governments. "It is always our desire to remove any feelings of unfair treatment."

**Public Cooperation**

Equally important in Nehru's outlook on administration was the role of public cooperation. He wanted the public to havé a sense of partnership in the great task of building up the new India. "Without active assistance and cooperation of the people" he felt "we can solve no major problems." "Great human achievements are always the result of combined efforts in which numerous people take part." "The success of development projects," he wrote to the Chief Ministers, "does not depend on governmental effort alone but more on the cooperation offered from the people and new atmosphere of cooperative and enthusiastic efforts." He, therefore, considered it absolutely important to raise the psychological morale of the people. He considered the human factor as extremely important for the success of programmes of governments. "It is men and women who create the necessities of life." Nehru often regretted that barriers between people and government were increasing and the 'flaming enthusiasm' among the people which was common in pre-independence days was very much missing in the years after independence.

**Administrative Reform**

Nehru attached great importance to improvement of administrative system and building of administrative machinery for discharging the new tasks of government. He believed that while administration during the British days was efficient for discharging limited tasks of colonial government, it was not suited to democracy and development of the post-independence India. "We have to change the whole tone of administration and give it different objectives." He, therefore, called on the services of several individuals to report on India's administrative system and make recommendations for improvement in administration. Among these individuals were Gopalswami Ayyangar, A.D. Gorwala and Paul Appelby. The recommendations of Ayyangar study led to reorganisation of the machinery of Central Government. It was on his recommendation that the system of cabinet committees was instituted. He commended the Gorwala Committee report to the State governments. He greatly appreciated the recommendations of Paul Appleby and himself recorded a long note on the Appleby Report. Five years after the recommendations, he recorded yet another major note on the subject.

He totally agreed with Dr. Appleby regarding the necessity of change on the whole outlook and methods of our administrative apparatus. "We have worked too much in the ruts and carried on old traditions which have little significance today. If we are to work for a welfare state, the whole of our administrative system has to work differently. It has to fit in with democratic and development urges. It must effectively deal with different economic and social problems and achieve results rapidly."

He felt that administration should be run as an organic whole and not compartmentalised. The different department of government should pull together. There should be national concensus on broad policies between the Centre and the State. There should be balance between centralization and decentralisation.

He felt that there was far too much of administrative proliferation after independence. The administrative machinery should not expand further so that it would not become unwieldy.

He desired continuous study of public administration, in order to throw up suggestions for continuous improvement in administration; that is why he readily accepted Paul Appleby's suggestion to set up the Indian Institute of Public Administration and remained its president till his death.

He felt that attention should be focussed on major issues so that too much time was not spent on small matters. "We must look at basic problems and not lose ourselves in a maze of detail or petty reforms which do not touch the main problems. We must be clear about priorities and as to what comes first."

He felt that the administration system was cumbersome and slow moving. Administrative responsibility was diffused and there was lack of accountability. Rules of procedures baulk action by creating innumerable traps. Far too many clearances were required leading to delay. He, therefore, suggested tightening up of procedures and delegation of financial and administrative powers and elimination of repeated notings on files and unnecessary examination that they entailed so as to lead to quick decisions and speedy implementation. He noted that development projects were delayed because of inadequacies of investigation before starting projects, cumbersome procedure of land acquisition, and delays in sanction. On completion of projects, there was delay in utilisation of benefits.

He thought that the system of chaprasis was a relic of colonial times and should be replaced by messengers.

In the area of personnel administration he wanted various reforms, the most important of which was giving importance to merit and eliminating class status and rank consciousness. He wanted greater contact between officers at various levels and an interchange between the Centre and the State so that the officers at the Centre would not lose touch with field administration. He wanted officers to keep abreast of modern thinking by reading books. It was in this context that he laid emphasis on training. But he was against officials going abroad for training. "It is more important that they should know conditions in India", since techniques and methods learnt there may not be applicable in India.

Nehru was keenly aware that "what our government are doing today will set the tone for future administration in India." He deprecated political interference in administration. "MLAs", he categorically told the Chief Ministers, "have no business to interfere with local administration."

Nehru reminded the CMS that "whatever course we adopt, we shall be judged by results." "The government of country", he wrote, "does not merely consists in issuing orders from high office but rather in reaching the minds and hearts of masses of people. Living in our ivory towers of government offices and dealing impersonally with files and papers, we are apt to forget that behind these files and papers lie human beings. Administration should earn the goodwil of the people since without it, Government cannot carry through any policy."

Having dealt with the general features of Nehru's approach to administration, we may now turn to his policies in specific areas.

**Political Policies : First Priority - Unity and Stability**

Nehru firmly believed that stabilization of Indian polity was imperative for the survival of India as a Democracy. First priority had to be given to unity, strength and stability of India. He noted that in most countries of Asia, politics has become a succession of coupd'e'tat and repeated changes of Government. Without stability, no sustained development is possible. "Our democracy is a tender plant which has to he nourished against numerous disruptive and fissiparous tendencies. In order to go ahead with the primary problems of India's economic ills, it is necessary to put an end to communal and separatist tendencies." He did not want India to "think in terms of some smaller group or the other, at the expense of the larger community." It is because of his leadership in formative years, that India stood out for her "orderly political and evolution organised attempts to bring about economic progress."

**Secular Approach : Anti-Dote to Communalism**

Nehru felt that threat to the Indian polity came from communal and religious forces. "Religion was exploited to break up our unity and now language, which should be binding ennobling factor is working in the same way. Caste remains to separate us and encourage narrow groupings... We have yet to develop a unified nation." He was determined that communalism is essentially a primitive and uncivilised type of thought and behaviour and if we are to advance, we have to get rid of this completely. Nehru's answer to communalism was administration with a secular approach. He desired that Hindus, Muslims, Sikhs, Christians and Parsis, all should feel that they are as good citizens of India as anyone else and have the same rights and previleges. While Muslim and Sikh communalism threatened the unity of the nation, even greater threat came from communalism of the majority community. Nehru felt that communalism of the RSS and Hindu Mahasabha resembled fascist forces. Nehru tried his utmost to create a sense of confidence among the minority communities. He felt that the majority community viz. the Hindus owed a duty to the minority to produce a sense of absolute security in the minds of Muslims and other minorities. His policy towards minorities was clear. "We are pledged to protect them and give them their full rights. We must honour that pledge." He wanted minorities to be properly represented in services-whether defence, police or civil.

In the early years of Independence, migrations of Hindus from East Bengal to West Bengal and Muslims from Uttar Pradesh to West Pakistan was indicative of a sense of insecurity amongst the minorities. In spite of the fact that Pakistan was out and out a religious State, Nehru believed that India should remain a secular State not only on grounds of humanism but also in the interest of political stability.

### Sikh Communalism

Nehru deeply regretted that inspite of the patriotic role of the Sikhs in the history of India, they often allowed themselves to be misled by rabidly communal leadership like that of Master Tara Singh who, Nehru felt, adopted the same approach as that of M.A. Jinnah and delivered irresponsible incendiary speeches demanding a separate land for Sikhs. Nehru had, therefore, reluctantly to put him behind the bars. The forces that triumphed in SGPC were intensely communal. Nehru was prophetic when he uttered the caution that if Sikh Communalism was not checked "there would be trouble for them and for us."

### Christianity

Nehru noted that there was a hangover of the old prejudice against Christian missions and missionaries. While missionaries have sometimes behaved objectionably from the political point of view, they have done great service to India in social fields and continue to give their service. They have often devoted their lives to people in tribal areas. They should not, therefore, be subjected to harassment or discriminatory treatment. That would be consistent with "Our policy of religious neutrality." He reminded the Chief Ministers that "Christianity is a religion of large numbers of people in India and came to India 2000 years ago."

### Civil Liberties vs Repressive Measures

Another threat to political stability came from the communists who in the years after independence resorted to disorder and violence. Various State governments introduced Preventive Detention Laws to deal with these elements. Nehru was not in favour of curtailment of civil liberties through harsh repressive measures. "To us who preach civil liberties on a thousand occasions, any suppression is painful. Repressive legislations has a bad odour about it and create a wrong mentality both in government and the people." And yet he persuaded himself to introduce Preventive Detention Bill in Parliament since he felt that rather than having varying State laws on the subject, it would be far better to have a carefully thought out piece of Central legislation which would bring uniformity in all the States. Such an Act was in his opinion necessary to deal with anti-social elements, black-marketeers, espionage and gang of dacoits supported by big jagirdars as in Saurashtra. Some varieties of communists indulging in violence - throwing bombs, killing people and looting had also to be dealt with under this law.

### Law and Order

Nehru considered law and order as an integrated all India problem. Law and order had to be maintained not by using repressive machinery but by evoking public support. A government which has to rely on shooting frequently ceases to command respect of the people. While police are essential to meet with any challenge to the State, "it is even more necessary to have a positive policy to remove grievances and keep in touch with the people." He did not favour more power to be given to police officers because they are likely to be misused. He laid down the convention that in every major case of firing, there should be a proper enquiry apart from the departmental enquiry."

He felt that preventive measures taken before the occurrence of an event or an incidence could greatly help in maintenance of law and order.

For such anticipatory action, Nehru felt important that country's intelligence services should be properly organised. He felt dissatisfied that "our Intelligence tells us only that there are rumours - not who the originators are."

Resort to agitational approach and collective violence to press demands, which pose severe challenge to the machinery of law and order and which have became such a common feature of public life, made their appearance even in Nehru's early years as Prime Minister. After the decision was taken to establish Andhra Pradesh, on a 'small issue' like Bellary taluk, rails were uprooted, trains stopped and attempts made to force the hands of Government in making its decision. A proposal for some change in educational system in Madras led to violent demonstrations and stoppage of trains. In Calcutta, increase in train fares by an anna led to violent disorders. On independence day students at Ranchi demanded that the flag unfurled by the Governor be flown at half mast in memory of those killed in police firings in Bihar. Even in the peaceful and disciplined State of Gujarat nurtured by Gandhiji and Sardar Patel rioting raised its ugly head and was followed in some places by police firing and death. That was on the issue of formation of Mahagujarat and against the decision about the composite State of Bombay. A proposal to appoint a Commissioner for North East Frontier Agency was construed as a diabolical move in Assam leading to lot of excitement. Nehru felt that such reactions betrayed "immaturity and certain continuing tendency towards disintegration" which ill becomes a nation. In a democracy "controversial issues should be decided after full discussion by some kind of majority opinion through representative precesses and not decided in the streets by bludgeoning people and comitting arson." But Nehru did not want the government to respond to violence with violence. If we do so, we play into the hands of those who want trouble and we widen the gap between the government and the people.

### Linguism

Nehru conceded that the demand for rectification of provincial boundaries on linguistic basis was a perfectly legitimate a demand which must claim attention, but he was reluctant to concede it soon after independence because he felt that arguments about new provinces give rise to strong passions. "This business of linguistic provinces is like pandora's box. We do not encourage this trouble when we have to face major problems all over India and the world." Eventually, however, in the face of persistent demand backed by strong feeling amongst the people he had to yield to these pressures starting with Andhra Pradesh.

In course of the debate in Parliament on Andhra Bill, members demanded immediate formation of Kannada, Marathi and Punjabi speaking States, disintegration of Hyderabad and "Chopping and cutting up India all over the place." These demands Nehru considered as an inherent tendency towards disintegration, but decided to appoint a high power commission to consider reorganisation of States and to consider the subject "from its all India aspect, keeping in view all the factors such as linguistic, cultural, economic, administrative, defence and security." However he was anxious that the linguistic conflicts should cease and with that in view suggested that primary education should be given to every child in the mother fongue. The state should run primary schools in a variety of languages. He did not like 'narrow and ungenerous attitude towards Urdu - a language of India which has enriched Indian culture and thought.' He wanted to be "absolutely fair to every language and give it freedom to growth." He laid down the following principles in this respect : (1) decisions regarding use of Hindi as a national language will be largely by consent and not imposed by majority over minority (2) every language should be given full scope and (3) in services nothing should be done which puts a person from a non-Hindi area at a disadvantage. At the same time he felt humiliating to adopt a foreign language like English as the official all India language.

**Provincialism**

Responding to the suggestion that army units should be raised provincially, Nehru felt that "we have enough provincialism as it is" and should not encourage separatist tendencies. Indian Army cannot be a collection of provincial armies. We should rise above provincial and linguistic urges and desires and consider the problems of India as a whole."

**Press Freedom**

Nehru felt sad about irresponsible journalism and unworthy newspapers publishing false statements and making scurrilous propaganda which often led to inflaming popular passions and flaring up of the communal situation or public disturbance.

Nehru's advice to the CMs was to get the cooperation of the press in dealing with communal situation through informal chats. He did not favour curtailment of press freedom. And yet when newspapers writing amounted to Something approaching blackmail he felt the need for taking legal action. "We must have fresh legislation to deal with the spread of communal hatred by newspapers."

**Media and Development**

Nehru was keen that Information Departments of Central and State Governments and Film Division should cooperate in putting about numerous development activities going all over the country-great works like Damoder Valley, Bhakra Nangal and Hirakud as well as community projects and numerous small projects built by voluntary labours.

**Relationship with Judiciary**

Nehru always upheld the independence of the judiciary. When it struck down preventive detention legislation in the name of civil liberties on one hand and land reform legislation in the name of constitutional provision of compensation for property at the market rate on the other, he introduced constitutional amendments. "The executive and the judiciary" he wrote, "have to pull together even though they function separately and independently. While courts have the rights to interpret the constitution and we must accept and honour their decisions, the wider social policy of the country must be determined by Parliament and State Legislature."

**Appointment and Role of Governors**

Governors, according to Nehru, should be eminent men and women whose talent and experience should be utilised by State government before coming to final decisions. The role of the Governor was to help smooth over difficulties. Being above party, he can help bring people together and remove frictions between groups and individuals in government or assembly.

**Government and Parliament**

Nehru never forgot for a moment that in a system of Parliamentary Democracy government is accountable to

Parliament. He attached great importance to the work of Parliament and made it a point to remain present on all important occasions. He desired that the debates in Parliament should be characterised by restraint and dignity and was pained when an element of vulgarity sometimes crept in. "Delaying and obstructive tactics hampered the work of legislature; democratic functioning depends on the spirit of give and take."

**General Elections**

Nehru was keen that the first general election should be held soon after the Constitution was adopted. He wanted Ministers to so regulate their tour arrangements during election times as to avoid any criticism that Ministers are misusing their official position. For him, the importance of election lay in the Constitution of a strong capable democratic government. "Elections in a democratic country are important but far more important is the spirit of the country, ideals which we proclaim, the faith and hard work which we put in for their realisation, the standard of behaviour that we maintain and the minds and hearts of the growing generation."

**Appointment of Ministers**

He emphasized that Ministers should be appointed on grounds of necessity only and on merit and not to please this group or that. Junior Ministers could be appointed to gain experience in administrative work.

**Cabinet System**

Nehru attached great importance to the working of the Cabinet as a team and to the practice of frequent consultations, formally or informally with colleagues.

**Foreign Policy : Non-Alignment**

Nehru was the architect of Indian policy of peace, friendship and non-alignment. Non-alignment did not mean a passive neutral role in world affairs nor the creation of a third bloc. It meant an active and positive policy in pursuit of peace and cooperation. It was enshrined in Panchasheel or Five Principles which have been repeated and confirmed on various occasions during Nehru's times and long after he left the scene, thereby indicating the rightness of his policy. His outlook in formulating that policy was not that of any moral superiority. It was rather born out of his desire to keep India out of entanglements with the power politics of the super powers and their cold war so that the country could be left in peace to pursue the goals of economic progress and social change. He wanted to maintain friendly relationship with all the countries of the world more especially with the border states. His policy was of "avoidance of war in settlements of disputes since modern war does not solve any problems." He wanted to help, "as far as we can in the ending of colonialism and imperialism or any other form of domination by one country over another" and put an end to racial inequality. He was opposed to the involvement of the Asian countries in the military alliances like SEATO and M.E.D.O. sponsored by USA and UK "who continued to think far too much in terms of military power and bases." This policy Nehru was keen to point out had grown "out of our natural way of thinking with its roots in the long past" and he was not prepared to give it up under pressure from super powers.

India could not pursue such an indifferent policy without self-reliance. He was aware that whenever a country depends upon another for aid, a certain obligation comes in and a certain involuntary dependance. "If we are wide awake, we can avoid that risk." He realised that the strength of our foreign policy depends on our domestic progress.

Nehru consciously moved away from the position where "as a result of past history and circumstances, India's contacts were chiefly with the Western world." The medium of English language greatly contributed to this. Nehru tried to correct the position and develop closer contacts with the neighbouring countries. He gradually developed contacts with USSR and China, both India's neighbours with whom "in the long run, we are bound to have greater dealings." The visit of Soviet leaders Bulgarin and Krushcheve to India for nineteen days in 1955 not only brought India and USSR together but proved to be an event of "first class world importance."

**Pakistan**

With Pakistan he wanted to have extremely cordial relationship and solve mutual problems in a cooperative way. However, his efforts were frustrated by the war like postures of Pakistan over Kashmir issue. Nehru repeatedly assured that Pakistan need not be afraid of any aggression from India. He hoped that the issue would be solved through the good offices of United Nations but in that he was thoroughly disappointed thanks to the attitude of UK and USA who wanted to build up Pakistan as "the centre of Islamic block" so as to subserve their Middle Eastern policy. Declaration of Pakistan as an Islamic Republic by Pakistan Constituent Assembly on 2nd November 1953 and Pakistan's acceptance of military aid from U.S. indicated "the vast difference between our outlook in India and dominant outlook in Pakistan." Inspite of these tensions and political conflict, Nehru was successful in forming the Nehru-Liaquat Pact regarding the treatment of minorities and settling canal water dispute. He was deeply aware of the "fundamental commonness of our people with people of Pakistan." He wanted India and Pakistan to live in friendly cooperation so as to concentrate energies on nation building activities.

**Nepal**

Nehru felt that a country like Nepal, "although weak is more important to us in the long run than some distant country, however big and powerful it might be."

The political and economic situation in Nepal was extremely fragile and the country very backward. Nehru was keen to scrupulously keep out of interference in the domestic situation in Nepal or take any big brotherly attitude. However, he did help the process of transition from autocratic Rana rule to a more democratic regime under king Tribhuvan. Accepting the full independence of Nepal, India did not claim some of the rights that Britain had exercised. But it was clear to Nehru that "India had a special position in Nepal and their foreign policies had to be in line with each other." He entered into treaties of friendship,trade and commerce with Nepal despite the tendency on the part of the Nepal government "to be somewhat discourteous to us and not to follow our advice."

**Ceylon (Sri Lanka)**

Nehru felt that culturally and historically Ceylon was almost a part of India. Because of Buddha, the Sinhalese look up to India as their holy land. But Nehru was sensitive to Ceylon's latent fear of the 'big giant of a country overlooking them." He did not want to say or do anything which would add to Ceylon's fear complex. "Ceylon is like a little brother to us and it seems most unbecoming that we should take any steps which might estrange the people of that country". He took the position that "India had no clear right to claim citizenship for people of Indian origin there since they were not Indian nationals."

**Burma**

His relationship with Burma and her Prime Minister Thakin Nu were extremely cordial.

**China and Tibet**

Nehru noted points of similarity between India and China-enormous population and economic backwardness. "How the Chinese overcome backwardness, industrialize their country and produce more wealth and distribute it more evenly, is of great interest to us."

Nehru correctly assessed the emergence of a strong centralised regime in China under communist rule as of great moment to Asia and the world. He took lead in admitting China to United Nations even though it earned him hostility of United States. He wanted to maintain friendly relationship with China and cooperate as far as possible. "Two great countries of China and India should understand each other." The relationship between these two great countries of Asia was one of the factors on which future of Asia depends. It is an irony of history that while under Nixon, USA developed friendly relationship with China with a view to set her up as counter force against USSR, India was a victim of Chinese aggression in 1962. The Chinese attack was a great shock to Nehru who confessed that he was 'out of touch with reality.' But Nehru's understanding of the situation was quite hard headed. "There was always some uncertainty in my mind as to what Chinese Government would do."

From the very beginning Nehru realised that "Tibet was no longer secure." "It was clear that China would establish its sovereignty over Tibet. This has been China's policy for hundred of years and now that a strong Chinese State has been formed, this policy would inevitably be given effect to. We could not stop it in any way." He tried to persuade China to deal with Tibet as an autonomous people though under Chinese suzeranity. Chou En Lai agreed to do so assuring that China has no desire whatever to interfere with Tibet's customs or ways of life. Nehru was deeply disappointed when rudely brushing aside his friendly advice, China invaded Tibet and kept it under subjugation. He consoled himself by saying that "our efforts somewhat delayed Chinese invasion of Tibet." He concentrated on one point— "that Mac Mohan Line is our firm frontier with Tibet" and said so on the floor of Parliament and in his discussions with Premier Chou En Lai. In 1962, China violated this line.

### Indonesia and Asian Solidarity

Nehru gave great support to the cause of liberation of Indonesia whose leaders became his close friends. He noted that Indonesia had a background of ancient and highly developed civilization intimately connected with India. He convened the Asian conference in support of independence of Indonesia. This marked India's solidarity with countries in Asia. He played a leading role in the Asian-African Conference at Bandung, Indonesia which met for seven days from 18 to 24 April, 1955. While eager to cooperate with countries in Asia, Nehru made clear that there was no question of India's leadership of Asia, though her policies and pronouncements often represented the wishes of vast numbers of people in other Asian countries.

### Indians in Neighbouring Countries

Nehru was attentive to the cause of Indians in neighbouring countries like Burma, Ceylon and Malaysia, though, he advised Indians to be loyal to the country of their residence and live in full cooperation with the people of the country.

### Africa

With the countries of Africa, India under Nehru developed friendly relationship. He vehemently opposed racialism in South Africa. He correctly predicated that changes would take place fairly rapidly in the whole continent of Africa. "The big question for the future is whether problems of Africa will be solved peacefully and cooperatively or will result in terrific racial wars and blood baths."

### Commonwealth

It was a success of Nehru's practical approach that India could be a member of Commonwealth even though proclaimed as Sovereign Democratic Republic.

### Open Diplomacy

Under Nehru, India pursued the path of open diplomacy. Not for Nehru to indulge in secret negotiations or under hand dealings of diplomacy.

### India's Peace Keeping Role

Under Nehru's leadership, India played an important role in the United Nations Organization in dealing with different problems and removing deadlocks. Nehru was happy that in practical demonstration of India's policy of pursuit of peace and avoidance of war, India was entrusted by UN a peacekeeping mediatory role in Korea, and membership of the International Supervisory Commission for Indochina. Dr. Homi Bhabha of India chaired the UN conference on the peaceful uses of atomic energy. Even Bertrand Russell appreciated India's peace-making role. "In this situation in which nations march open eyed towards disaster but do not see how to stop, the neutrals can play a great part and among neutrals India can be the leader." Nehru was happy that "the prestige of India was high and large numbers of people in all parts of the world looked up to India as a nation working for peace for which they craved."

### Foreign Service and Missions

Nehru took great care in setting up foreign missions, in appointment of Ambassadors and building up the Foreign Service. He selected an eminent philosopher like Dr. Radhakrishnan to be India's Ambassador to Russia. When India started opening missions abroad there was a tendency to attach more importance to European capitals but gradually reflecting India's interests, Nehru set up first class embassies with experienced diplomats in Pakistan, Cairo, Nepal, Burma and Indonesia apart from the four in London, Washington, Moscow and Peking. In order to keep embassies in touch with thinking in New Delhi, Nehru held meetings of heads of missions. "Our Ambassadors and Ministers abroad, even though in constant touch with us by letter and telegram, tend to become isolated.

We at HQ also tend to take a partial view. Therefore, to meet together and discuss fully the important problems that confront us is helpful for both."

### Defence Policy

Nehru's defence policy was consistent with his foreign policy of developing friendly relationship with all countries. "Our defence apparatus is meant only for home defence and not for activities in distant theatres of war." He was opposed to the growth of military mentality or outlook in India. He kept a vigilant eye on defence expenditure ('a measurable dent on expenditure can only come from defence') without sacrificing the capability of defence forces, so as to release resources to meet growing demand of development schemes. "Few things have pained me so much as to spend large sums of money on the apparatus of defence." Nehru rightly held that "defence does not consist of merely uniformed men marching with guns; it consists of adequate resources, industrial background and high morale amongst people. The strength of the nation depends far more on its economic and industrial development than on arms purchases abroad. Ultimately our strength lies in our unity of purpose, firm determination and the progress we make." Unfortunately Nehru's expectation that India's friendly relation will make it unnecessary for her to build up a big military machine was shattered when China inflicted a humiliating defeat on India in 1962. That was a big set back to Nehru's Defence Policy which though rational unfortunately proved unrealistic.

### Economic Policy

For Nehru political democracy was an instrument of economic democracy. "If poverty and low standards continue, then democracy, for all its ideals, ceases to be a liberating force. It must, therefore, aim continuously at eradication of poverty and unemployment."

### Food and Agriculture

Nehru constantly reviewed the economic situation of the country which in the early years after independence was none too good. The legacy of war was one of shortages of food grains and other essential commodities and constant trend of price inflation. The situation was worsened by recurrence of droughts and floods in several parts of the country. Shortages led to hoarding and profiteering. Under Gandhiji's advice, the war time system of control was dismantled to eliminate corruption and black marketing but decontrol led only to ominous rise in prices and the policy of decontrol had to be reversed and tighter control reintroduced with Preventive Detention Law against the hoarders. As regards food subsidy, he felt that though it could give some temporary relief, it might be disastrous in the long run. Nehru laid great emphasis on strengthening food administration in charge of procurement, storage, rationing and controls. He also pleaded for avoidance of waste, change in food habits, use of subsidiary foods like sweet potatoes, tapioca and banana, not consuming polished rice and growing vegetable and foodgrains in the compounds.

Nehru realised that in the short run there was no alternative to import of food from all corners of the world to prevent scarcity and starvation. But the experience proved frustrating and even humiliating with US Congress taking its own time in approving the proposal of US Executive to send two million tonnes of foodgrains to India. Nehru, therefore, felt that "dependence on relief from outside will not help....We have ultimately to depend on ourselves and the first thing is to have adequate food production."

**Grow More Food**

The only real solution according to Nehru to meet the food crisis was to concentrate national effort on the Grow More Food campaign which to his disappointment did not show adequate results. "Our food production per acre is terribly low and can be increased greatly." He started constantly monitoring the progress of GMF campaign. He found that the very first hurdle was lack of statistical data. A proper statistical machinery had to be instituted. He set up the CSO-Central Statistical Organization and supported the Indian Statistical Institute which pioneered sample surveys to provide accurate information. Also a Census of land holdings was undertaken on a quinquennial basis. For simplification of statistical work he took a lead in introducing the metric system which "like the zero symbol originated in India."

Nehru accorded priority to agricultural development. For

him, "sound agricultural system was the basis of industrial advance." It was "the keystone of planning." He initiated a number of schemes and programmes for boosting agricultural production like crop competitions, promoting Japanese method of paddy cultivation etc. These did help to increase agricultural production and productivity. Nehru wanted that increase in agricultural production had to be brought about not just by increasing area under cultivation but by raising agricultural productivity. For this he initiated the policy of announcement of fair prices and price support to foodgrains as also the system of organised supply of agricultural inputs and credit to farmers. Hence the importance he attached to the establishment of network of village cooperatives all over the country. He wanted cooperation to be part of development. "Cooperative should be non-official and develop people's capacity. It should not be just credit giving institution but something with life and spirit in it." The village multipurpose cooperative together with Panchayat and the school should be the "foundation of democracy and self reliant growth." "We should lead ultimately to cooperative commonwealth." The cooperative approach had to be extended to cooperative farming as well. Since he considered it "essential both from economic and social points of view." At his initiative the Congress passed a resolution in favour of cooperative farming. Unfortunately, the atmosphere was not in favour of the revolutionary change and the experiment of cooperative farming failed.

**Policy and Implementation**

Following the recommendations of Boyd Orr, Nehru started laying emphasis on filling the implementation gap. "Many of our policies are excellent but the real snag lies in implementing them. Somehow or the other they lose themselves in some places between the policy forming authority and the man in the field. Unless he is brought into the picture and made actively to cooperate, results will be limited." Nehru also emphasized the need for unity of purpose between the provinces and the centre in this vital matter. He appointed Shri R.K. Patil, as Commissioner, Food Production, to energise GMF campaign.

**Development Projects**

Nehru thought of a number of development projects to increase India's agricultural production. One such initiative was the starting of the Community Development and National Extension Service Projects all over the country on the model of Albert Mayer's Etawah project and S.K. Dey's Nilokheri project. He wanted these project to spread the gospel of selfhelp and cooperation and play a special part in increasing agricultural production through intensive cultivation. It should reach down to the village and indeed to each family. There should be closest possible integration of community projects and national extension service with States' agricultural development scheme.

Nehru promoted irrigation projects like Bhakra Nangal and DVC, Thermal Power Stations like Bokaro, Reclamation Projects as in Tarai and Dairy projects like the Array colony which he called the temples of modern India. He was delighted at the discovery of underground water in Rajputana which he felt could be harnessed to halt desertification. He thought that simple agricultural machinery as in Japan could be introduced with advantage. He wanted that such machinery be manufactured in India. He preferred use of organic manure and composts to chemical fertilizers. Nehru felt happy as the development schemes and projects progressed. He saw India with her great vitality going ahead with constructive work. With some experiences of development, he started feeling that we should "concentrate in future on small schemes spread all over the country." He hoped that the policy of land reforms apart from removing the burden on the actual tiller would spread income from land more evenly among the peasantry, thus giving them more purchasing power.

## Land Reforms

Nehru attached great importance to land reforms. "It has been our declared policy that all intermediaries should go and the peasant who tills the land himself should become the proprietor of his patch." It came as a shock to him that taking advantage of the loopholes in Law, the landlords resorted to eviction of tenants. "Even now people hold many hundreds of acres of land, sometimes even a thousand acres or more. This result is not what we had looked forward to." Nehru looked beyond abolition of the Zamindari System which was only the first stage. The next stage in Land reforms is to have ceilings and cooperatives.

**People's Agencies**

Nehru underlined the role of voluntary agencies and workers in the success of development projects. He encouraged the activities of Bharat Sevak Samaj. He gave great support to the development of PR institutions. "Let them make mistakes" he said but they would learn. He felt that the village panchayat, the cooperative and the school should be the basic institutions in every village and cooperative activities should be universal in rural areas. He wanted to convulse India with cooperation.

**Coordinated Administration**

Nehru felt that the departments of food and agriculture are so closely related that they should be brought together and so important that they should work under the personal direction of Chief Minister.

As Nehru grappled with problems of agricultural and rural development exacerbated by droughts and floods he realised that the basic problems in rural areas was lack of purchasing power, underemployment and undernourishment and thought of a large scale works programme to create the purchasing power in rural areas.

**Industrial Policy Resolution**

Nehru believed that the country would not progress without industrialisation. "In order to put an end to unemployment we have to develop our industry–heavy, light and cottage industry— in a very big way." The industrial growth required the support of infrastructure—power, steel, skilled manpower. He commended Japanese model of rapid industrialisation. But he desired a balanced approach to industrial and agricultural development. He wanted cottage industries to be made efficient by application of scientific methods. He set up All India Handloom and Handicrafts Boards and Khadi and Village Industries Commission to promote cottage industries. Nehru was the architect of the Industrial Policy Resolution which embodied the concept of a mixed economy with the public sector occupying commanding heights. "We look forward to the progressive growth of the public sector and developing a socialist pattern. The basic industries should be more and more under State ownership or control." The existing industries need not be nationalized.

The available resources could better be utilised for setting up new plants to be owned by the State. Capitalism would not have an unbridled sway since it leads to concentration of resources in few hands. Therefore, some measure of Central control over industries was essential. Nehru was greatly pleased by his visits to the newly set up public enterprises like Sindri Fertilizer Factory, Chittaranjan Locomotive Works, Bharat Electronics. Unfortunately the performance of public sector in later years did not fulfil Nehru's expectations.

### Railways

Nehru was aware that the country would not progress without sound infrastructure. Railways constituted an important part of it. War times had taken a heavy toll of the Railway system which was badly run down. Nehru entrusted Railways to the efficient hands of Gopalswami Ayyangar and was largely successful in restoring Railways to health and strength.

### Housing

Nehru was worried about tremendous housing difficulties in big cities. "Large number of people are living in miserable hovels which were a disgrace to our country." He was exasperated by the spread of slums in the cities and said that they better be burnt down. Since bricks, cement, iron and steel were expensive and in short supply, he encouraged the approach of large scale manufacturing of pre-fabricated structures so that cheap or low cost housing on a large scale could be provided expeditiously to the teeming millions in clean environment with the necessary sanitary facilities. Nehru wanted prohibition of luxury construction and cinema houses so that essential housing was not starved of building material. He disfavoured expensive schemes with good deal of money spent on expensive structures without giving thought to the social services that go with them.

### Planning and Controlled Economy

As Nehru started grappling with various economic problems before the nation, he keenly felt that there should be a coordinated approach to policies in different sectors of the economy. With this in view, in the first few years he set up Economic Committee of the Cabinet, a committee of economists and statisticians and the office of the economic advisor and statistical advisor. He believed that the coordinated approach could be developed only through planning. He was himself the Chairman of the National Planning Committee appointed by Congress before independence. Dr. Trone's view further encouraged him to think in the direction of planning. He was convinced that the planning must be comprehensive and the Planning Authority should deal with the whole of India though the plan execution should be left to the provincial governments. That is how the Planning Commission was conceived and born. Nehru gave great importance to the work of Planning Commission in building up new India. He presided over its activities and felt happy when the first Five Year Plan was formulated. For the Second Plan, he adopted the Mahalanobian model with stress on heavy industry without which "We can never make India a modern, prosperous and strong nation." But it also provided for wide spread organisation of village industries without which "we shall not be able to go far in providing employment."

He looked upon the Plan as a "mighty cooperative effort of all the people of India." Though planning had to begin at the top, the smallest units, viz. village, must be involved in evolving the Plan.

In Nehru's concept of planned economy, there was scope for the operation of the free market and the private sector but within the framework of the control at strategic points. Petty controls need to be removed. He thought planning in a democratic society inevitably implied some kind of a mixed economy. He believed in the ideal of the welfare state—which meant productive gainful employment for all and removal of grave disparities in income and standard of living.

Nehru requested the Chief Ministers to constitute planning agencies on smaller scale at the State level, so that planning activity could be carried out in coordinated manner at the Central and State levels.

Nehru believed in democratic process of planning. He conceived of planning in the widest sense of the term aiming at the advancement of human welfare not only in terms of raising the standard of living but also promotion of cultural, spiritual and human side of life. For him planning was not only a "a question of allotting priorities" but a 'coordinated view of the Indian scene and basic policies and objectives." He wanted vast majority of people to know about Plans and asked simple pamphlets in Hindi on Plan to be made available to them and to every school so that teachers could read them to the classes. He also suggested making documentary films on development projects which could leave a visual impact.

**Environment**

Even in the early days of planned development, Nehru underlined the importance of protection of environment. "We want both to exploit as well as conserve our natural resources. Sometimes desire to exploit them outruns discretion and we forget the part of conservation. There is a certain interdependence between man and environment and any upsetting factor may bring about harmful consequences. If trees are cut down and forests removed, then this might affect the rainfall and even convert a fertile area into a desert."

**Labour**

"Labour must be treated with all friendliness. We have to aim at cooperative action for production. While real difficulties of labour should be attended to, attempts to cause disruption and chaos to gain political advantage must be resolutely opposed."

Nehru was greatly worried by irresponsible strikes by workers in Railways and Textile mills. He did not like to ban strikes or to curtail legetimate trade union activity, but he wanted trade union leaders to be more responsible so that they do not cause loss to the national economy. Nehru's attitude to labour was very sympathetic. "We have to deal with labour in a spirit of frankness as well as equality. If we carry in our minds some relic of old ideas about the working classes being some kind of inferior grade citizens who trouble us from time to time, then we are bound to produce adverse reactions.

**Economy in Expenditure**

Nehru felt that "we are a poor country and must always avoid unnecessary expenditure, remembering that it is all at the cost of millions of people of India." India should not compete with other countries in ostentatious display. In order to keep government's spending within means Nehru directed all government departments to avoid any expenditure not considered absolutely essential. He wanted utmost economy whether in defence or foreign missions or on tours and public functions. In ruling out use of alcoholic drinks at official functions he had saving in expenditure in view apart from the moral aspects. He made a rule at the Centre that no one should be sent abroad on government business without special permission of the Prime Minister.

Mobilizing resources he felt that a great country like India should not look to others for help but should be self reliant and herself save resources—in money or in labour. There was, in his view, considerable scope for raising money by loan. In order to give incentive to savings, he thought of utilizing money saved for particular area concerned. Small savings schemes should be encouraged. A large number of rural banks should not only loans to farmers but also should attract small pools of money, which in aggregate may amount to a very big sum.

### Social Policy

Nehru felt that economic progress should go hand in hand with social change. He felt that "our social structure is far too uneven and there are too many difficulties between those at the top and those below." "We cannot go ahead on the economic plane without changing our social background and breaking through restrictive social customs." Hindu society greatly suffered from all kinds of social disabilities. To remove some of them, Nehru was instrumental in passing of the Hindu Code Bill and Special Marriages Bill. He gave greater representation to women in Parliament and made them eligible for appointments in all branches of public service.

### Social Welfare

Nehru set up the Central Social Welfare Board under the Chairmanship of Smt. Durgabai Deshmukh and encouraged the activities of the Welfare Extension Project.

### Culture

Nehru encouraged cultural traditions of India—"so strong and so deep." He felt deeply about festivals in different parts of India. He liked the spirit behind them and the place they have in the hearts and minds of the people. They promoted gaiety and spirit of fellow feeling. He wanted that popular enthusiasm for these festivals should be harnessed to the cause of building up a new India.

He was so attracted by the wonderful variety of dress of both men and women that he suggested that the Ministry of Education should set up a museum of Indian dresses.

He was very happy that the Republic Day had established itself as a great popular festival "a folk dance festival" and was proud of it as "the spectacle of India on the march." To him it seemed to represent "India in miniature, the unity of India in its great diversity, India confident and on the march." For preservation of ancient manuscripts he suggested the building up of proper Indology Institute.

## Educational Policy

Nehru appointed Radhakrishnan Committee to examine India's educational system. He commended its report to the Chief Ministers. He desired that the methods of removing illiteracy must be closely connected with habits and interests of the people. Education must aim at quality and not just quantity. The educational system should promote dignity of labour through manual work and social service projects for students. NCC should be extended to all the schools and colleges in India.

He was concerned about rapid decline in educational standards and student indiscipline. He regretted that the universities had become battlegrounds of political parties. The Vice-Chancellor and Professors could neither control nor inspire respect. He wanted the appointment of Vice-Chancellor to be taken outside the sphere of party politics. A new atmosphere had to be created amongst students and teachers.

## Health and Medical Policy

Nehru promoted an integrated health policy with proper scope for modern as well as the traditional Ayurvedic and Unani systems.

## Prohibition

Nehru was not particularly enthusiastic in pressing ahead with prohibition since it involved great loss of revenue to the State. He also feared that it may encourage illicit distillation and boot-legging.

**Astrology**

Nehru did not want public functions to be governed by astrological predictions.

**Backward Castes, Scheduled Castes and Scheduled Tribes**

Nehru appointed Scheduled Castes and Tribes Commission with M.L. Shrikant as the first commissioner. He was keen to break down caste barriers.

Nehru enunciated a clear-cut tribal policy. "They form a large part of India's population. They greatly vary amongst themselves. Their way of life is very different from that of others". "While helping them, we have to take special care not to impose ourselves or our ways of life upon them, nor allow them to be exploited by others. Isolating them and treating them as museum pieces is even worse." They should be allowed to retain their own cultural traits and habits and develop along their own lives.

**Sports**

Nehru gave full support to the organisation of Asian games in India. He regretted that our sports standards are far below the international standards and do not come up even to the best Asian standards. He, therefore, took up the development of sports, games and athletics in India. He gave the lead in setting up the Institute of Himalayan Mountaineering.

**Science and Technology**

Nehru was concerned about the narrow base of science and technology in India. "Though the country had some first rate scientists, very little research was being done." Nehru laid the foundation of scientific and technological development in the country by setting up a chain of laboratories like the National Physical Laboratory in Delhi and National Chemical Laboratory in Poona. He set up the Atomic Energy Commission to harness the atomic energy for national progress.

**Conclusion**

The basic problems of Indian administration identified by Nehru continue till today and the basic policies that he laid down have stood the test of time. The departure from those policies has only created difficulties and distortions in the post Nehru era.

He ceaselessly strove for India's progress on all fronts—political, social and economic.

He laid a sound foundation for the country's progress. That was the supreme achievement of Nehru, the administrator.

# 19

# Indira Gandhi and Public Administration : Some Reminiscences

Jawaharlal Nehru was the founding President of the Indian Institute of Public Administration which was established in the year 1954 and continued to be its President till his death i.e. for a period of ten years. Every year he used to make a point to be present on the occasion of the Annual General Body meeting of the Institute held in October and in the course of his addresses, talked on those aspects of public administration which were uppermost in his mind. The Institute has published all his ten addresses in the publication entitled 'Jawaharlal Nehru and Public Administration.'

Indira Gandhi was the President of the Institute for two years- 1970-72 and 1971-72. However, she did not continue to be President thereafter because she thought that she could not spare the necessary time. However, even while declining to be President of the Institute, she gave expression to her feeling that she wanted the Indian Institute of Public Administration to be an "institution of excellence." After she ceased to be the President of the Institute, the opportunities for her visit at the time of the Annual General Body meetings were no longer available and therefore it appeared as though the direct contact between her and the IIPA was lost. We, therefore, felt that there should be some point of contact between the Prime Minister and the IIPA and thought that the best way would be for the participants in the Advanced Professional Programme in Public Administration (APPPA) to meet her and hear her views on different aspects of public administration. The Advanced Professional Programme in Public Administration is a unique long term course in public administration for the senior civil servants belonging to All India and Central Services and indeed is the only course of its kind.

The course begins with a series of lectures on various social and management sciences relevant to public administration. This is then followed by a series of exercises including dissertation, term papers, socio-economic studies of villages and visits to neighbouring countries for a comparative view of administration.

When I approached Mr. Sharada Prasad, Information Adviser to the Prime Minister, with our request for meeting with the Prime Minister, I was not sure whether it would be granted since after all, Prime Minister is such a busy person. But we did get an appointment with the Prime Minister which took place on March 23, 1983. The meeting was fixed at 8.30 a.m. at 1 Akbar Road. We went well ahead of time so as to reach the gates of 1 Akbar Road before 8.00 a.m.

It was spring time and the weather was pleasant-cool but not cold. Since our appointment was fixed, we were expected by the security men who let us in and we took our positions on chairs arranged in a small shamiana. By about 8.15 a.m. everybody was on his seat. I was feeling a bit nervous as to how the meeting would go; how much time the Prime Minister would be able to spare and whether she would be talking directly or would respond to questions put to her. Since we expected a question and answer session, rather than a brief lecture, I asked the participants to be ready with important questions covering a wide spectrum of problems of public administration and our preparation proved to be quite what was needed.

I was waiting at the entrance to Shamiana with a bouquet in my hand. Even before the scheduled time of 8.30 a.m., at about 8.25 a.m. itself came the Prime Minister of India briskly walking followed by her aides and security men. She appeared to be in a very cheerful mood. She stood in front of all us, and at once announced that she would spare one hour for us. This at once removed all our fears as to whether the Prime Minister would be able to spare sufficient time. We were ready for 15 minutes or half an hour, but here the Prime Minister was giving one full hour; we felt relaxed.

I gave the Prime Minister, in a few words, the information about the current work of the IIPA in general and APPPA Course in particular. She seemed to be listening attentively. Then she suggested that rather than giving a brief talk, she would like to respond to questions. The Prime Minister listened to every question carefully and responded fully.

All the time when she was responding to our questions, while we were all comfortably seated, she was standing, railing against the chair in front.

She never gave a feeling or impression of any hesitation on her part to reply to any question nor did she show any kind of resentment though one of the questions did refer to the emergency period. There was not a trace of a feeling that it was the Prime Minister talking to the civil servants. We felt that we were on the same wave length. All the time she made us feel at home as though we were her guests.

**Her Goal - Strong and Self Reliant India**

The most important of all the points that she made was that her goal was to make India strong and self-reliant. This appeared to be the uppermost thought in her mind and the essence of her endeavours as the Prime Minister of India.

**Development and Change**

She gave a very interesting analysis of change which is required for progress of Indian society. She said that change would take place only if people feel that change would be in their interest. She gave the example of a bus conductor in a British bus who was extremely polite to the passengers not because he considered politeness to be a virtue but because he felt that being polite made things easier and better for him: Any way for being polite he got his prize in the shape of a fortune left to him by an unknown passenger who remembered him for his politeness! Apart from making a point in a telling manner, this also exhibited her sense of humour.

She emphasized the importance of flexibility and discipline

both of which were required for introducing change. In a large country like India change and communication to people regarding change must take into account local situations and even local manners. She recalled the plight of the late Mrs. John Mathai when she was working in all sincerity for the refugees who came to Delhi after partition but was misunderstood by them because she addressed them as 'TUM' rather than 'AAP'. She meant no offence but was misunderstood because of her lack of familiarity with the Hindi language! The refugees took offence.

**Social Discipline**

As regards discipline the Prime Minister conceded that Indians are less disciplined than Malayans or the Chinese. She recalled her journey on board the ship to Burma when she observed this herself. But she added that when faced with adversity, Indians could be very disciplined: While making change, some distortions take place and certain corrections have to be introduced though they may slow down change.

The Prime Minister underlined the importance of primary education which she thought should be given more attention. Women had to come out and development has to be managed better.

Seventy minutes-ten minutes more than the time she gave us-had passed and we thanked her for meeting us. In our moments of exhilaration regarding the wonderful manner in which our meeting with the Prime Minister went on, we forgot to take a group photo with her. We requested her aides and they said that would not be any difficulty and that the P.M. would come back. The P.M. did come back and looking at me, she said "Are you still here?" with a twinkle in her eye. I said that we want a group photograph with her. She immediately obliged.

Our second meeting with Prime Minister, Indira Gandhi, took place on 7th February, 1984 when we went with the next batch of APPPA participants to meet her. This time after the experience of the previous year, I was less nervous and more relaxed because I knew how exhilarating the experience would be of meeting her. However, 7th February was colder than 23rd March and the Prime Minster had covered herself with a long black overcoat. She also looked to be little pre-occupied and even tense because she was to meet the opposition leaders on the Punjab problem. She gave some instructions to her aide regarding the meeting but once she came in, she gave all her attention to us. She warmly welcomed us. We saw the Prime Minister's concern for us when she remarked to her staff that it was cold and better heating arrangements should have been made for us. This time there was a difference in the manner in which the meeting progressed. The Prime Minister first gave a direct address on some matters and thereafter she responded to questions.

**Administration Relevant to Indian Situation**

She began saying that she was not going to talk to us directly about administration because "that is your job", but said that the goal of training in administration was to enable administrators to face up the difficulties which beset our country and our people. However, training was often based on thought and literature derived from the Western countries which was related to their social systems and had very little relevance to conditions in India. We have to keep the Indian situation before us all the time.

**Positive Atmosphere**

She laid a great deal of stress on the need for development of proper atmosphere in the country. This would, firstly, depend on a greater emphasis on our obligations and responsibilities rather than on rights and privileges. She cited the experience of some doctors who told her that they went to villages to do free medical work over the weekend but people did not very much appreciate their work and felt that it was their right to get such a free treatment. Those who were at the end of the queue even got upset that they were not attended to even though the doctors wasted no time in attending to the patients, So this exclusive emphasis on "trying to get what I can from top to bottom", had to be changed. Democracy is a good system but it means both responsibility as well as opportunities. It means a sense of partnership and cooperation. It is not correct to go on running down every thing. This tendency is developing even among the school children but such a negative tendency leads to the erosion of the authority of the Government. We have to create a positive climate so that India becomes strong and self-reliant.

**Self Reliance**

India is too large a country with too large a population to be bailed out of any difficulty by any other country. India must have the freedom to develop in her own way and not be pushed around.

We go on laying blame on others all the time. We should not go on saying what we could get from the country but what we can give to country. It is simply not possible for any government to do every thing for the people. We ought to be self reliant. The press also gives news about disasters and quarrels but not about development of achievements because they are not news. This creates an impression specially outside that India as a country is no good. On the other hand, we have to create a climate that India can do things. NAM, CHOGAM Conference, and the Asiad gave a feeling to the outside world that India can do things and every thing can go on smoothly.

Talking about our economic system,she said that we had preferred the Indian type of socialism or mixed economy but somehow we seem to have got ills of both the systems-Capitalism and Communism.

**Discarding Old Rules and Methods**

Talking about administrative change, she said that while sticking to basic values, we must have flexibility of outlook but we seem to be tied up in some old rules and methods, which do not work. We had to evolve rules and methods of work that are most appropriate to our country.

We stick to programmes even though they did not give desired results. Also many things cannot be done because somebody picks up the letter of the Law and insists on rigid interpretation.

We have to inculcate in our administration a feeling for social service and for regarding people as equals. The administrators should not go about as masters but rather as workers in the service of the public. It is because of this feeling in lacking that some of our institutions like rural banks are not functioning properly. There has to be a sense of popular participation and involvement. The Government cannot govern unless it is there.

**India's Diversity**

Talking about India, she talked about its diversity. India

is one country and there is an Indianness about it but we have many personalities and we have not tried to suppress any of these personalities unlike U.S.A. where everybody comes to conform to one standard. Here we speak different languages and there are differences from State to State and even between districts within a State, each having its own personality.

### Thinking People

Administration should not be in a closed shell. We need people in this country who are thinking people. We need an administration that has its feet on the ground and is in touch with common people and their problems and yet is thinking ahead. We are living in a world where science and technology are advancing very fast. The challenge of the future is becoming bigger and bigger and therefore more difficult for countries like ours. Life is not going to be easy but an easy life is not a satisfactory life. We must face hardship and adventure. She was not advocating a difficult path for the sake of difficulty because in the long run, this path leads to success in work, to greater achievement and more personal satisfaction.

### Disparity in Development

Answering various questions after her address, she said that the benefits of programmes of development are often captured by the dominant groups of people. Some States advance more rapidly than others. She cited the example of some Punjabi youth who organised a camp in U.P. They were astonished that those areas were not going ahead because the people there just did not work as they did in Punjab. Similarly when a special programme is chalked out for Harijans, others feel that they are becoming aggressive and take counter move against them. If business people are asked to take up industries in backward areas, they are reluctant and put off the projects altogether. So we have to do balancing all the time. However, we must realise that the poor are the very base in India and if the base is not strong, neither the middle classes, nor the higher ones are going to develop very much.

### Land Reforms

Replying to a question regarding land reforms, she said that they are important but have come up against political opposition as well as court cases which have delayed their implementation. Besides, if small plots are allotted to the landlords, they are not often able to develop them because they do not have resources. Consolidation of holdings is one of the most important programmes. Fragmentation of land holding has to be prevented. We have not given up land reforms but there are limitations including those of shortage of funds and resources.

### Unemployment

In response to a question on rural unemployment she said that one of the causes is the tendency to hanker for degrees. Nobody wants to become rural mechanic or foreman for which there is employment.

### Forests

She expressed a concern about deterioration of forest areas. She cited the King of Bhutan who told her that large areas are turning into "mountain deserts." We have to lay stress on trees not only because they are beautiful but they are also absolutely essential for regeneration of earth. Our droughts and floods are largely due to lack of forest cover. We have to lay importance on development of forest, animals and birds all of which are parts of the development of natural resources.

### Growth of Monopoly

To a question regarding the need for restriction on some persons holding position of Director in several companies, she said that she was not in favour of this type of monopoly and the point needed to be looked into. But she said that the minute we touched any industry, they raised objections. We want the Indian industry to develop rather than import things. We want small and medium industries to grow. We had hoped that each big industry would lead to a lot of ancillary industries but the main industrial group becomes so powerful that the smaller industry also belongs to them and this is a problem.

Finally, she underlined the basic importance of education which has not received as much attention as it should have.

Both the visits were for us a memorable experience.

# PART III

# BUREAUCRACY

# 20

# Bureaucracy

Max Weber, the German sociologist was the first to make a scientific study of the institution of bureaucracy as an 'ideal type'. He described it as a rational-legal institution of the twentieth century. It exists in government, both central and local; as well as in other large scale organisation in different fields like commerce, industry and banking, health and social services and in the educational system. In the setting of the modern State, bureaucracy as defined by Weber, is the most characteristic form of governmental administration. He defined the characteristic features of bureaucracy as an institution as follows:

1. Members of bureaucracy are personally free and subject to authority only with respect to the impersonal obligations of their office.
2. The offices are organised in hierarchical form.
3. Each office has a clearly defined sphere of competence.
4. The office is filled by appointment after selection of the person best fitted for it, and his relationship with the organisation is contractual.
5. Selection is on the basis of technical qualifications.
6. Rumeneration is by fixed salary, perhaps with pension rights, but there may be a salary scale.
7. The office is usually the sole occupational position that the incumbent may hold.
8. There is promotion according to seniority and

achievement as judged by superiors.

9. The official cannot appropriate his position and does not own the means of administration.
10. The official is subject to discipline and a control in the conduct of his office.

Bureaucracy with such formal characteristic is considered essential for running any large modern organisation.

The institution of Bureaucracy has evolved over a long period of time. Structures approximating Weber's definition of Bureaucracy have existed from time to time in different parts of the world. Ancient Egypt, the Roman Empire, ancient and medieval China, the Mauryan empire in India had their own bureaucratic system.

Military bureaucracies have existed for centuries before. In China, recruitment to Civil Service on the basis of examination has existed for more than 2,000 years.

No modern State can function without an instrument of bureaucracy. Indeed, bureaucratic proliferation has become a noticeable phenomenon of many countries and one of the concerns of administrative reforms today is how to regulate the size of bureaucracy. The size of bureaucracy in the modern State is inevitably expanding because of the expanding agenda of State activities. When the activities of the State were limited, bureaucracy was confined to a few departments but as the State undertook large responsibilities the size of bureaucracy inevitably expanded. After Second World War, Britain introduced the concept of the "welfare state", as the result of which the State had to set up the machinery for the provision of medical services, for unemployment insurance etc. This inevitably added to the strength of bureaucracy. It is now said that the State looks after the citizens "from womb to tomb" or from "cradle to grave". The State can look after these responsibilities only through the instrument of bureaucracy. Another factor responsible for increasing the size of bureaucracy was the assumption of the responsibility for direct economic managment by the State. These brought into being "public enterprises" which had to be manned by the bureaucrats, though they are distinguished from the normal bureaucracy by being termed as "technocracy" or "manager class".

In the developing countries also, there is a rapid bureaucratic proliferation after Independence because the State took up responsibility for forcing the pace of economic development and social change. During the colonial times bureaucracy was concerned mainly with the maintenance of law and order and collection of land revenue. But the assumption of responsibility by the independent Government after the attainmet of independence for planning and development in the comprehensive sense, meant coming into existence of new departments and organisations. They had all to be manned by the bureaucrats. Thus, bureaucracy has now become ubiquitous.

It is extremely important from the point of view of citizens that the bureaucracy is efficient, competent, honest, incorruptible, fair, just, objective and responsive. Bureaucracy has to maintain high standards. The very concept of bureaucracy is intended to maintain high standards. The opposite of bureaucracy is the "spoils system" when there is no formal system of recruitment by an independent agency through a prescribed procedure and based on prescribed qualifications. In the spoils system, appointments are simply made at the will of those who are in position of authority. Obviously, such a spoils system could be infinitely worse than the modern bureaucratic system.

However, bureaucracy is under attack. Bureaucracy has become a pejorative word. Bureaucracy has come to be identified with red tape, delay, circumlocution, lack of imagination, excessive rule mindedness, lack of responsiveness to the people, internal jealousy etc. Above all, there is a charge of the Parkinson's Law under which bureaucracy goes on proliferating for its own sake rather than for the sake of work to be done for the people.

Administrative reforms is mainly intended to check these bureaucratic evils. However, there is a feeling that these bureaucratic evils are not easily curbed. In country like Japan, the law itself has laid down an absolute restriction on the size of bureaucracy. In England, under the drive for economy initiated by Margaret Thatcher, the size of bureaucracy was reduced by 10 to 20 per cent. Even in India, restrictions have been imposed on fresh recruitment.

In order to improve the quality of bureaucracy, programmes

of training have been introduced.

Institutions like Indian Institute of Public Administration, New Delhi, the Lal Bahadur Shastri Academy of Administration, Mussoorrie and State Institutes of Administration provide training to members of bureaucracy, belonging to All India and Central Services, State Services and local government employees.

Public relations wings have also been opened in several bureaucratic organisations to help the citizens in obtaining the services from government departments. In order to make bureaucracy answerable to democratic institutions, it has to appear before Committees of Parliament and Legislative Assemblies like the Public Accounts Committees and the Committees on Public Undertakings. At the field level bureaucracy is answerable to elected local government institutions.

In order to curb the evil of corruption in bureaucracy, vigilance machinery has been set up. (Though it has also to be inevitably manned by bureaucracy!) Inspite of all this, it is not certain that bureaucracy has been rid of its evils.

Bureaucracy is a matter of tradition. In a country with a democratic tradition bureaucracy tends to be more responsive to the people than in other countries with a feudal and authoritarian traditions. Some people may look upon bureaucracy as a "necessary evil" but no modern State can function or progress without bureaucracy. Bureaucracy is, therefore, to be looked upon as an essential institution in the modern State and has to be nurtured and strengthened to play its role effectively but in a manner responsive to the people.

# 21

# Bureaucracy
# The Challenge of Change

It was Max Weber the sociologist who described bureaucracy as the rational institution of the twentieth century. He thought that it was an integral part of the modern urban industrial society. The latter is characterised by large scale organisations with their attendant administrative structures. These are to be found in every part of the modern society and economy in government, as well as in industrial, commercial and financial establishments.

The bureaucracy as a rational institution has certain characteristics; first, the recruitment to bureaucracy is on the basis of selection of person on merit and according to prescribed qualifications; second a member of bureaucracy holds office with clearly defined sphere of competence, with a definite role and responsibility; thirdly, for discharging the duties of the office, he is remunerated on the basis of a salary scale and pension rights; fourthly, a member of bureaucracy does not have any personal interest or obligations in relation to his office; fifthly, promotions are according to seniority and achievement; and sixthly, a member of bureaucracy is subject to discipline and control in the conduct of office. These special characteristics are expected to impart to the work of the members of bureaucracy qualities of objectivity, impartiality, efficiency and orderliness.

When India became independent, she already had an apparatus of bureaucracy at the level of Central, State and local administrations. A decision was taken not to do away with the pre-independent structure of bureaucracy but rather to re-fashion it for achieving the goals and tasks of independent India. The re-fashioning had to be in two directions. First to make it a fit instrument for the new objectives of the State which was no longer a mere law and order State but what was described as a Welfare State inaction. India launched a series of Five Years Plans and various programmes for economic development and social change like programmes of rural development, modernisation of agriculture, industrialisation, development of infrastructure including expansion of health and education facilities, power and irrigation projects and roads and communication facilities, and building up of institutions like panchayati-raj and cooperatives. The bureaucracy with traditional orientation and training in the task of law and order was expected to acquire the new skills that were attendant to the new programmes and process of economic development and social change.

The second change in bureaucracy was called for by the need for bureaucratic functioning in the framework of democracy. Before independence, the bureaucracy could function on its own through its own hierarchy . After independence, not only was bureaucracy answerable to the democratically elected Central and State Governments, but was also exposed to a number of democratic pulls, pressures and influences. This democratic transformation fundamentally required a change in attitude of bureaucracy to the common citizen of India. Democracy implies that the people are sovereign and therefore bureaucrats had to be constantly aware that people are their masters and bureaucracy is there to serve them.

To what extent has this twofold change been brought about? Has bureaucracy, by and large, been a fit instrument of economic development and social change? Has the bureaucracy really been in harmony with democracy? These questions are basic to the solution of bureaucracy in independent India.

Unfortunately, bureaucracy all along and especially of late has been subjected to widespread criticism. It is pointed out that neither development nor democracy has been well served by bureaucracy. At the same time, no alternative to bureaucracy has been conceived or devised even though induction of outside elements in the bureaucratic structure has also been attempted from time to time though considering the size of the bureaucracy as a whole, this may be considered only a marginal change.

While bureaucracy has been exposed to carping criticism, the criticism has been rather one-sided and not very constructive. The credit that is due to it has not always been given. The role of bureaucracy in holding the country together, in carrying out the day to day tasks and functions of the government and in formulating and devising a number of new programmes of development has not always been well appreciated. If only the conditions in India are compared with conditions in other countries which emerged to freedom in Asia and Africa in the post-World War II period, the bureaucracy in India would certainly come out with flying colours.

India adopted the Westminster model of parliamentary democracy of which the essential feature was the political neutrality of bureaucracy. India has tried to stick to this principle though it has always been threatened by the process of politicisation and by the potentially dangerous tendencies of identifying the government with the political party in power and with unconstitutional sources of authority. Recently, many examples of deviations from the strictly politically neutral character of bureaucracy have come to notice. However, what threatened to be almost a crisis seems to have passed over. But that does not mean that as yet the tender plant of political neutrality of the bureaucracy is completely free from any such danger. In fact, the threat to that principle is ever present. Political neutrality is undoubtedly necessary for an objective impartial and rational bureaucracy. But temptations to political alignment are always great and the demacles sword of punishment for refusing to toe the political line may always be dangling. Clearly there is a need for erecting a bastion of bureaucracy to protect it from illegimate political compulsions to take palpably illegal administrative action. At the same time Bureaucracy as a professional body must itself evolve and adopt a code of conduct consistent with the highest standards of administrative behaviour.

In some newly independent countries of Africa, the doctrine of political neutrality of bureaucracy has been given up. That is because these countries have accepted the system of one party State. In the apparatus of administration in these States, there has been on one side a system of political appointments to many top jobs and on the other hand, the members of bureaucracy have been called upon to perform the task of propagating the political ideology. Indeed the distinction between the political work and the administrative work itself seems to have been given up since it is felt that in the task of economic development and modernisation, the administrative tasks themselves involve political mobilisation.

We have not adopted such system in India so far, though it has been urged time and again that bureaucracy must show greater commitment; but it has been shown that commitment has its own dangers and can degenerate into sycophancy, illegality and even tyranny. Bureaucracy, therefore, has to combine dedication to development with impartiality and objectivity in administration. This is by no means an easy task. Even the great poet Bhartruhari has observed

"Even yogis would find it difficult to play the role of a (civil) servant!"

Some people have compared bureaucracy with horses. They have stated that if there are proper people to ride, bureaucracy can be made to deliver the goods. This is not an apt comparison. Bureaucrats are not horses. They are human beings with volition of their own. The idea of riding bureaucracy can also be quite dangerous. Nor is it correct to compare bureaucracy with a machine or an instrument; a mechanical simile is as bad as the biological simile. If bureaucracy degenerates into machine, it would be completely drained of all the human element which is the most valuable element in the system of public administration.

We already took the decision at the time of independence that we will not give up bureaucracy lock, stock and barrel; even today, more than forty years after independence, though unfortunately, there seems to be widespread dissatisfaction with bureaucracy, in India, there is yet no concept of giving up bureaucracy as it exists today altogether. On the other hand it is constantly felt that bureaucracy in India must be reformed. That it should be more prompt, more human and humane, more efficient, more objective, more imaginative, more enthusiastic in serving the cause of democracy and development.

How nice it would have been if bureaucracy in India had earned for itself a good name and had endeared itself to the people of India! But while criticizing bureaucracy, let it not be overlooked that the defects of bureaucracy in the ultimate analysis reflect the defects of India as a nation and as a people. Inspite of the notable achievements of the last forty years, one cannot help feeling that India as a nation could have accomplished much more than what it has done given all its assets and possibilities. Our society has again and again betrayed some basic traits which detract from achievement- traits like "each for himself and devil take the hindmost" attitude, the tendency to help oneself without having any regard to the social good, tendencies towards corruption and nepotism, inability to take impersonal and objective view, the incursions of narrow considerations like caste and community, lack of sensitivity to surrounding, inability to appreciate and respect merit and achievement and a deep-rooted slackness and lack of initiative. All these defects were luridly and harshly brought out by V.S. Naipaul in his book "India, the Wounded Civilization". Shri Naipaul seems to have worked himself in a frenzy and one may not like to go whole hog with him, but there is an element of truth in what he says and if the future of India is to be bright, the nation must rid itself of some of the traits mentioned above and in this bureaucracy must take the lead. That in fact must be the constant concern of the movement of administrative reform in India.

# 22

# The Decline of the Civil Service

There is widespread concern in the country about the decline of a vital institution of a modern State, viz., the civil services. The concern is not so much about fall in efficiency or rise in corruption, though undoubtedly these are extremely worrisome matters, as the fact is that civil service as an institution is not playing the role it is expected to play.

The expected role is that first, as public service its conduct should be governed by rule of law. Second, it is expected to work solely in the public interest. Third, in the framework of parliamentary democracy it should work in a politically neutral manner. These three are mutually reinforcing attributes of civil service as an institution. The lament is that the civil service has lost all these attributes.

## Above All Rules

It is generally believed that it is the function of the judiciary alone to uphold the rule of law. Actually, it is equally the responsibility of the civil service and the political executive. Rule of law requires that no one is above the law, or an exception to the rule of law. Law includes rules, regulations and procedures laid down under the law. In practice, in big matters and small, we seem to have gone back to the feudal concept that the rulers are above all rules; rules and regulations are meant for the governed, not for those who govern.

Indeed some people in authority seem to believe that power and authority have no meaning if the wielders of power cannot violate rules with impunity, whether these relate to simple matters of rules of traffic and parking or not so simple matters like attestations of documents or conduct of elections in respect of both of which cases of blatant violations of the rule of law by civil servants have recently come to notice.

In one case, a Foreign Service officer attested without insisting on the presence of the person whose signature was attested just because the Foreign Minister had asked for the attestation without delay. In another, a District Magistrate and an SP made themselves unavailable to receive complaints just because they were against those working for the then Prime Minister. Similar failure to discharge their duties as impartial returning officers was noted in Muzzafarpur in Bihar and Meham in Haryana.

Administrative actions are as much governed by the rule of law as judicial pronouncements, every administrative action is or has to be as much a judicial act as a judicial pronouncement. But while the doctrine of the independence of the judiciary makes judicial pronouncement immune from interference of authority (though even here in recent times there is ground for suspicion that this may not be quite so) administrative actions of civil servants are not expected to be protected by any corresponding doctrine of independence of administration. That is because while judiciary is an independent limb of the State, administration is not. Civil administrators are subordinate to the political executive. Subordination takes a heavy toll of the rule of law in administrative action.

Not only postings and transfers but the entire career of the civil servants is at the mercy of their political masters—the higher the rung of the career ladder, the more this is so. What Boris Yeltsin has said about the political bureaucracy in USSR is equally true about civil service in India—"the higher you climb up the professional ladder, the more are the comforts that surround you and the harder and the more painful it is to lose them. One becomes, therefore, all the more obedient and dependable". Subordination, therefore, soon leads to subservience and sycophancy. Prize posts are the reward for compliance and pliability; for independence and insistence on the law, there is only marginalisation, obscurity or even the dog house.

No wonder, a former Central Minister in charge of Personnel is said to have observed at a meeting that when they appoint Secretaries what they are looking for "is not genius or brilliance but the qualities of domestic servant, viz., loyalty". No wonder, "not service but servility" becomes the motto of the civil servant.

**Domestic Servant**

The criterion of loyalty was upheld by the Supreme Court Judge M. P. Thakkar in J. C. Jaitley case. When Mr. Jaitley, an IAS officer of Bihar Cadre, was overlooked for promotion to the post of Secretary, he went to the Central Administrative Tribunal which observed that Government should lay down clearcut criteria and procedures for appointment to the post of Secretary. But in appeal, the worthy Supreme Court judge upheld the doctrine of the "domestic servant". "If I want to appoint a cook, I would appoint any one of whom I like. Same applies to Government appointing anybody as Secretary".

The pernicious doctrine of the "domestic servant" removes all distinction between private and public administration. Its consequences on morale and quality of the civil service over the last two decades or so have been disastrous. While honest, upright and straightforward civil servants have been sidetracked, the clever and the ambitious have vied with each other for sharing the plum posts. They have become past masters in sycophancy and PR. This has helped them to smoothly glide from the favours of one set of political masters to another, though new rulers come with the express determination to clean the Augean stable left by their predecessors. This is the irony and tragedy of the civil services in India.

In such a climate it is no wonder that the rule of law becomes casualty. There is more to administration than merely upholding the rule of law. Administration has to deliver the goods. And the goods are to be delivered to the masters. If the rules come in the way, it is for the civil servant to see that they are got around. Therein lies his merit. A civil servant who at every step invokes rules for not doing things would be branded as one with a negative attitude and an obstructionist.

Once this kind of thinking becomes common, it becomes a habit for the political master to expect compliance from the civil servant, even when it would go against the rules. And the civil servant, given to habitual obedience, starts crawling when he is asked to bend. Political interference extends even to quasi-judicial matters handled by civil servants when they sit as courts of law. The area of interference gets continually extended to serve party, partisan, private and personal interest. The distinction between public and private interest gets totally obliterated.

**Honest Advice**

The secretariat manual and conduct rules lay down instructions for the civil servants. A Secretary is Secretary to Government, not to individual Ministers. He has to give his advice without fear or favour. Experience has shown that a civil servant who acts on these instructions does so only at his own peril. If he cares for his career he has to care for both fear and favour of his political master. He should master the art of knowing in advance the mind of his Minister and tender his advice accordingly.

Notes by Secretaries to the Government are expected to discuss exhaustively the pros and cons of any issue and give honest, unambiguous advice on each matter at issue. Such notes are fast disappearing from secretariat files. Civil servants have realised that unambiguous noting can be hazardous. Much better to discuss the matter with the Minister and write down his instruction for compliance. Better still to get them carried out without reducing anything to writing which may later cause needless embarrassment.

In the wake of the new tribe of powerful Special Assistants to Ministers and Secretary to Prime Minister, things came to such a pass that orders and instructions of Prime Minister were recorded under their signature and were complied with by departmental Secretaries without questioning. When the appointments of Secretaries themselves depended on outcome of a a interview with the Special Assistant such automatic compliance, no wonder, was taken for granted. Such Secretaries avoided confrontation.

In such an atmosphere the old doctrine of civil service neutrality was easily replaced by the new doctrine of committed bureaucracy-committed not to the Constitution or public interest, not to the Government in power, but to the personality of the Prime Minister. Committed bureaucracy embodied the concept of loyalty.

Unfortunately, Ministers realise how transient and indeed deceptive this loyalty is only after they lose power. They see the loyalists readily shifting their loyalty to their arch enemies, succeeding them in positions of power. When will the Ministers learn the lesson that the so called committed and loyal servants are far less dependable than others who proclaim no such personal loyalty but are steady in the pursuit of their professional commitment, give disinterested advice to Ministers solely to public interest, and at the same time carry out orders of Government in an impartial manner.

The basic issue of commitment of public servants to public interest is not free from ambiguity. Who has to define "public interest" not in any general manner but in specific, concrete cases ? The issue came to a head in the famous Dr. Ponting case in UK. He was a Deputy Secretary in the Ministry of Defence in Britain. In the Belgrano sinking affair during the Falkland war, he found that the Government of Margaret Thatcher was misleading Parliament, and in "public interest" he released public documents to an Opposition MP. When this was found out, he was dismissed from the government and prosecuted in the court of law under the Official Secrets Act.

**Public Interest**

The Cabinet Secretary, Armstrong, issued a clarification on what constituted public interest. Public interest, he said, was what the government in power thought to be so and it was not for public servants to take on themselves to define it and act in such public interest. Dr. Ponting thought that revealing full facts to Parliament was in public interest. Withholding such facts from Parliament was against public interest. And in giving secret documents on the Belgrano affair to an Opposition MP he thought he was acting only in public interest. The juries in the court of law gave the verdict of "not guilty" under the Official Secrets Act. But Dr. Ponting had to undergo a great deal of suffering in course of the hearing of the case.

Every nation gets the civil service it deserves. If India wants an honest, upright, impartial civil service, the atmosphere in which it functions has to change. The constitutional protection of punishment only on the basis of a proper enquiry is hardly enough to give security and independence. The civil servant must feel that his career would not be sacrificed at the altar of political patronage.

In Australia the public service commission has a role in the posting of civil servants. In UK, until the Thatcher era, civil servants could not be arbitrarily transferred. In India there is need to lay down impartial and open criteria and procedures for postings of civil servant. And a tradition needs to be established, on the basis of an all-party consensus, that these criteria and procedures would be scrupulously adhered to.

# 23

# Generalist vs Specialist

The controversy generalist-vs-specialist, has gone on for several years. Indira Gandhi once said, "she had great respect for engineers many of whom were brilliant. But for that reason it was not right to say that the generalists were of no account. Different types of people were needed for different situation." She spoke in the same vein but some-what more elaborately in her address to Indian Institute of Management Bangalore. She said, "the last few months have seen a vigorous controversy raising over the relative importance of generalists and specialists. I have declared time and again that, in order to achieve progress, we should learn to make better use of our specialists. I do not respect hierarchy nor have I hesitated to appoint specialists as administrative head of Ministries and place them in positions of authority. All generalists are not mere revenue and law and order people. The very complexity of administration is compelling them to gain new kind of competence. The test is to find the best person for any job. The present controversy is somewhat sterile." Quoting from an article by Mr. Krishina Pillai she said, "Dr. Johnson was asked, who is more intelligent men or women". Dr. Johnson replied, "which men "and" which women". We may say the same about the generalists and the specialists. This is not a question of a particular class or group of people but the individual within them. Our experience is that the generalists and the specialists both tend to be somewhat bureaucratic when they come into the system. The specialists are not more assiduous than the generalists when suggesting new approaches to administration, new way of getting things done, new methods of mechanism. Both are subjected to human feelings, feuds, hatred and jealousies and narrow-mindedness and these are not diminished in new institutions headed by specialists. There should be an interweaving of the competence and administrative abilities of trained generalists and of skills of specialists. In a fabric of a modern administration the two are like the warp and the woof. The important issue is to evolve a system by which we are able to get the best out of our personnel and to ensure that the entire administration and specially the level at which the administration comes in direct touch with people are imbued with a sense of service and undertaking."

The controversy between the generalists and the specialists has been conducted in our country at two levels— the academic and the agitational, the spiritual and the mundane level, somewhat like the discussion on Hindu religion itself which at the spiritual level is concerned with the ultimate reality and at the mundane level about sharing of offering to God and ritualistic precedences.

At the mundane and the agitation level, the controversy gets reduced to a rat race for securing higher posts, more facilities and emoluments, greater power, control and authority, a higher status. But at the theoretical or spiritual level, the level at which the Prime Minister Indira Gandhi considered the issue, it becomes a matter of brining the best in human talent for fulfillment of the goals and objectives of public administration.

It is important that all concerned including the parties to the controversy consider the subject clearly and dispassionately and not clouded by prejudice or pre-conceived notions or purely with a view to achieve selfish goals. Identification of the so called generalist with revenue and law order functions is an example of deliberate distortion to achieve partisan goals.

The so called generalists are concerned with general administration i.e. with general administrative tasks in various subject matter areas. This does not mean that the general administration is either disfunctional or does not require knowledge, skill, experience or training. Indeed the administration of public affairs is a specialised function requiring techniques and skills of its own. One of the ways of building such experience in men concerned with administration, is to provide them experience in various fields dealing with different matters, men and institutions. Thus administration becomes a body of specialised knowledge, skills and techniques with a general application. There is certain amount of transferability of administrative skill and knowledge from one field to another.

The persons specialised in administration would not of course be technically specialised and may not know much of the technical intricacies of the field in which they function. This is as much true of the field of public administration as of private business. The Fiat Auto Company has a world-wide reputation. It owed its success to its Manager, Agnelli who has shown that he knows to run an auto company although he concedes that, "I have not the slightest idea how to build a car." Under him the Fiat Company greatly broadened its product line, introducing several new models in the past two years and increasing Fiat's international reach.

What is true of construction of automobiles is also true regarding administration of a hospital or of a University. The administrator of a hospital may not diagnose human diseases but he must diagnose the ailments in the organisation of the institution which gives medical relief.

It is not as though the concept of generalist administrators conceived only in India. It is a familiar concept everywhere. For example Mr. McNamara who was the distinguished Chairman of the General Motors Company and then the Defence Secretary later provided dynamic and innovative leadership as the President of the International Bank for Reconstruction and Development. Similarly the French Civil Servants starting from being inspectors du finance have risen to the position of the Foreign Minister like Couve de murville and Finance Minister like Giscard Estang who later became President of that country.

It should not be difficult to give examples of the need for the generalist administrators in specialised fields. One example is the irrigation development. This is a field for many specialities-construction engineers, agricultural engineers, agricultural scientists, cooperative executives, marketing specialists etc. But the integration of these activities into a coordinated plan of action is a field in which generalist administrator would be needed. Without his role, coordinated planning and team work may not be possible. Coordinating diverse talents and programmes for a single objective is a special task of the generalist administrator.

Construction of Hydro Electric Project is another example where many specialists have to make their contributions including construction engineers, electrical engineers, accountants, land acquisition officers etc. But the coordinated planning of a huge hydro electric project would require not only scheduling of plans and programmes but also ensuring their success by getting requisite funds and materials through contact with numerous agencies whose cooperation is required in the execution of mighty project. This is not a work which engineers engaged in the construction activities can do, since all their energies would necessarily be concentrated on the technical job of construction.

These are two typical examples of what the Prime Minister Indira Gandhi had called the interweaving of the talents of the generalists and the specialists. As economic development becomes more advanced and diversified, the scope for the activities for generalist becomes more and not less since advancement and development requires more effort of planning and coordination. This work can hardly be neglected and indeed must necessarily occupy the focal position.

At the same time, person occupying the central position in administration would have to develop an adequate appreciation of the technical and subject matter contents of various projects and programmes and would have to make a special effort to get along with the specialists and get the best out of them.

In most cases, the coordinating generalist administrator would have to be placed in a strategic position. But this does not mean any devaluation of the position of the technical specialists. At the same time, occupation of strategic position gives no right to the incumbents to score over his technical colleague or ride rough shod over his opinions.

If this is realised by all concerned and if the generalist administrators and the technical specialists cooperate with each other malice towards none and respect for all, it would help a great deal in enabling the public administration as a whole to reach its goals.

# PART IV

# TRAINING

24

# Training System of Civil Servants in India

Training is rightly considered as an investment in human resource development (HRD). It helps in developing the human potential and in raising the level of efficiency and performance. Training of civil servants is particularly significant in the field of public administration and is accorded a crucial place in the agenda of administrative reforms.

In India, the entire training of civil servants received increasing attention after the country became independent. A variety of training institutions have been established to enable civil servants to play their new and diverse roles in Independent India.

Training of public servants in India has a long history of its own. During the last thirty years there has been considerable expansion of training activities all over the country. Institution building in administrative training has been a noticeable phenomenon leading to the establishment of Central, State and autonomous training institutions. The creation of the Department of Personnel and Administrative Reforms with additional new responsibilities in the fields of training, career management, personnel policy, planning etc. is an outcome of Government's keenness in promoting personnel development and efficiency in public service. There is no doubt that in recent years training of public servants has acquired a sharp focus.

The civil service today has a role completely different from that it had in the pre-independence era. It then played the role of the instrument of a colonial government. Collection of taxes and maintenance of law and order were the two major goals of the colonial administration. The civil servants serving the colonial regime generally kept themselves aloof from the people who feared them. But since then, things have changed vastly.

Building up a new nation became the most challenging task facing India when it became independent in 1947. The regulatory functions of the government were certainly important but planning and implementation tasks for development with a view to raising the levels of living of masses immediately outpaced them in both magnitude and priority. The State became an active agent for the promotion of socio-economic change and development.The State became a Welfare State rather than a Police State as it was before independence. The civil servants in the Welfare State were increasingly called upon to shoulder responsibilities for promoting socio-economic change and development. The civil servants are now expected to enlist the cooperation of the people in pushing forward the development plans and projects in the most distant village in the interior. There is a growing feeling that civil servants who deal with complex economic, political and social problems, must be provided with necessary knowledge about the changing environment and new challenges, must be imparted new skills needed for promoting development and must be attuned with proper attitudes in enlisting the confidence and cooperation of the people. These became the aims of training.

The methods of training have also undergone changes. Institutional training is coming to occupy an important place. This is evident from the fact that a large number of training institutions have now come into existence. On-the-job training is certainly essential but it is not enough. It has to be supplemented by institutional training and both preservice and inservice. Institutions are assuming greater responsibility for supervising training in the field as well.

Independent India needed the establishment of new civil services for shouldering the new responsibilities in the sphere of development. The Government of Independent India took decisions to create the new services as well as to recognize the existing ones. A major decision was taken to establish the

Indian Administrative Service (IAS) as successor to the Indian Civil Service (ICS) but the IAS was not to be a carbon copy of the ICS. It was expected to play a new role in the new environment.

The civil servants in India at the national level are divided into a number of services. The services which are common to the Centre and the States are called All India Services like Indian Administrative Service, Indian Police Service and Indian Forest Service. Besides, there are a number of Central Services for well defined functional areas like Indian Foreign Service, Indian Audit and Accounts Service, etc. The members of the Central Services work throughout their career for the Central Government in the respective fields of specialisation for which they are recruited and also in the Central Secretariat.

In the changed context of proliferating governmental functions undertaken to promote socio-economic development at a fast pace, the questions regarding the size and the calibre of civil service personnel naturally came to the fore. The First Five Year Plan (1951-1956) stated "that an efficient administrative set-up with personnel of requisite capacity and quality was one of the essential conditions for successful planning." In specific terms this implied.

> "The higher civil service must have basic knowledge of what is happening in the country, of the history and working of the contemporary social revolution and of the history of comparable revolutions elsewhere, and that they must have the right outlook and the right attitude to fulfil the many demands of public service. Basic knowledge does not imply cramming of the mind with facts of all sorts, mostly unrelated to one another. It implies the development of the capacity of the mind to collect, analyse the related facts to draw correct inferences, to encompass the total range of a problem and to be methodical and straightforward.With such a mind, one could go in any field of activity, however, varied and new and perform with confidence and success."

In sum the civil services had to be geared up for a different role in the post-independence era.

The effort to produce civil service personnel of the requisite capacity and quality necessitated the redesigning of existing training programmes and the institution of several new ones. The IAS Training School at Metcalfe House, New Delhi was set up in 1947 to provide training to the members of the Indian Administrative Service. Another IAS Staff College was set up at Shimla in 1955 to provide in-service training and to meet the training requirements of those selected through special recruitment processes in addition to the annual intake. In 1959, it was decided to merge the two institutions and to set-up the National Academy of Administration at Mussoorie.

**Role of Lal Bahadur Shastri National Academy of Administration, Mussoorie: Induction Training at the Academy**

The Lal Bahadur Shastri National Academy of Administration, Mussoorie is the apex training institution responsible for imparting induction training to the officers of the All India and Central Services (Class I, now called Group A) recruited through a competitive examination conducted by the Union Public Service Commission.

The induction training to the probationers of the Indian Administrative Service (hereafter referred to IAS) at the Academy is in two parts, viz. a Foundational Course followed by a professional course. In the case of probationers of the Central Services (Group A), the Academy only imparts the initial segment of their induction training through the Foundational Course. The Professional Course for these officers is organised in their respective training institutions, e.g. the Indian Police Service Officers are imparted professional training at the Sardar Vallabhbhai Patel National Police Academy, Hyderabad, the Indian Revenue Service Officers (Income Tax) at the Revenue Service (Direct Taxes) Staff College, Nagpur; the Indian Revenue Service Officers (Central Excise and Customs) at their Training Institutions at New Delhi; the Indian Postal Service Officers at Posts and Telegraph Training Centre, Saharanpur; officers of Indian Audit and Civil Accounts Service at the Indian Audit and Accounts Service Staff College, Simla; officers of the Railways at the Railway Staff College, Baroda and so on.

The Academy conducts two courses for probationers

recruited to the All India and Central Services - A Foundational Course and a Professional Course.

**Foundational Course**

The Foundational Course at the Academy has been basically designed to promote a common outlook and common understanding and build up right attitudes and values in the organised civil services. It attempts to instil a sense of unity and a spirit of comaraderie amongst the participants from the various services. This is based on the recognition of the premise that although members of different services are required to perform different kinds of jobs, there has to be unity of services to achieve the objectives of administration and that the attitudes and value system of the civil services have to be geared to the requirements of a democratic welfare society, with its main focus on the rural people, the minorities and on the weaker and under-privileged sections of the society. The specific aims and objectives of the course are to:

1) give the probationers, a basic understanding of the constitutional, political, economic, legal and social framework within which they have to work;

ii) impart basic knowledge on the 'core subjects;

iii) promote a common outlook and common understanding so that the probationers could appreciate each others' role in administration;

iv) help in building up right attitudes and values and the qualities of leadership and organisational skills which make a civil servant proficient in his duties.

**Professional Course**

The Professional Course at the Mussoorie Academy for the IAS officers is structured into a sandwitch pattern under which the IAS Probationers come to the Academy in two-spells. The first spell is after the Foundational Course for a period of five months after which the probationers are sent to the States of their allotment for district training for a year to study the district administration, both developmental and regulatory including the maintenance of law and order. After this, they report back at the Academy to round off their second phase of the professional training for a period of three months.

The main objective of training in the districts for the IAS officers is to familiarise them with the working of the totality of Government or the aggregate functions of the Government at the district and local levels. For this purpose, they are placed under a senior colleague-a District Collector/Deputy Commissioner for practical understanding of the administration in action, of the complex problems involved, of dealing with people, sub-ordinates, colleagues and seniors.

The district training briefly consists of:

(i) Under study period;

(ii) On-the-job training;

(iii) Attachment to district and lower level officers; and

(iv) Institutional training.

With a view to groom properly the directly recruited officers of the Civil Services in terms of helping them to acquire the knowledge and skills and to develop the correct attitudes, it is necessary to impart 'Induction Training' to the officers. The need and importance of induction training has since been accepted by all concerned. This training has to be so structured that it provides a broader view of the environment and administrative set-up so that it widens the horizon and perspective of the officers. There should be adequate stress on intellectual accomplishment and building up of sound character. It should also be as comprehensive as possible to provide knowledge and skills for specific jobs which these officers will be required to hold in the coming years.

For equipping these officers for their responsibilities during the initial years of their service, it is necessary to give them an understanding of the constitutional, legal, political, economic, social and administrative framework within which they have to work. They have to be acquainted with the organisation and processes of government, and the principles and practices of public administration and management. In addition to help them to acquire necessary knowledge and skills, there has to be a stress on civil service ethics and proper attitudes relevant to the prevailing political and socio-economic system and general fabric of the society and the expectations from the administration.

Most of the Central Services have by now come to have

their own professional training institutions. The few which do not have facilities for institutional training follow a blend of on-the-job training and attachment to specialised institutions, punctuated by some special lectures by subject-matter experts.

**In-Service Training Programme**

Apart from the induction training to the new recruits to the All India and Central Service Officers (Group A), the Academy also runs a number of in-service programmes for senior officers. These are not just refresher courses, but advanced programmes keeping in view the progress of modern management techniques, impact of science and technology on administration and development of behavioural sciences relevant to public services.

**Institute of Secretariat Training and Management**

The ISTM conducts post-entry foundational, professional refresher as well as specialised training programmes for different grades of officials working in the Central Secretariat and its attached offices upto and including the Middle Management Level, as well as employees of some levels in State Governments, Union Territories and autonomous organisation. Its training courses could be broadly classified as follows:

— Foundational and Refresher Programme

— Management Programme

— Specialised Programmes

— Training of Trainers Programmes

— Behavioural Science Programmes

— Secretariat Programmes

**Other Training Institutions**

In addition to the National Academy of Administration, several Ministries and Departments in the Government of India took steps to establish full-fledged institutional facilities for the professional training of members of services under their control.

**State Training Institutes**

The States did not lag far behind. A number of them set up training institutions for the training of State Civil Services which were newly created in some cases.

### Specialised Autonomous Training Institutions

In addition there are a number of autonomous/private training institutions in the country to meet the training needs of the experienced higher personnel. Indian Institute of Public Administration is the premier apex institution in the field of training and research in public administration.

### Specialised National Training Institutions

The Training Division of the Department of Personnel has invited a scheme of collaboration with various specialised training institutions in the country such as Indian Institute of Public Administration, Indian Institute of Management, Ahemdabad, Administrative Staff College of India, Hyderabad, Institute of Economic Growth, Delhi and Institutes of Development Studies, Bangalore and Trivandrum. Specific research and teaching programmes are built up with the faculty of these institutes and funds are provided to them to develop suitable case studies and teaching and technical notes.

### Department of Personnel With Particular Reference to Training Division

The need for a central personnel agency entrusted with personnel functions in the Central Government has been felt for quite some time, particularly in the context of rapid expansion in the number of civil services after independence. The Estimates Committee of the Third Lok Sabha recommended that the ever expanding role of the Government in a Welfare State with its natural concomitant of a large civil service calls for effective personnel control through a single agency. The Administrative Reforms Commission (ARC) also emphasized that it was necessary to set up a central personnel agency with overall responsibility in all important matters and manned largely by specialists and would be able to devote concerted attention to formulation of new policies, set new standards and raise the quality of administration. The Central Government accepted this recommendation and as a consequence, the Department of Personnel was set up in August 1970 and placed within the Cabinet Secretariat.

In the beginning, the Department of Personnel was set

up as part of the Cabinet Secretariat and thus functioned directly under the Prime Minister. In 1973, the Department of Administrative Reforms hitherto located in the Ministry of Home Affairs was transferred to the Department of Personnel and latter's name was changed to the Department of Personnel and Administrative Reforms.

The Department has the following six divisions :

(i) Policy and Planning Division

(ii) Training Division

(iii) All India Services Division

(iv) Establishment Division

(v) Vigilance Division

(vi) Establishment's Officer Division

The Department of Personnel and Administrative Reforms which was previously one of the Departments of the Union Ministry of Home Affairs is now upgraded to the Ministry and its new nomenclature is Ministry of Personnel and Administrative Reforms, Public Grievances and Pension, which is under the overall charge of the Prime Minister.

**The Training Division**

The Training Division was established in April 1968 in pursuance of the recommendation made by the Committee on Administration dealing with the progress of implementation of the Cabinet decisions on administrative improvements. The Officer on Special Duty was appointed the Director of the Training Division. Since then, the functions and responsibilities of the Training Division have grown manifold.

The ARC in its Report on Personnel Administration made comprehensive observations and recommendations concerning training. It observed that training of the various functional cadres should be the responsibility of the individual departments and ministries. However, the Training Division should have the overall responsibility for training in headquarters work as well as preparing personel for entry to senior management. It should also be its task to formulate a national policy for civil service training, ensure its translation into operational plans and oversee their implementation.

These recommendation have since been accepted by the Government and have provided useful guidelines for the organisation of the Training Division and its work programmes.

**The Indian Institute of Public Administration**

The Indian Institute of Public Administration has been in the forefront of inservice training in public administration and is considered to be the premier institution in the country for the training of senior level civil servants of both Central and State Governments and executives of public sector undertakings.

The training courses at the Institute fall into two broad categories:

**(A) Sponsored Programmes:** including (a) those sponsored by the Training Division, Department of Personnel and Administrative Refrom, Government of India (b) sponsored by Ministry of Works & Housing in relation to programmes of Centre for Urban Studies and (c) sponsored by other Ministries and agencies such as Department of Rural Development, Central Electricity Authority etc.

**(B)** Those conducted by the Institute on its own and for which participation fee is charged.

In each course, the accent is on some particular facet of broad areas like rural development administration, urban administration, financial administration, personnel administration, social policy and administration and application of quantitative and other techniques in the field of administration. The Institute conducts about 50 to 60 such courses every year with the participants numbering 1200-1500. The training programmes are designed in a pragmatic way to see that the course content is closely related to the problems of the day-to-day working of the participants. The training methodology and techniques include lectures, discussions, workshop sessions, presentation of case studies and discussion thereon, library work etc. Full interaction among academics, policy makers and administrators in an intimate and objective environment of the Institute is a special feature of the training programmes.

Since 1975 the Institute has been conducting an Advanced Professional Programme in Public Administration. The course running over one academic year commencing from Ist July and concluding on 31st March, is intended to train middle and senior level government officers of the Centre, States and Union Territories and public sector undertakings. It is a post-graduate course, designed to promote effective administrative leadership.

The Institute continues to take initiative in identifying and designing new courses. Some of the new courses established in recent years are those on Management of Motivation, Attitudinal Changes in Administration, Ethics in Administration, Vigilance in Administration, Report Writing, Develop-ment through Participation, Management for Agricultural Marketing, Quantitative Methods in Management, Economic Analysis for Public Sector Management, Multi-level planning, Public Administration and Environmental Management. Recently, the Institute has taken up the responsibility for conducting courses on Policy Formulation for officers of Indian Administrative Service in purşuance of the direction of the Prime Minister that the civil servants of all categories must compulsorily undergo training programmes.

**Training in Local Self Government**

The local government, since independence has been serving as a partner in the process of nationwide development, searching out, creating and developing areas of cooperation between the people and their government by administering a variety of services of local nature on behalf of Central Government as well as on its own self.

Local Government employees account for about two million persons. This truly constitutes a big numerical force. It has to be trained to live up to the responsibilities of the modern local government.

So far as rural local government is concerned, varied training programmes were organised at the initiative of the Central Ministry of Community Development and Panchayati Raj by a number of institutions at Central, State and regional levels. At present, the National Institute of Rural Development supported by the State institutes conduct programmes in the field of Rural Development and Rural local government.

For municipal employees in India there are not many

institutions. The All India Institute of Local Self Government has done pioneering work in the field of municipal training. It was established in 1951 having its headquarters at Bombay and various permanent as well as peripatetic centres spread all over India. The Institute conducts various training programmes regularly at its different centres providing its training services to people from all parts of the country.

The Central Government appointed in April 1963 a committee to examine the available facilities, if any, for the training of municipal employees of all categories and suggest the structure of the training programme required for such employees as well as the courses and training period for such category of officers. In pursuance of the recommendations of this Committee, the Central Government established a training institution at the national level known as Centre for Training & Research in Municipal Administration. Its main objective is to stimulate and strengthen municipal administration and to create a national awareness about the problems of urbanization and urban administration.

The Central Government also agreed to establish the Regional Centres for Research and Training in Municipal Administration. These Centres have been established in places like Calcutta, Bombay, Hyderabad and Lucknow for imparting training to the municipal personnel in the region.

It would be pertinent here to mention the Centre for Urban Studies of the Indian Institute of Public Administration which was established in December 1966 with full financial support from the Central Government. Its main objectives are:

1. to organise training courses in urban and municipal administration;
2. to hold seminars and conferences on urban and municipal problems;
3. to undertake research relating to urban and municipal affairs;
4. to develop a documentation unit and organise a clearing house of information on urban administration; and
5. to collaborate with other regional centres and academic institutions in training and research in urban administration.

The Centre organises a number of short-term specialised courses for senior officers from the municipal corporations, municipalities, urban development authorities and state government departments dealing with urban administration on subjects such as financial management, personnel administration, valuation and assessment of property tax, urban plan administration, solid waste management, urban management, shelter for urban poor, information system in urban planning, vigilance in urban authorities, urban research methods, integrated development of small and medium towns scheme management, etc.

Mention may also be made of the National Institute of Urban Affairs which is an institute for urban research in India.Its main aim is to assist and strengthen the decision-making process by making available to policy-makers, a critical and objective analysis of the urban situation, as well as alternative sets of approaches to the urban problems faced by them. Training with the object of building up planning capacities of mid-career, senior level functionaries involved in urban and human settlement development programmes is among the newly-added activities of NIUA.

The Institute has three major training assignments :

1. Training of functionaries engaged in the planning, implementation and management of Urban Basic Service Programme.
2. Training in Human Settlement Planning
3. Urban Development Workshops.

NIUA started functioning in 1976 as per the decision of the Ministry of Works and Housing.

**Training and Civil Service Development**

At no time training of civil servants has received more attention than it has been receiving now. Prime Ministers have been stressing the need for the creation of a new administrative culture for service of the masses. To achieve this end, there is a greater need for the training of civil servants of all categories to develop their competence and commitment to the basic values of our society. Training in Government has thus to be perceived and designed with a higher purpose and responsibility.

Under the direction of Prime Minister Rajiv Gandhi a meaningful programme of training of officers of the IAS related to the important phases in their career path had been worked out. The first phase is the early nine or ten years when the officers belonging to the Indian Administrative Service have to work in the field implementing various programmes. During this phase the officers will participate in the training courses related to programme implementation. During the next phase, from nine to 18 years of service, the officers will have opportunity to participate in the courses related to techniques of management which could be applied in dealing with problems of public administration. Finally, at the beginning of the senior phase of career, when the officers start getting opportunities to contribute to process of policy formulation, they will undergo training programmes related to policy analysis.

Though there has been an increase in expansion and diversification of training programmes during the last few years, the three-tier programme of training for officers belonging to the Indian Administrative Service marks a new beginning in the approach to training for civil servants related to the new emphasis on administrative reforms, with the objective of building up an efficient, clean, goal-oriented and result bound administration. There are four assumptions underlying the new approach to training. First, that as an officer advances in his career, it becomes necessary for him to assimilate new concepts, ideas, techniques and skills. Secondly, that these can be assimilated not only through experience on the job but also through intensive programmes conducted at the institutions like the Indian Institute of Public Administration. Thirdly, the new concepts, ideas and techniques can be put to use in the actual process of administ-ration and fourthly participation in the training programmes is not a matter of individual inclination or a chance occurrence but a compulsory condition of career advancement. What is visualized is a training ladder which must necessarily correspond the career ladder of the civil servants. It is to be hoped that the civil servants themselves will became more aware of the place of training in improving the calibre of civil servants and standard of public administration in our country. We are living in a fast changing world and we have to continuously update ourselves if we are to be of any relevance.

# 25

# Training for Transformation : Tasks Ahead

After the attainment of Independence, India embarked on a planned process of community development and social change. For the task of development, the traditional concept of adminis-tration had to undergo a change. In the colonial era administration was mainly concerned with law and order and collection of land revenue which was the principal source of revenue. The State was a police State. After the attainment of independence, the State had to be a welfare State and its administration, a development administration. This, of course, did not mean that a welfare State could do without the police machinery nor that development excluded regulation. But there was a definite shift of emphasis and administration had to be full of initiative and dynamism in order to stimulate and promote economic development and social change.

The principal agenda of administrative action included the following components:

(i) building up of infrastructure, both social infrastruc ture consisting of health and education as well as economic infrastructure in the shape of roads, transport, communication, irrigation, electrification and marketing.

(ii) modernisation of agriculture and rural development including revival of rural industries.

(iii) economic diversification and promotion of industrialisation and the tertiary sector in the shape of banking and insurance.

While development leading to bigger GNP was important, it was necessary to ensure that the benefit of development was not reaped only by the privileged section of the society but percolated or trickled down to the masses of people. Increased production should go with equitable distribution. Also development had to manifest itself in the improvement of the quality of life of the people. Another formulation was that development should bring the people above the poverty line. At the same time , development should take place without damaging nature's life supporting system, called the eco-system.

New policies, organisation, systems of management and personnel had to be built to perform the administrative tasks of economic development and social change.

From the organisation point of view, it should be realised that the centralised or top-down approach is not adequate. There has to be people's participation and this requires decentralised organisations and institutions in which people can play their role. Without such grassroot organisations and a system of communication reaching from the centralised administrative structure to these grassroot organisations, development would not take place adequately and people would not be able to participate in the process of development. We have to evolve and promote various types of grassroot organisation including local government institutions, autonomous organisations and field agencies.

Development and decentralisation also call for change not only in the bureaucratic structure but also in the bureaucratic attitude and orientation. Bureaucrats need new techniques like those of community mobilisation and extension. The bureaucrats have to ensure that the delivery system reaches the door of the citizen, whether farmer or the artisans. Great deal of importance is now being given to the training of bureaucrats to improve their skills of management as well as skills of evoking popular participation. Training of people themselves to enable them to participate in the process of development should also receive attention.

How far have we been successful in building up the new

administrative structure and ethos to fulfil the goals that we have set before ourselves, is the main question to which we would like to address ourselves.

Attention may be drawn to some of the major deficiencies to which thought has to be given by us during the early years of the 21st Century.

(i) The goal of homogeneous economic and social development has not been attained. Development has come to be concentrated in a few centres or areas like the metropolitan centres, capital region or the irrigated areas. Distant rural hinterland deprived of accessibility to public services have languished. A deliberate attempt to reduce economic disparities would, therefore, have to be one of the major economic responsibilities in the years to come. Economic infrastructure and delivery system will have to be built in the backward and remote areas.

(ii) The Second important problems that may continue to provide anxious time to us is that of demographic pressure on agricultural land. The availability of per capita land is continuously declining and therefore the only hope is of continuously increasing productivity of agricultural lands. Hybrid seeds, use of chemical fertilizer, insecticides and pesticides and irrigation have been the main instrument of increase in agricultural productivity during the last few decades. But the question before us is whether the upsurge of the 'green revolution' would continue or peter off with the agriculture suffering stagnation if not actually declining. The 'green revolution' has not yet become universal and there is continued scope for carrying forward the momentum of 'green revolution'. But how far we can go in this direction, is the main question.

(iii) And this brings to the third main task namely, restraining the growth of population and its pressure. Some of the developing countries have been very successful in halting the population growth by adopting the norm of one child family but others have not been so successful. There is an inverse relationship between economic development and education on one side and population growth on the other but it takes time before this relationship gets established. In the meanwhile the flood of population growth may well engulf our fragile resource base.

(iv) The population pressure not only exhibits itself in the shape of smaller agricultural holdings but also in the shape of tremendous growth in population of the urban and metropolitan areas. Urban life has suffered from tremendous pressures on different services like water and sewerage. Slums and shanties have proliferated and metropolitan areas have almost become ungovernable. It is obvious that the management of metropolitan areas is the concern of not only metropolitan authorities but also of the provincial and national governments. Spatial or regional planning has to be a part of national planning and national administration.

(v) Science and technology can come to our rescue in grappling with these tremendous problems but the technology has to be appropriate. Capital intensive technology adopted from the West may well lead to unemployment and the remedy may be worse than the disease. What is required is the appropriate technology which can make full use of human and other resources and which can promote both development and employment. Technology which destroys traditional skills without creating new skills may well prove to be counter-productive. Promotion of indigenous and innovative appropriate technology is the need of hour. We may have .o devote greater attention to the evolution of appropriate technology.

(vi) Development has already come up against the hazards of environmental destruction. Pressure on population and economic development has started seriously damaging the life supporting system in the shape of forest and water resources. Obviously, greater attention needs to be given to environmental preservation and economy in the use of finite resources. In planning and project management adequate attention may have to be given to environmental consideration.

(vii) And then there are external problems of development in the shape of deteriorating terms of trade available to the products of developing countries and the possible decline in the flow of resources from international financing agencies like the World Bank and the IMF. Developing countries may have to combine in order to promote the concept of a new international economic order and south-south cooperation so that the colonial economic pattern is not perpetuated but is modified for the benefit of the developing countries. An important aspect of south-south cooperation is the exchange of administrative experience between the developing economies. Under the umbrella of many organisations of the Third World countries, it might be possible to arrange for a regular exchange of experience between public administration institutions of the developing countries.

In the context of the above analysis, the following would emerge as the priority areas of training for the performance of tasks ahead:

(i) Training must focus on better implementation of Plan programmes and strategies aimed at elimination of poverty, problems of development in backward and remote areas and reduction of disparities.

(ii) Training should concentrate on skills and techniques required in administration for eliciting popular participation

(iii) Training programmes must concentrate on micro planning and decentralised planning, especially for backward areas

(iv) Greater attention must be paid for training for social service sector including family planning. Delivery system in the social service area can be improved through sustained training of personnel working in this area.

(v) Training must concentrate on the tremendous problem of slums and over-crowding in the cities.

(vi) Management of environment should be an important part of training in public administration. It has to be realised that preservation of environment is not only a problem of technology but also of approach to development.

(vii) There should be a greater exchange of experience between various developing countries. Indian Institute of Public Administration has already formulated a proposal for the establishment of the Third World Institute which needs to be fully supported.

# 26

# New Dimensions of Training in Public Administration

As socio-economic situation becomes more complex in our country and new problems emerge, the tasks of public administration are also becoming more and more difficult and complicated. It has become necessary to continuously gear up the administrative manpower to face the new situations, to deal with the problems effectively and to introduce innovations in administration involving even radical departures from the past practices.

More than twenty years ago while inaugurating a course on training in administration, a senior ICS officer who later on became a Governor, observed that in his view there could be no such thing as training in administration since the administration has to learned on the job. We have come far away from this outlook and it is now almost universally recognised that training is one of the essential input for improving the administrative performance. To this end, training has to constantly take note of the emerging challenges of administration and equip the administration continuously by providing new knowledge, developing new skills and techniques and reorienting attitudes. In other words, training has to ensure continuous administrative renewal.

The IIPA has introduced in recent years a number of new courses for the administrative executives in the Central and State Governments as well as the executives in public sector enterprises functioning at the middle and higher levels.

One group of these courses is connected with the Project Implementation. Monitoring and Evaluation of various projects in the field of agriculture, industry, tertiary sector and urban development. The techniques of Project Planning and Appraisal have been established somewhat earlier in the field of industrial development but they were comparatively recently introduced in the field of agriculture, tertiary sector and urban development. In a sense project management is the same in agriculture or urban development as in the field of industrial development. Everywhere it partakes the nature of investment of a chunk of searce resources of the country for promotion of a stream of goods and services and if these resources are to be productively utilized, then the investment must be based upon careful identification of the projects, their scientific formulation, vigorous appraisal, effective implementation and close and continuous supervision and monitoring. The proposals for such investments or enterprises must be based on cost-benefit analysis and project budgeting. The economic aspects of the project report must be integrated with the technical aspects as well as the organisational and managerial aspects. These principles of project formulation, appraisal, monitoring and evaluation apply to all types of agricultural projects-whether production and distribution of hybrid seeds, supply of fertilizers, storage of inputs, marketing of agricultural commodities, construction of irrigation wells, installation of pump sets, command area development, or dairy, poultry or seri-cultural projects. In the past all that we had in the field of agriculture were "schemes". The concept of "project" is far more advanced and scientific than the old concept of a "scheme". In the wake of massive assistance of the World Bank for projects of agricultural and rural development, this skill in project formulation has become an essential part of the equipment of administrators working in the field of agriculture, irrigation and rural development. In the field of urban development also, the technique of project formulation and appraisal has to be followed while undertaking a variety of projects such as water supply, sewage disposal, provision of house building sites, public housing, developing marketing complex, provisions of public utilities like library or a park. In the tertiary sector, infrastructure development, irrigation and power projects or modernisation of the irrigation system, are some of the major areas for project management. The technique of project management has to deal with physical as well as economic aspects. For physical aspects, techniques like net work analysis have to be understood and used by all administrators connected with these projects.

Slightly removed from project management is the area of micro planning. This is important in the field of development administration. A number of development projects in the rural areas have to be planned on a decentralized basis. Rural development administrators were hitherto responsible for this work. Now the bankers have joined them since the bankers have to prepare credit plans for field areas. These local development plans have to cover various sectors and different sections of the society. They have to lay special emphasis on the weaker sections of the society like small and marginal farmers, landless labourers and artisans. To work out programmes which could make them viable is an extremely difficult task which should be attempted through a series of measures which form part of micro-planning. Inspite of years of experience in this field in connection with a variety of programmes starting from the community development projects on to intensive agricultural development programmes, drought prone area programme, command area development and integrated rural development, techniques of micro planning have neither been perfected nor the field workers adequately trained. This is, therefore, the second important area of training in public administration to which IIPA has given attention in recent years. Development officers, bankers as well as technical officers of various departments have participated in these courses.

Apart from the specific sectors of administration, there are certain general techniques of administration which have emerged as the most important requirements of modern administration. Administrative decision-making today cannot be based on some intuitive judgements. They must be based on scientific analysis often quantitative in nature. The administrator must possess not only literacy but also numeracy. Hence the importance of quantitative methods in administration such as cost benefit analysis, discounted cash flow, PERT & CPM network analysis, survey and sampling, operational research etc. The Institute organised the course of this kind for the first time recently which was found extremely useful by a wide variety of civil servants working in the secretariat, in public sector enterprises, as in the field areas; all of them found the quantitative methods a definite addition to their repertoire.

A closely connected course was on economic analysis for public sector enterprises. The public sector enterprises which participated in it included such diverse organisation as the Engineers India Ltd., Oil and Natural Gas Commission, the Bharat Heavy Electricals Ltd. Training in economic analysis was given with reference to the commercial criteria as well as the social criteria, financial criteria as well as the productivity criteria of the functioning of the public enterprises. Besides these courses, specialised courses have been conducted on specific techniques like operational research, management information system and the use of computers.

Management information system is an essential pre-requisite for efficient implementation. Without management information system, effective monitoring is impossible and yet the fact remains that most of the programmes and projects do not have a comprehensive management information system. The course conducted on the subject sought not only to provide essentials of a sound management information system but also gave the participants an opportunity to evolve during the duration of the course itself, concrete management information systems for the organisations from which they came.

The use of computers is still a novelty to Indian administration. However, recently, IIPA has undertaken consultative projects for the introduction of computers. These are in respect of the treasury system in Gujarat and personnel system of the department of education in Rajasthan. In the introduction of computers the software is as much important as the hardware. The installation of a computer is probably the least important part of the introduction of computer technology. What is more important is a system for feeding the data, processing the data and interpreting the data for decision making and this is possible only if the personnel are properly trained in computer information system. The courses were conducted at Udaipur in Rajasthan and Ahemdabad in Gujarat to provide this specific training to the participants in the computer based information system.

Administration is concerned with man management, materials management and financial management. In respect of all these, new skills and techniques have to be developed. The most important aspects of man management relate to building up of morale, motivation and leadership. The test of leadership lies in development and sustenance of morale and motivation and they are thus closely related. In a recent socio-psychological study conducted by the IIPA of the middle level executives of Delhi Administration, it was discovered that the work motivation was rather low because organisational climate was stiffling rather than stimulating. Most of the personnel are lost into the dreary desert of dead routine. There is a little initiative and less freedom. There is neither reward nor recognition, resulting in alienation and antipathy. IIPA conducted a seminar for Senior Civil Servants of Delhi Administration to sensitize them to these factors which account for the low work motivation.

Good administrative leadership can inspire work motivation. Administrative leadership is the art of inspiring confidence and cooperative effort. However, Administrative leadership might be inhibited by political constraints. However, administrative leaders have to be promoters and facilitators of public interest and cannot just follow the line of least resistance. These behavioural aspects are all important in the courses on administrative leadership.

Material management is still comparatively a new subject in the field of administrative training but the administration today consumes more material than administration in the past. An institution like the Food Corporation of India has to handle enormous quantities of foodgrain. All departments and enterprises use enormous quantities of building material like steel and cement; transport enterprises, airlines or State transport use and require spare parts of machinery. How much stock of material should be maintained so that there is neither over-stocking, nor stock-outs ? This is the basic issue which the course on material management handles. Financial and economic aspects of material management are as important as the physical aspects.

In the field of financial management, performance budgeting is a new technique which has been introduced in a rather ritualistic way in public administration but has not yet served the purpose in the sense that it has not been used as a technique of planning public expenditure. Expenditure control is still exercised through the old technique of *ad hoc* cuts rather than regulating it in proportion to performances which is the essence of the technique of performance budgeting.

The impact of these innovative courses conducted at IIPA in recent years may not be readily felt but they are bound to be of long range significance and make their own contribution in improving administrative performance and productivity. In the year 1982, which is declared as the year of 'Productivity', this contribution of IIPA is of national significance.

# 27

# Training of Trainers in Public Administration

## Dimensions of Training

In-Service training on a comprehensive basis in all departments of public administration has yet to be established in most of the States. The States which have state academies or institute of public administration have, of course, much better arrangements for in service training than the other States which have yet not established such institutions. Yet the over-all picture still leaves much to be desired. The legitimacy and indeed the crucial importance of in-service training through suitably designed courses is yet to be recognised in most of the States. The procedures of recruitment of various departments stipulate minimum educational qualifications which are provided by the Universities and other academic institutions. The products of the Universities, however, have to be deliberately moulded and developed in order to fulfil the more specific requirements of jobs and assignments in the departments. Such specific equipment has to be technical as well as managerial and administrative. Unfortunately, there is as yet no comprehensive attempt to provide, in a deliberate manner, this additional technical and administrative training through "ladder-type courses" to match the career development of the Government officers who are left in the main, to pick up what they could through day-to-day experience. Apart from the fact that this "Catch as Catchcan" approach is a time consuming arrangement, it may also be extremely costly in terms of the mistakes committed by untrained functionaries. Moreover, administration has to keep pace with the changing technology and organisation. We are living in a period of "explosion of knowledge" which is said to be doubling every five years. A continuous mental retreading or refreshing of knowledge of administrative personnel is very badly required if it has to cope up with the "revolution of raising expectations" of the people from the agencies of Government. In a period of rapid economic development and social change, the Government is required to undertake the tasks which are of non-traditional nature. These can not be discharged without a deliberate attempt to impart new skills and knowledge to the functionaries in charge of the tasks. Even the traditional tasks of Government have to be discharged in a new manner, in the new contexts and situations. Unfortunately, it has become a rule rather than an exception, for public administration to rush into new responsibilities without even giving thought to the adequacy qualitative no less than quantitative of the personnel. What is badly required is a carefully advanced manpower planning and training.

We have, therefore, to accept the following propositions as basic to any attempt to make public administration a fit instrument of the responsibilities that the Government have to discharge.

(1) In-service training has to be provided to different types of personnel in different departments.

(2) For new tasks and programmes, specific courses will have to be designed and provided.

(3) Training has to be both initial and refresher- the latter to avoid man-power obsolescence.

(4) Training has to be both technical and subject matter as well as organisational, administrative and managerial.

The administrative personnel working for technical programmes must have an appreciation of the technical requirements. On the other hand, the administrative personnel cannot be indifferent to the requirements of organisation, personnel, finance and management.

A more specific area in which senior administrative and technical personnel need training is in the processes and techniques of planning. In a planned economy, such as ours, the programmes and schemes of departments should fit into the overall planning. At the same time, project formulation and evaluation should be a built-in future of our public administration. The Ford Foundation has recently entered into an arrangement with the Planning Commission for strengthening the planning personnel and procedures in the States. Training in the process of planning should obviously form an important part of this new arrangement. Training institutes will have therefore to design special courses in Economic Planning, Programme Planning, Project Formation and Appraisal.

**Training Arrangements**

For mounting a training programme of such nature, there are two essential minimum requirements in every State. (1) A well organised State Academy or Institute of Public Administration providing both technical and managerial administration for administrative courses and (2) A training organisation built through the gamut of public administrative system. As regards the first, the training institute or academy of every State has to build up, a faculty with the capability of organising both technical and administrative courses. It is not necessary that all the technical competence required for such courses should be available within the faculty. The services of guest-lecturers could always be availed of. But the faculty must have a nucleus character and should be able to identify the specific technical requirements of a course, design such a course, work out its syllabus and locate and identify personnel whose services could be drawn upon for the conduct of such courses. Such an institution should be headed by a senior civil servant with not only wide experience in a fair cross-section of public administration but also with a professional as well as an academic outlook on public administration and its place in the modern world. He must combine within himself administrative experience, academic inclinations and a perspective over the future. A prior experience in training would also be essential.

The training organisation might consist of the principal training officer or a Director of Training in general administrative department working directly under the Chief Secretary with better links with training officers in every department and area of public administration. It should be the work of training organisation to link up the programme of recruitment of various departments with the task and responsibilities to be discharged by them. They should ensure a careful man-power planning in every department and a phased programme of training of all the functionaries in the different departments.

Obviously there should be a very close contact between the institute of training and training organisation in the department. It may even be desirable to designate the director of the institute as the director of training or the principal training officer.

Every State will have to take stock of its present training arrangements and to work out the manner in which they could create the training organisation described above. Most States do not have any arrangements to refresh the technical competence of their officers. It may be necessary for the State Training Institute to make use of the academic institutions and the institutes of technology to provide periodic refresher training in various technical subjects. In the field of general orientation, the orientation and study centres started by the Ministry of Community Development did provide a general orientation in development administration to not only the administrative personnel like the BDOs but also the technical officers of various departments. Such orientation course also exist in departments like Cooperation and Health. It is, however, doubtful whether anything of that sort is provided for in the older departments like Revenue and Home which nevertheless have to introduce new schemes and programmes from time to time.

## Trainers and Their Training

It would be appropriate to include the faculty of the training institutions and the officers of the training organisations in the category of trainers. If, however, training is a continuous process, then every superior officer has the responsibility for the training of his subordinate and must have the outlook of a trainer. It is the specific responsibility of the faculty of the training institutes and the officers of the training organisations to promote and stimulate such an outlook throughout public administration. While considering the training of the trainers, it is however necessary to concentrate on the faculty of the training institutions and the officers of the training organisations.

The need for the training of these two types of personnel is somewhat different. The faculty of the training institutions must have a thorough professional knowledge of their specific areas, be they agriculture, rural industry, personnel management or financial management. They should also have the skill in teaching which requires knowledge of the learning process, communication skill, etc. On the other hand the officers of training organisation must have a sound knowledge of personnel management and man-power planning.

In the ultimate analysis, the trainers must train themselves. They must be constantly engaged in the intellectual pursuit which is an unending process. The library of the institute of training should be its strongest asset. It should provide them with upto-date literature in the form of books, journals and reports published in India and abroad. Secondly, the faculty of the institute must have opportunities to participate in seminars and courses in India and occasionally abroad. Thirdly, they should be constantly engaged in research to sharpen their faculty and to link their knowledge from books with the field situation. Fourthly, they should keep close contact with the academic institutions. Fifthly, they should have close liaison with the different departments. The training organisations can provide such liaison.

The officers in the training organisation must frequently visit the training institutes. They must have a live contact with them as well as with the various administrative departments. In the specific subject of man-power planning, the officers of the training organisation should undergo specially designed courses at the Institute of Man-power Planning and the Institute of Public Administration.

We are now gradually developing in this country National level training institutions in various fields of public administration. The Indian Institute of Public Administration is engaged in training and research in Public Administration as a whole. The National Academy of Public Administration conducts initial and refresher courses for officers of the All India and Central Services. It is possible to develop the scope of activities of these two institutes in various ways. One such development can take place in the direction of training of trainers. A regular programme of Short Courses, Conferences, Seminars and Workshops could be developed for the trainers in the general areas of public administration at these two institutions. In specific areas, however, there would be need for additional subject matter courses. These have to be organised at the National Training Institutions in the special fields. For instance the Vaikunth Mehta National Institute of Co-operative Management has been conducting courses for the training of trainers in the field of co-operation in which there could be greater participations from the faculty members concerned from the State Institutes and Training Centres. There could be similar participation in institutions like the National Institute of Community Development, National Institute of Health Administration, National Institute of Banking Management, National Institute of Labour and Employment, etc. There should be a close nexus between training institutes and trainers at the State level and the National Training Institutions and their faculty. Moreover, between training institutions in public administration as a whole and the training institutions in the private sector or in the Universities like the Indian Institute of Management or Institutes of Technology, there should also be closer links and sharing of knowledge, experience and activities.

# PART V

# POLITICS ADMINISTRATION AND PUBLIC INTEREST

# 28

# Role of Bureaucracy vis a vis the Political Executive

The question of the roles of the bureaucracy and the political executive in the process of public administration and the relationships between them in playing their roles has been the subject-matter of discussion, not only in India but also in other countries, specially those with the system of liberal democracy, such as United Kingdom, France, West Germany, Denmark, Sweden, U.S.A. and Australia. While U.S.A. has a Presidential form of government, the rest are parliamentary democracies. Of these, the Westminster model of United Kingdom is considered to be closest to our own system of parliamentary democracy.

To pose the subject of relationship as one of bureaucracy *versus* political executive, is however, perhaps to start from an assumption which may not necessarily be correct. The assumption that the relationship between the bureaucrats and the political executive is one of antagonism, may be contrary to the normal day-to-day experience and practice of public administration where the two have to work together as interdependent participants in discharging the tasks of government. These tasks cannot be discharged satisfactorily without close and smooth relationship between the bureaucrats and the political executives. When such is the case, the matter scarcely receives any attention. But it is only when conflicts and resultant tensions arise between the two that the subject becomes a matter of discussion, debate or even controversy.

Such became the situation following what has come to

be known as "Ponting case" in the United Kingdom. Mr. Ponting was civil servant in the Defence Ministry. He felt so much dissatisfied with the government regarding the sinking of the "General Belgrano" ship during British-Argentina War over the Falkland Islands, (he felt he was being instructed to mislead the Parliament) that he leaked out the facts by anonymously sending papers to a Member of Parliament Mr. Tam Dalyell. Mr. Pontig was proceeded against both departmentally and in the court for leaking out secrets. He was found not guilty by the court but was discharged from service.

It was the case of Mr. Ponting that his loyalty to truth, to the nation and to the Parliament was above that of the loyalty to the Government of the day and to his Minister, and he felt that his action was fully justified in terms of the higher loyalty to "Public interest."

The case became a touchstone of bureaucratic behaviour and led to the examination of the whole subject and the issues involved therein by the head of the British Civil Service, Sir Robert Armstrong. On the basis of his examination, he issued a memorandum to serve as a guideline for the civil servants in dealing with their Ministers. In this memorandum, Sir Robert Armstrong put together certain "inarticulate major premises" governing the relationship between the bureaucrat and the Minister which though unwritten were understood or taken for granted and formed the basis of the functioning of the British government for about a century. The memorandum dealt with both the constitutional position of the civil servants and the practical code of conduct. The memorandum evoked a lot of public interest. The sequel to the memorandum was the appointment of a Committee by the House of Commons known as the Treasury and the Civil Service Committee, on "Civil Servants and Ministers: Duties and Responsibilities." The report was released on 12th of May 1986. The report, while commending the Armstrong Memorandum, found it inadequate in some respects and came out with some of its own recommendations. It would be worthwhile to discuss the main issues arising out of the Armstrong Memorandum and the suggestions made in that connection, since they might be of relevance to the Indian conditions.

The first issue is regarding the constitutional position of

the civil servant. Sir Robert Armstrong's memorandum makes it quite clear that the civil servant is wholly accountable to the Government in power and to the Minister. "The duty of the individual civil servant is first and foremost to the Minister of the Crown." Civil servants of England are "servants of the Crown" but for all practical purposes the Crown is represented by the government in power. In other words, the civil servant has no independent constitutional position "separate from the elected Government of the day." He has, no doubt, to provide his own independent advice without fear or favour to the Minister on policy formulation but once the policies are decided by the Minister and the Government, he has to faithfully carry them out without any reservations. The subject of disclosure of information is related to this basic position. The civil servant cannot give out any information except with the authority of the Minister nor can he do anything which will, in any way, compromise the position of the government and the Minister.

But is there any way out for a civil servant when he feels that he cannot carry out the orders of the Minister? One such case may be when he thinks that the orders of the Minister are *illegal*. Armstrong memorandum suggests that in such cases the matter should be put before the Permanent Secretary who should refer it to the Legal Department so that the proper legal advice is obtained and brought to the notice of the Minister. If necessary, the matter may go to the Cabinet Secretary, and to the Prime Minister. In any case, the question of civil servant, carrying out the illegal orders of the Minister should not arise.

There may be other cases, however, where the civil servant may, as a matter of conscience or as a matter of principle or on moral grounds feel that he is not in a position to carry out the orders of the Minister. In such cases again, he can take up the matter with the Permanent Secretary who is head of the Department who may even take it to the Cabinet Secretary. If, however, civil servant is overruled, he has no alternative but to either carry out the orders or resign.

The position regarding the remedies available to a civil servant as indicated by the Armstrong Memorandum was not fully endorsed by the House of Commons Committee. They had some other suggestions to make. One was that the work of the Cabinet Secretary and the head of the Department should be bifurcated. The responsibilities of the two positions are too many for any one individual to do justice to them. They have, therefore, recommended a separate and distinct position of the head of the civil service. The responsibility of the incumbent of the post is to wholly attend to the grievances of the civil servants particularly relating to the relationship with the Minister. This alone would ensure the morale of the civil service is maintained at a high level. The other recommendation made is the creation of the post of an Inspector-General of Civil Service who would not be removable by the Minister and would hear in a judicial capacity, complaints by a civil servant who feels that a Minister is acting in an improper way. This would be thus an external mechanism of appeal available to the civil servants. A view was also placed before the House of Commons Committee that if a conflict arose between the Minister and civil servants, the way of resolving it was through Parliament because it was Parliament to whom Ministers were responsible.

While the Armstrong memorandum dealt with the duties and responsibilities of the civil servants in relation to the Ministers, it did not deal with "corresponding responsibilities which Minister has in relation to civil servants." Sir Robert as a civil servant was unable to instruct Ministers on their duties and responsibilities in relation to civil servants. However, the House of Commons Committee went into this question. Appearing before the Committee as witness Sir Robert stated that the responsibility of Ministers to their civil servant was "to read and digest the information and advice that the civil service has to offer, to take it seriously" and consider it along with whatever information and advice they have from the sources. Another witness making the same point regarding the duty of the Ministers to give a fair hearing to the civil servants added that "they should not merely overrule the civil servants on political whims." The official who speaks his mind should not be put in a disadvantageous position as compared with the sycophantic or the timid. Ministers should not ask the civil servants to act in ways which are immoral. Their power of appointment should not be used for partisan purposes. The House of Commons Committee recommended that the Prime Minister should issue a note containing guidelines such as above for Ministers setting out what Ministers may or may not require their civil servants to do in proper course of their duties.

The position in India regarding the role of civil servants is somewhat similar to that in U.K. However,India has a written Constitution and what has been a matter of convention and tradition in U.K. is in India governed by the provisions of the Constitution. In India, under the Constitution, the executive power of the State vests in the President (Indian counterpart of the Crown). However, the President exercises these functions according to the aid and advice of the Council of Ministers headed by the Prime Minister. Similar position obtains in the State where the executive power is exercised in the name of the Governor who acts according to the advice of the Council of Ministers. The advice of the Council of Ministers is according to the policy of the government which reflects the mandate and ideology of the political executive. Articles 308-328 of the Constitution make specific references to the civil services in India. It is said perhaps there is no other Constitution in the world which makes provisions relating to civil services in the fundamental law of the land. This gives civil servants in India a distinct role to play. In the discharge of their duties they are protected by the Constitution.

However, constitutional protection is one thing and practice is quite another. In practice, it is alleged that the civil servants are unwilling to render unpalatable advice to Ministers and succumb to pressure in the implementation of policies. Civil servants, it has been said, behave in a supine and pliable manner and examples are given when the civil servants even commit illegal or improper acts to satisfy their political masters. The Prime Minister Rajiv Gandhi in his address to the nation soon after assuming office laid emphasis on the crucial importance of administrative reforms. One aspect of the reform, he observed, related to excessive politicisation of bureaucracy which demoralised it and adversely affected its performance.

While the accountability of the civil servants to Ministers and to Government cannot be questioned, it does not mean that the civil servants should not feel free to discharge their duties of advising the Minister and the government on policy formulation without fear or favour and carrying them out in an impartial manner. The whole civil service institution exists for this purpose. If the civil servants have any inhibitions in discharge of their duties, they will cease to be professional civil (public) servants. They may become sycophants or mere yes-men and the very *raison d'etre* of the civil service as an institution may disappear.

In the light of the foregoing, it is suggested that the code of conduct for the civil servants should be as follows: (1) that the civil servant should be master of his own work, apply himself thoroughly to the issues under consideration and give his advice on the basis of a thorough examination of the issues involved, alternative courses of action and the consequences that follow from the adoption of the various alternative courses; (2) having given his advice, he should accept the decision of the Minister and carry it out faithfully; (3) however, if the policy decision or any other decision is illegal or financially improper, he will be well within his rights to refuse to implement such an order or decision. He should represent in the matter to the head of the civil service and ultimately to the Chief Minister or to the Prime Minister.

The statement of the constitutional position and the conduct it enjoins, does not, however, finally dismiss the moral and ethical issues involved in terms of higher loyalty of public servants (which includes both bureaucrats and political executives) and the related code of ethics (not just code of conduct).

• No doubt the *immediate accountability* of civil servants is to the government in power. But in the *ultimate* analysis, their loyalty has to be the "public cause",to "public interest" and the national goals and objectives. In India they have been clearly laid down in the Directive Principles of the Constitution and the Five Year Plans and other documents. They include, to mention only the more important ones, commitment to raising the level of masses of people, abolition of poverty, national integration, preservation of unity and freedom of the country and protection of environment. Here it may be proper to draw attention to the code of ethics for government servants in U.S.A. which requires them to "put loyalty to the highest moral principles and to the country *above* loyalty to persons, party or government department."

The same applies to political executives also. Their *immediate loyalty* may be to their party but, in the ultimate analysis, their loyalty has also to be to the "public interest" as a whole, transcending limited party or sectional interest.

Thus, both the civil servants and the political executives have to dedicate themselves to the steady, long-term interest of the nation as a whole. In the short run the political executives might well be under the pressure of party interests or interest of certain groups. But a politician becomes a statesman when he places the interest of the nation above the interests of the party or particular sectarian interests. However, if the national interest at large is sacrificed at the altar of partisan interests then difficulties are likely to arise in the discharge of duties by the civil servants.

Shri Dharam Vira has drawn attention to his experience which is relevant in this connection. In the early years after independence the stalwarts like Pandit Nehru, Sardar Patel, Dr. Rajendra Prasad and Rajaji were at the helm of government. They were statesmen, who stood for national interest. They were broad minded enough to allow their civil servants to give their frank advice even though contrary to their own views and perceptions. Dharam Vira feels that after the first generation of stalwarts disappeared from the scene, their standards were not maintained. Long-term public interest was often sacrificed at the altar of narrow short-term considerations. Fearless, frank advice of the civil servants was often not relished and such civil servants who dared to give free and frank advice were cold shouldered or sidetracked if not punished. Frequent transfers of civil servants who refused implicitly to carry out the wishes of politicians in power, became the rule. This phenomenon of so called "political interference" has constantly created problems for the civil servants in the discharge of their duty.

The problems can only be resolved if both the bureaucrats and the political executives as public servants make disinterested pursuit of national interest the sole touchstone of their actions. Of course, even then conflicting interpretation of public interest is bound to arise in policy formulation and decision-making. But these could be bonafide differences and it is obvious that interpretation of public interest by the political executive must prevail in the ultimate analysis.

The above discussion leaves out certain fundamental questions about the role of the bureaucracy itself and the extent to which it is able to play its role properly, particularly in the context of the working of the modern government. The Armstrong memorandum throws no light on this since it is no more than a formal document explaining the formal position of the civil servant in relation to Minister.

However, in the thinking and literature on public administration, it is a subject which has received great importance. The view about the role of bureaucracy has undergone a change over the last several years.

In the earlier years, a sharp distinction was made between the spheres of politics and administration. Woodrow Wilson wrote, "Administration lies outside the proper sphere of politics-Administrative questions are not political questions; the field of administration is the field of business, it is removed from the hurry and strife of politics. Expression of the public will is the sphere of politics while execution of that will is administration." Luther Gulick observed that "politics and administration were heterogeneous functions, which cannot be combined without producing inefficiency."

A similar distinction was later on made by Herbert Simon between matters of interest and values and those belonging to facts and knowledge. Politicians are concerned with the former whereas the civil servants are concerned with the latter. Thus, while the civil servants are concerned with technical efficacy and feasibility, politicians are concerned with responsiveness to the relevant constituencies of the people. The latter may involve politicians in patronage, log rolling and pandering to special interests.

Yet another distinction is in terms of policies and their execution. While political executives take policy decisions, bureaucrats merely implement them. This view is not accepted because bureaucrats do take part in the process of decision-making and policy formulation.

Yet another formulation regarding division of labour between the bureaucrats and the political executives is that while bureaucrats are concerned with continuity and stability, the politicians are eager to introduce innovative or even radical change flowing from their ideology. If the bureaucracy provides *equilibrium* to the machinery of government so that it remains at an even keel, political executives introduce *energy* required for change. "While politicians articulate society's dreams, bureaucrats bring them gingerly to earth." While politicians energise the policy system, bureaucrats do the backroom work, managing incre-mental adjustments. While the civil servants are content with incremental change,the political executives are concerned with policy initiatives of broad scope, and dealing with controversial questions. The politicians go beyond the organised clientele and articulate unorganised interest. Ministers make major changes while proposals generated by civil servants are of the nature or 'status quo' or 'safety first." It was said that during the period of political instability in France, the bureaucrats smoothly carried out the business of administration but another view is that the bureaucrats did not really govern the country but simply carried on routine functions and maintained the status quo.

It is in this context that in recent years, a change has been taking place both in thought and practice regarding the division between administration and politics. It is felt that for pushing forward innovative changes desired by the political executives, something more than the routine minded administration is required. The vital support needed by the political executive to carry out change has to be provided by experts from outside directly assisting the Ministers. This trend of outside experts was seen in the political appointments made by Prime Minister Harold Wilson (Sir Thomas Balogh, Prof. Nicholas Kaldor and others) and recently by the Prime Minister, Mrs. Margaret Thatcher (Lord Derek Rayner of Marks & Spencer). The French have the system of "cabinets" consisting of personal staff to support Ministers and his policies. The House of Commons Committee looked into this issue. Many witnesses appearing before the Committee stated that political advisers in small numbers as the members of the Minister's staff have proved their worth and the civil servants have been able to work with them. Even Sir Robert Armstrong felt that these outside experts played a useful role. These outside experts can constitute 'policy units' for the Minister. On the other hand, the appointment of such policy units of outside experts might create a wall between the Minister and the Department and would downgrade the role of the permanent civil servants.

In India, the experiment of Special Assistants to Ministers was tried but later on given up as not a very happy institution. However, the point still remains. Can the routine minded, maintenance oriented, filepushing, pedestrian bureaucracy provide adequate support for a bold, forward-looking, dynamic and innovative administration required by the new leadership to usher India in the twenty-first century? If not, are not some changes needed in the administrative system? Bureaucrats need to be "Social Scientists in action." It is necessary to pick up those in the civil service who have a deeper understanding of the economic, political, social and environmental system out of which administrative issues arise and which provide means for effectively dealing with those issues. Procedure oriented civil servants who have only superficial understanding of these issues can hardly provide needed support. Nor are of any use the bureaucrats whose forte is only manipulative skill mainly used for the self-serving purposes to jockey themselves into strategic positions. In this context proper selection and placement is of vital importance.

A question may be raised whether such an approach would not lead to the concept of "committed bureaucracy", and whether it would be compatible with the doctrine of "political neutrality" of the civil servant. The system in U.K. as in India is based on the assumption that civil service is expected to serve governments of different political complexions with the same sense of devotion to duty. Hence it has necessarily to be politically neutral. The Committee of House of Commons felt that the non-political character of the career civil service should be preserved and it should not be politicised. On the other hand, in U.S.A., higher administrative posts are held by political appointee. Even in West Germany political alignment had become a factor in the selection of civil servants for higher positions. In France also the distinction between politics and civil service is blurred as witnessed by the fact that civil servants emerge as political leaders, the most outstanding being Giscard D' Estaing who rose to be President of France.

In India too recruitment to political executive is undergoing a change. Instead of the old style politician, persons with managerial, professional or technocratic background are emerging as political executives. This would require similar change on the civil service side also. Neither the traditional political executive nor the traditional bureaucrat can be equal to the emerging concept of politico-administrative hybrid required for dealing with complex issues and challenges faced by India today. The trend is for a growing convergence of the role of the bureaucrat and the political executive.

To sum up, the relationship between bureaucrats and political executives is not fundamentally one of zerosum conflict. Their mutual relationship should neither be of collision nor collusion.; it should rather be one of creative cooperation, based on a sense of shared responsibility. They have to work together in facing multiple challenges before the government and in fulfilling the aspirations of the people. The bureaucrats and the political executives should reinforce each other so as to augment their diverse capabilities. However, it might well be necessary for a forward looking system of public administration to go beyond the traditional concept of the politicians and the bureaucrats and be prepared to introduce innovations, so as to bring about a politico-administrative symbiosis required by modern government.

# 29

# Public Accountability and Ethics in Administration

Public accountability is a feature which distinguishes public administration in a democratic set-up as against that in an autocratic set-up. An autocrat is accountable to none whereas in a democracy, the public administrative authorities are, in the ultimate analysis accountable to the people.

In a system of Parliamentary democracy, the Parliament represents the people and Government is accountable to the Parliament. The Government itself consists of the political executive and administrative executive. The administrative executive is accountable to the political executive, which in turn is accountable to the Parliament.

The administrative executive is arranged in hierarchical order and subordinate public servants are accountable to their superiors.

Various mechanisms have been evolved to enforce accountability. Before the budget is passed by Parliament, there is a full-fledged discussion on the annual reports of the departments and in the course of discussion, the Members of Parliament raise several points regarding the working of the department and the Minister incharge is required to provide explanations and clarifications of the points raised. It is only after the Parliament is satisfied on the points raised, that the grants of the department are passed. It is true that almost every year for want of time, demands for grants of executive department get passed, without discussion by applying gillotine but the remedy for this would be either more time allowed for discussion on demands for grants or better rationing of time.

Even after this, Parliament enforces the accountability of every department through various devices like parliamentary questions, call attention motions and discussions in the consultative committees.

Public Accounts Committee makes a thorough review of the work of various departments on the basis of the audit report presented by the A. Gs in States and the Comptroller & Auditor General at the Centre. Secretaries and their senior colleagues appear before the Public Accounts Committee to explain the lapses pointed out in the audit report. However, more often than not, the matters are reviewed several years after their occurrence when those responsible for the lapses might through retirement or transfer not be available to answer the questions.

Individual members of the Cabinet while being responsible for the departments in their charge are also accountable to the Cabinet and its committees which review from time to time several aspects of the working of the departments.

Administrative executive is, as stated already, accountable to the political executive. All important decisions are, of course, taken by the political executive with the help of Secretariat officials and within the policies laid down, the line departments carry on their day to day work, reviewed from time to time by the Minister or the Secretary who helps the Minister in such reviews. It is through such reviews that field administration is accountable to the ministry. Through annual confidential reports, the work of public servants is assessed which affect their future career. Except for the work of the Parliamentary Committees, there is no direct inter-face between the Parliament and the administrative executives. Vis-a-vis Parliament, it is the Minister who shoulders the entire burden of accountability. For every act of omission or commission, it is the Minister who assumes the constitutional responsibility. By convention, the individual officials are not expected to be mentioned by name on the floor of the Parliament, since no one should be personally criticised who has no opportunity to be personally present and reply. This does not mean that individual responsibility cannot be fixed on a public official — it can be but through the administrative process.

The Committee on Subordinate Legislation keeps a watch on rules and regulations issued by departments and satisfies itself that they are within the four corners of laws passed by Parliament or Legislature.

The public enterprises while being accountable to their Board are in the ultimate analysis accountable to the Minister and the Parliament. The Parliamentary Committee on Public Undertakings reviews the work of public enterprises and draws attention to deficiencies and suggests improvements.

Whenever serious administrative lapses take place, enquiries are held to enforce accountability on those responsible for their serious lapses. Such enquiries often show that it is difficult to pinpoint responsibility. Decisions are taken in such a manner that responsibility cannot be fixed. Files pass through several stages, meetings are held which spread the range of accountability so wide that no one individual could be held responsible for any lapse. Sometimes, action is taken on the basis of oral instructions and this adds to the difficulties in fixing accountability. Circulars have therefore been issued to the effect that all oral instructions should be followed by orders in writing.

If any action by any administrative authority causes loss to a citizen, he may go to the court of law for redressal of his grievances. However, no public official can be criminally prosecuted without the necessary permission of Government authority. It is felt, however, that for any lapse in the shape of any unconstitutional or illegal act of public servant, the accountability of the individual civil servant must be enforced in course of law and he should not take shelter behind the protection given by law.

Ombudsmen or vigilance authorities are also agencies through which the public citizens can get their redressal against corrupt or illegal acts of public servants.

But public accountability is not just in the negative sense of holding public servants responsible for his lapses. It has a positive connotation. Public servants have responsibilities to discharge which are of tremendous public significance and indeed can make all the difference between the survival and progress of the nation. To fulfil these responsibilities, a public servant needs stability of tenure and necessary administrative support.

Given these pre-conditions, he must be held accountable. This often does not happen because of constant transfers and diffused responsibility.

The positive aspect of public accountability in terms of achieving results is far more important than the negative aspect in terms of avoiding lapses. Unfortunately the latter is often highlighted while the former is neglected. If this happens, public accountability may prove to be even counter-productive. Public servants would like to err on the safe side rather than take decisions which could expose them to errors and public enquiries. Public servants should have the full confidence that bonafide mistakes would not expose them to persecution while positive achievement would be recognised and rewarded.

Finally, public accountability is a matter of attitude of public servants towards the public. Very often public servants tend to forget that public administration is not an end in itself but a means to an end - and the end and indeed the sole *raison-de etre* of public administration is public service and this should be reflected in every act of every public servant from top to bottom. It is only then that the public will have the feeling that public administration is accountable to the public. To an extent, training can promote and foster such attitude amongst the public servants.

# PART VI

# ADMINISTRATION OF PUBLIC ENTERPRISES

# 30

# Politico-Social Environment and Public Sector Enterprises

Every enterprise functions in an environment — political, social and economic and we should consider all of them because they affect the working of an enterprise.

## Public Sector Enterprises as a Means of Economic Development

We had public sector enterprises even much before Independence, notably, railways, post offices and ordnance factories which were run on departmental lines. But it was only after Independence that the public sector enterprises started coming up in a big way. The economy was backward and underdeveloped. Entrepreneurship was limited. Basic industries were not existent and hence it was felt that public enterprises were needed as pace setters of economic development. Thus, public sector enterprises in fields like steel, oil, natural gas, petroleum, atomic energy were set up in response to a pragmatic need. They provided the foundation and precondition of a sustained diversified process of economic development.

## Public Sector and Economic Philosophy

However, there was also an ideological basis for the establishment of public enterprises. That ideology was sometimes known as that of a socialist pattern of society, some times as that of a mixed economy and some other time that of a planned economy. In the philosophical statements regarding such an economic system, it was asserted that the public sector should gain the commanding heights of the economy.

### State and Public Sector

However, it has been sometimes characterized that instead of becoming the commanding heights of a socialist economy, the public enterprises have taken the shape of State Capitalism. The State has been dominant and it is stated that this has acted as a damper to the development of the autonomy of public enterprises. It is often stated that there is much back-seat driving of public enterprises by ministries and departments. Also, while the ultimate accountability has to be to the Parliament in a democratic system, it has affected the capacity of public enterprises to act as autonomous commercial enterprises.

### Goals and Criteria of Public Enterprises

This raises further point as to goals and criteria of public enterprises. Should the commercial goals be prominent or the socio-political goals like development of backward areas or provision of employment opportunities, or the State acting as a good employer?

### Philosophy and Ethos of Public Enterprises

Then there comes the question of the philosophy and ethos of public enterprises themselves. It is complained that there is sometimes too much of bureaucratic ethos governed by literary adherence to rules and regulations, what is inconsistent with flexible decision-making needed by commercial enterprises. On the other hand, it is also sometimes stated that the public enterprises sometimes are no different from private enterprises and are without any distinct public sector philosophy.

### Management-Worker Relationship

This is particularly relevant in employer-employee relationships or management-employee relationships. The managers of the employees do not consider themselves as co-workers in a national endeavour. The trade unionism persists in public enterprises as much as in private enterprises.

### Relationship with the Public

Finally, comes the relationship with the public. The public are not treated in such a way as to make them feel that public enterprises are their own. People do not have a sense of belongingness. Often, the public sector enterprises like railway or state transport or post and telegraph pay scant attention to public conveniences.

# 31

# Public Enterprises— State Policies and Managerial Improvement

## The Changing Role of the State as an Economic Agent

The role of the State in India before the attainment of Independence in 1947 was confined to the maintenance of law and order and perpetuation of the colonial regime. The State was called the 'Police State' or the 'Night-watchman State', and its attitude to economic affairs was *laissez-faire.* The collection of land revenue and other taxes was meant to provide resources for carrying on the so-called sovereign functions mentioned above.

After the attainment of Independence, there was a radical change in the role of the State. With the attainment of Independence, the national attention was focussed on rapid economic development for raising the level of living of the masses of people. It was felt that rapid economic development was not possible in *laissez-faire* State. It rather called for ambitious plans and programmes of economic development in whose formulation and implementation the State had to play a main role.

## Pattern of Economic Development

There were two alternative models of economic development before India. One was the path of capitalistic development followed by the western democracies and the other of socialist development followed by Russia and other eastern European countries. The path of capitalistic development was not acceptable to a country like India because it was felt that it would lead to monopoly inequality and exploitation, and may not be instrumental in bringing about development at as rapid a pace as desired. On the other hand, the socialist path to economic development was also not acceptable because it was feared that the simultaneous ownership of all the means of production, including land by the State brought about through revolutionary measures would only lead to totalitarianism with all its attendant problems. It was, therefore, decided to follow the third way, the way of mixed economy, with following clear-cut features:

(a) There would be an overall frame of national planning with aggregate goals regarding the rate of increase of Gross National Product and developments in the major sectors of the economy.

(b) In the national plan, there would be scope for private, cooperative as well as public sector.

(c) The private sector would continue to make its contribution to the economic system, particularly in the field of consumer goods industries as well as in agriculture. But the private sector would have to conform to the goals of national planning as well as national policies aimed at control of monopoly, dispersal of economic activities, etc.

**Scope for Public Sector**

(d) The Public sector would enter in those fields where the private sector would not be forthcoming, but which were considered to be essential for national development. These would include basic and heavy industries like steel, nonferrous metal, petroleum, coal and mining, fertilizer and chemical complexes, building of aeroplanes, ships, locomotives, passenger coaches, heavy engineering and machine tools etc. These were described as the "commanding heights" of the economy. Insurance and major banking institutions would also be nationalised. As a part of its regulatory framework, the State would also undertake a major role in the public distribution system through organizations like the Food Corporation of India. In the field of infra-structure like irrigation, electrification and power generation, the State would also have a major role. The Public Sector was to make also investments in consumer goods industries like drugs and pharmaceuticals, cement, fertilizer and sugar partly for nursing sick units taken over by Government. The progress in the establishment of the public sector enterprises in the country could be judged from the following statement:-

| *Successive Plans* | *Date* | *Total investment in crore or 10 million rupees* |
|---|---|---|
| Ist Plan | 1.4.51 | 29 |
| 2nd Plan | 1.4.55 | 81 |
| 3rd Plan | 1.4.61 | 953 |
| Annual Plans | 1.4.66 | 2415 |
| 4th Plan | 1.4.69 | 3902 |
| 5th Plan | 1.4.74 | 6237 |
| Annual Plan | 1.4.79 | 15602 |
| 6th Plan | 1.4.80 | 18225 |
| | 31.3.81 | 21126 |
| 7th Plan | 1.4.85 | 42,673 |
| | 31.3.86 | 50,362 |
| | 31.3.87 | 61,643 |
| | 31.3.88 | 71,213 |
| | 31.3.89 | 85,628 |
| | 31.3.90 | 99,329 |
| | 31.3.91 | 1,13,234 |

| *Year* | *Number of enterprises* |
|---|---|
| 1971-72 | 93 |
| 1972-73 | 101 |
| 1973-74 | 114 |
| 1974-75 | 120 |
| 1975-76 | 121 |
| 1976-77 | 149 |

| | |
|---|---|
| 1977-78 | 155 |
| 1978-79 | 159 |
| 1979-80 | 169 |
| 1980-81 | 168 |
| 1981-82 | 183 |
| 1982-83 | 188 |
| 1983-84 | 214 |
| 1984-85 | 215 |
| 1985-86 | 225 |
| 1986-87 | 228 |
| 1987-88 | 225 |
| 1988-89 | 232 |
| 1989-90 | 244 |
| 1990-91 | 246 |
| 1991-92 | 246 |
| 1992-93 | 245 |

Besides there are a large number of public enterprises in the State sector.

**Form of Public Sector Organisation—Typology of Public Enterprises**

Before Independence, there were two outstanding public enterprises in India, namely Railways and Postal Services including Talephone. These were managed as departmental enterprises. The public enterprises which were taken up after Independence have mostly been undertaken as public limited companies under the Companies Act. Only a few are corporations under specific Acts passed by Parliament. The rationale for *not* accepting the departmental form of organisation was stated as follows in the First Five Year Plan-"The drawbacks of departmental management of public enterprises are well known. Successful conduct of such enterprises requires a good deal of initiative and power to take quick decisions on the part of executive incharge and these can hardly be secured if the enterprise is under government department."

The original choice of the Government of India was in

favour of Corporation as the appropriate form of public enterprises. The Industrial Policy Resolution of 1948 had stated that "Management of Public enterprises will, as a rule be through the medium of public corporation under the statutory control of the Central Government." In pursuance of this, Damodar Valley Corporation, the Industrial Finance Corporation of India, and the Employees' State Insurance Corporation were created in 1948. However, due to unsatisfactory experience which Government had with the DVC, the public corporation device was used sparingly after 1948. In 1953 the two air corporations, the Indian Airlines Corporation and Air India were created under the Air Corporations, Act. The State Bank of India was established in 1955, the Life Insurance Corporation in 1956 and the Oil & Natural Gas Commission in 1959.

The Corporation device was also used for enterprises of a banking nature like Deposit Insurance and Credit Guarantee Corporation. Enabling laws were passed to set up statutory corporations in various States e.g. Road Transport Corporation Act 1950 and the State Financial Corporation Act 1951. Two other acts which established Central Public Corporations and also permitted the State Governments to establish their own statutory bodies were - the Warehousing Corporation Act 1952 and the Food Corporation Act 1964. The 14 commercial banks which were nationalised in 1969 were also made autonomous organisations under the Banking Companies Act 1970. The International Airport Authority of India was established as a statutory Corporation in 1971. Government of India has not established statutory corporation for its enterprises after 1971.

The adoption of the form of public limited company for the management of public enterprises owes its origin to the decision of the Union Cabinet to that effect taken on 12th November, 1950 on the basis of a paper submitted to it by the Ministry of Industry & Supply. It was on this basis that the first fully owned Central Government Company viz. Sindri Fertilizers & Chemicals Ltd. was established in December 1951. One great advantage of the companies against corporations was that the Government could obviate going to Parliament each time. The Company form is therefore, continued as one which avoids constitutional responsibility which a state owned enterprise should have to the legislature. A Government company unlike, the statutory corporation is created by executive as against legislation thus avoiding Parliamentary accountability and control. Government, therefore, prefers company form as against public corporation because of the ease of floating. A public company is autonomous in the sense that its objectives and rules of internal management are governed by its Memorandum and Articles of Association.

The Estimates Committee as well as the Administrative Reforms Study Team, have pointed out that no well defined principles or set of criteria have been followed in determining the form of organisation of the public enterprise. While air transport is managed by a Corporation, sea transport is the responsibility of the company. Life Insurance Corporation is also a company.

The Administrative Reforms Commission proposed setting up of Sector Corporations. The idea was that these will do much of supervision and coordination, leaving Government control to a few strategic and vital points. The Government rejected ARC recommendation but introduced a concept akin to sector corporation viz. The Holding Company called The Steel Authority of India (SAIL) in 1973. But the SAIL concept gradually disintegrated.

A Government company, according to Section 617 of the Companies Act is that in which not less than 51% of the paid up share capital is held by the Central Government or the State Government or jointly by the Centre and State Governments. A subsidiary of a Government company is also a government company. Most of the Central Government companies are fully owned by the State. But a few like Madras Fertilizers Ltd. or Madras Refines Ltd. have foreign participation, a few like Fertilizer and Chemicals Travancore Ltd., the Praga Tools Ltd. and Natural Newsprint and Paper Ltd. have private Indian participation.

## The Rationale of the Public Sector

The major reason for the establishment of public enterprises in the country is that they are looked upon as pace-setters of economic development of the country. Without them the economy would not get modernised and the basic infrastructure for development would not be available. The public enterprises have also to mobilise the natural resources like the oil and gas resources which otherwise could remain untapped.

Thus while most of the public enterprises owe their origin to the initiative of the State, an enterprises like the Textile Corporation of India is the result of nationalisation of sick private textile mills. It was felt that unless they were taken over by the State, there would be wide-spread unemployment.

### The Objective of Public Enterprises

As would be apparent from what has been stated in the introduction, the very objective of public enterprises was to serve the larger purpose of economic development. They were to provide the basic infrastructure without which the economy could not develop. Steel and coal, railway and shipping, oil, natural gas and energy were considered to be part of this basic infrastructure.

### Commercial Criteria vs. Subserving Public Purpose

This does not mean that the public enterprises do not have any commercial criteria of success. They have to be run on commercial lines in the sense that they have to operate in the market and have to make optimum use of their resources, exercise economy in all aspects and make reasonable profits so as to contribute to the surplus resources available for further development. They have to be run according to sound business principles and prudent commercial practices. In order that the enterprises are run on commercial lines, it is acknowledged that they must have the necessary operational autonomy. But this autonomy has to be reconciled with their accountability since they are responsible for the fulfilment of the objectives of the national Plans. Thus the Sixth Five Year Plan observes- "The justification of the public sector lies in its contribution to fulfilling certain broader socio-economic objectives." It attributes major structural changes witnessed in the Indian economy to the public sector. Public interest need not necessarily conflict with business principles.

In order to reconcile fulfilment of *national objective* along with the realisation of the *commercial objectives* of the public enterprises, there is a need for the *quantification* of the *social objectives*. The Committee on Public Undertakings has observed that the Government should clearly enunciate economic, financial and social responsibilities of public undertakings. Moreover, as the Sixth Five Year Plan observes, Government should judge the performance of public enterprises on the basis of overall results rather than in relation to individual citizens.

The means at the State's disposal will ensure that the activity of public enterprises complies with their objectives. As mentioned above, the public enterprise has to possess the necessary operational autonomy. This means that it should be able to take quick decisions regarding all aspects of its activities connected with the production of goods or provision of services. If the public enterprise does not possess the operational autonomy and has to look to the Ministry or Department of Government for every decision, the decisions would be delayed and, in the meanwhilé, the economic situation might undergo a change, and the working of the enterprise itself would get immobilized. The traditional decision-making procedures in Government tend to be somewhat dilatory since several authorities and several limbs and agencies of public administration have to be consulted before decisions are taken. Obviously, it would atrophy working of the public enterprises if their decisions are dependent on the decisions taken by Government in the Departments and Ministries.

At the same time, the Government is responsible for the public enterprise to Parliament. Parliament would hold the Government responsible for the satisfactory performance of public enterprises. Government is also required to place the annual reports of the public enterprises on the Floor of Parliament, and its annual reports are open to criticism and comments by the Parliament.

Sometimes, it is argued that beyond a point discussion on the floor of Parliament regarding public enterprises might exercising those responsible for public enterprises who start exercising on excessive caution in their decisions and this might prevent the growth of the enterprise.

It is, therefore, argued that the Parliament must discuss only the overall performance of the public enterprises in relation to their national and other objectives. But individual internal decisions should not be exposed to the Parliamentary debate. Nor should the Government interfere in its day-to-day matters.

It should lay down general guidelines to public enterprises but leave the working of an individual enterprise to its board of management.

Those guidelines could be in terms of the general level of performance, the remuneration to top management positions and certain norms of expenditure. But these should never be rigid and there should be adequate flexibility. The monitoring of the progress of the enterprise should be at reasonably long intervals so that the management of the public enterprise is not worried all the time of convincing the authorities in Government.

### The Legal Instruments which Determine the Objectives of Public Enterprises

India's Constitution lays down the Directive Principles according to which the ownership and control of the material resources of the community have to subserve the common good, and the operation of the economic system should not result in the concentration of wealth and means of production to the common detriment. The public enterprises have, therefore, to subserve the common good. A public enterprise may be set up through an Act of Parliament creating a corporation. However, it has recently been felt that most commercially-oriented public enterprises could conveniently be set up under the Companies Act.

The State has set up the Bureau of Public Enterprises to lay down the general norms.

### Parliamentary Control

This is a control of ultimate accountability. The Parliament has its Committee on Public Undertakings which makes an examination of selected public enterprises. The existing rules regarding Parliamentary questions in India recognise the concept of autonomy. According to these rules, the question regarding autonomous P.Es. will either relate to a matter of policy or raise a matter of public interest. However, in practice the distinction between policy and day-to-day management is not maintained. In the case of one corporation viz. LIC investment in some shares became a public scandle and the cover of autonomy was not acceptable to the House. In the case of public companies audit and accountability to Parliament is secured as provided under sections 619 & 619A of the Companies Act which relate to audit and submission of annual reports. As regards Parliamentary Questions wider latitude is allowed in the case of questions on companies while the same in respect of corporations is determined by the provisions of the Act concerned.

**The Prime Minister**

The Prime Minister as the head of the Government is responsible for steady progress in all economic sectors. PM is, therefore, kept informed by periodical progress reports regarding the working of public enterprises.

**The Cabinet**

The Cabinet has its Sub-Committee on Economic Affairs as well as a Committee on Infrastructure. Recently it was felt that the weaknesses in infrastructure were mainly responsible for holding up the economic goals of the Government. Sub-committee on Infrastructure monitors the progress of various public enterprises.

**Sectoral Ministries**

Each Ministry is responsible for proper progress of public enterprises which fall within its jurisdiction. Thus the Fertiliser Ministry monitors the progress of fertilizer factories, the Steel Ministry of the steel mills and so on. The corporations are required to obtain prior approval of Government for regulations regarding terms and conditions of service of their employees. Government have powers to issue directives to corporations which are bound by the same. Capital expenditure of corporations beyond the limit laid down in the Act need Government's approval. The corporations are not allowed to raise their resources without the Government's approval which in practice is not granted. The heavy financial dependence makes the corporations subservient to Government.

**Bureau of Public Enterprises**

This was established in early sixties to act as a friend, philosopher and guide to public enterprises and also to monitor their performance, keep Government informed and render independent advice taking into account both the policies of

Government and views of public enterprises. It has been suggested that the Bureau needs to be replaced by a more independent and professional Public Enterprise Commission with full-fledged manpower, monitoring and evaluation divisions.

In the case of Government company also, funds are obtained from Government (and if not fully owned by the government from private shareholders) and through revenues derived from the sale of its goods and services. Since the Government is the sole shareholder in most cases, the autonomy of the undertakings is largely dependent on the controlling Ministry which writes and can revise the Articles of Association. The managers of Government companies, therefore, feel that they are autonomous only in name and operate as adjuncts to the Ministries. As the Government company never formally secures its autonomy from Parliament, it can never have privilege of autonomy from it. Its legal form gives far-reaching powers to Government which can reduce the Government company almost to the status of a Department.

Mr. Paul Appleby in his report on public enterprises stated that the corporation and the company are essentially the same and differ only in their basis of legal authorization. The Government appoints the Board in both the cases and no difference exists in regard to the appointment of personnel and incurring capital expenditure. The Comptroller & Accountant General has effective way in audit of both the cases. Government has the powers of issuing directives and Parliament in practice makes no differentiation in regard to control on the basis of organisation.

The Minister exercises control over public enterprises through discussions, negotiations, pressures and directives over various matters including prices of products and services charged by the public enterprises. The Government officials on the Board can also effectively use their presence to dominate the decisions to reflect Government wishes and desires.

The various ways in which Government influence public enterprises are:

(1) **Prior approval** : Before certain important decisions are taken e.g.rules governing the foreign collaborations.

(2) **Powers to issue directives** : In case of government

companies, it is generally stated in the Articles of Association that the President may from time to time issue such directions or instructions as may be necessary in regard to finances, conduct of business and affairs of the company. The directives may be general and applicable to all the public enterprises or specific to a particular P.E. In the former category are those relating to the reservation of posts for Scheduled Castes, Scheduled Tribes, Ex-servicemen or dependents of those killed in action.

**(3) Circulars or office orders** : These are issued by Government mostly through the Bureau of Public Enterprises in the Ministry of Finance. Public Enterprises receiving such guidelines cannot ignore the mandatory elements involved in them, though the legal or formal value of those documents may be doubtful. Some examples of these are-the Financial Adviser to be the Principal Adviser to Chief executive on the financial matters and should invariably be invited to attend the Board meetings; avoiding retrenchment of labour when computers are introduced; architectural and town planning design work to be given to public agencies only; PES to keep accounts with public sector banks; PEs not to increase conveyance allowance; norms for entertainment allowance to the Chairman and Managing Directors; fixing remuneration payable to consultants adoption of network techniques and budgetary control, effective communication system and quality control, economy in residential telephones, scale of amenities for residential control, integrated reporting systems.

**(4) Appointments:** All Board level appointments have been approved by the Appointments Committee of the Cabinet. Besides on the Boards sit a representative each of the Ministry of Finance and the administrative Ministry concerned.

**(5) Reports, returns, statements** received by Government to keep it informed about the working of PEs and enable it to exercise supervision and control. Often the purpose is not fulfilled because they are not in a meaningful form or do not receive the necessary attention in the Ministries.

**(6) Meetings:** Performance review meetings are held in the Ministries.

(7) **Powers to supersede:** If the enterprises fail to carry out the obligations imposed by the Act, or are unable to discharge their functions and duties or act in public interest.

### Planning Commissions

The Planning Commission takes into account programmes and plans for total economic development, including that of public enterprises.

### Office of the Comptroller and Accountant General

Except in the case of Banks, financial institutions and LIC where chartered accountants are auditors, in all other corporations the audit has been entrusted to the Comptroller & Auditor General of India. A specialised wing of the CAG viz the Audit Board looks after PEs audit. A government company is exempted from accounting and audit laws and procedures applicable to Government departments. However, section 612 of the Companies Act of 1956 gives statutory recognition to the CAG's right with regard to audit of Government companies.

### Political Parties

These are ever watchful about the conduct of public enterprises and raise issues from time to time on the Floor of Parliament. Members of political parties are members of the Committee on Public Undertakings.

### Government Participation in Internal Bodies within the Enterprise

The managing board of the public enterprise has the nominees of the various departments and ministries concerned. The board level appointments are made by Government on the basis of the recommendations of the Public Enterprises Selection Board.

### The Type of Control

The control is mainly performance control rather than legal or management control. There is a feeling that the excessive public control has led to the stultification of the decision-making processes in public enterprises. It has been observed that "most of the autonomous enterprises operate as extensions of government departments and the autonomy envisaged for them is an exception rather than the rule." As early in 1951 Mr. A.D. Gorwala in a report to the Planning Commission entitled, "The report on the efficient conduct of State enterprises" observed with reference to the Damodar Valley Corporation, the first autonomous Corporation established after Independence-"There is no point in having a corporation and treating it as an administrative department subordinate to the secretariat. If it is desired that the Corporation should work, its autonomy must be respected. The Corporation's time should not be wasted in continuously having to defend its existence." In 1955,the Estimates Committee of the First Lok Sabha (Parliament) in its 16th report on the "Organisation and Administration of Nationalised Industrial Undertakings' stated-"The State undertakings have become adjuncts to Ministries and are treated more or less on the same lines as any subordinate organisation or office. The Committee deplores this tendency which has a harmful effect on the productive activity of the undertakings as these have been subjected to all the usual red tape and procedural delays common to Government departments with serious consequential effect on production."

Government, however, is on the horns of a dilemma. Many public enterprises "have such a critical and strategic position in the economy that the Government has got to concern itself with their operation at various points." However, this has to be reconciled with the fact that the enterprise does require the necessary autonomy, initiative and flexibility to secure results.

The autonomy of the Damodar Valley Corporation became an object of dislike in Government circles. Uncordial relations between the DVC and the Government were brought to the notice of the Parliament in March 1952 by the Estimates Committee_"The DVC developed strange conception of its autonomy and tried to bypass the authority or advice of the Government." The Minister announced on the Floor of Parliament that in the light of experience it was decided by government that there should be less autonomy and more financial control."

### Social Control

Workers' participation in management is encouraged. Consumer and social groups could also be represented on the Board of Directors.

## International Public Undertakings

There are not many examples of other government's collaborating with the Government of India in the establishment of enterprise.

## Managerial Improvement for Public Enterprises

Managerial improvement for public enterprises is a matter of constant concern in India. In her interview given to the Times of India (August 14, 1983), Prime Minister Indira Gandhi herself dealt with the subject when she was asked by the interviewer whether the public sector continues in her opinion, to perform badly. To this the Prime Minister replied "the public sector is neither better nor worse than the private sector. Some enterprises have done very well, others poorly. But on the whole the public sector performance has been improving. The overall net profit is now Rs. 600 crores ($600 million). Between last year and now, the turnover has risen from Rs. 36,443 crore to Rs. 41,512 crores (or 14 per cent) and the profitability ratio in terms of gross profit to capital employed is up from 12.33 per cent to 13.13 per cent."

The interviewer further asked the Prime Minister whether one reason for the bad performance of the public sector was supposed to be too much interference by Ministers and lack of adequate power with the managers. The Prime Minister replied "it would be wrong to blame all this on Ministers. Not all Ministers are culprits nor are all managers and technicians angels. We want to establish good working relations between the two and also see to it that our engineers and industrial managers are kept on their toes, ever alert, avoiding what is known as the bureaucratic outlook. Much of the improvement in the better enterprises is the result of the changes we have introduced."

The extensive quotation from the interview of the Prime Minister indicates the concern of the Government of India for raising the efficiency of public enterprises, the causes of less than satisfactory performance of some enterprises and the direction in which effort is to be made to improve performance.

It may appear as though the efficiency of the public

enterprises is judged only by profits. While profits provide a ready criterion for measurement of efficiency, it has to be understood that the public sector enterprises have to fulfil other criteria as well. For example, in India's system of planned economic development, public enterprises are considered to be engine of growth. They provide sinews of economic diversification and industrial advancement. They are the means of locating and developing natural resources. They promote development of backward areas. They contribute technological progress and training of skilled manpower. They provide employment opportunities; they provide essential services to the public. It is necessary to take all these factors into account in measuring efficiency of public enterprises.

Among the various factors responsible for managerial performance of the public sectors, is its personnel. When public sector enterprises were newly established, managerial personnel were largely drawn from the existing pool of administrative cadres in the country. Thus the Managing Directors came from the members of the Indian Civil Service and the Financial Managers from the members of the Indian Audit and Account Service. However, it came to be pointed out that administrative experience did not always correspond with the needs of managerial performance nor had techniques of Government accounts and audit relevant to commercial and managerial accounting. Personnel, therefore, were drawn from amongst the managers of private sector as also qualified Chartered and Cost & Works Accountants. More recently, a concept of development of management from within has also been promoted. Following the decision taken by Government that no officer of Government could be on deputation to public sector enterprises beyond two years at the end of which he should either agree to get himself permanently absorbed or return to Government, it has become all the more urgent for public enterprises to be self reliant in respect of their managerial personnel.

The Public Sector Selection Board has been especially constituted to recruit higher management personnel in public enterprises. All the appointments at the Board level require the approval of Government of India.

The Public Sector Selection Board has to do a lot of talent hunting to locate suitable candidates for holding senior management positions.

For the training of managers of public sector enterprises facilities in institutions like the Indian Institute of Public Administration, Administrative Staff College and Institutes of Management, are availed of. In addition, various public sector enterprises have set up their own training institutions.

Every enterprise has its own norms of efficiency. The Bureau of Public Enterprises also has laid down general norms and is responsible for general monitoring in addition to detailed monitoring done by the subject matter ministry concerned with the public enterprise. The Department of Economic Coordination in the Cabinet Secretariat tries to remove bottlenecks. The Cabinet Committee on Economic Affairs has also an infrastructure reviewing the performance of the public sector enterprise from time to time.

The efficiency of public enterprises depends not only on its inner functioning but also on its environment and general policies of the Government like the priority given to the public sector in supplying the various requirements of public agencies.

Resources for public sector enterprises come from Government in addition to internal generation of resources and funds available from Industrial Development Bank of India and the Finance Corporation of India. Recently public enterprises have been asked to raise deposits.

In the Indian system of planning, public enterprises are given an important place and are in charge of commanding height of the economy. They, therefore, receive constant support from Government.

Parliament also takes a great deal of interest in the efficiency of public enterprises. The Committee on Public Enterprises reviews the performance of public enterprises from time to time and makes important recommendations which the administration has to follow up and see that they are properly implemented.

From the analysis given above, the following appear to be the measures required for improving the efficiency and performance of public enterprises:

1. Clear cut definition and criteria for performance appraisal;
2. Careful corporate planning in order to reach those objectives;
3. Adequate autonomy to public enterprises to pursue the corporate planning;
4. Elimination of backseat driving from Government authorities;
5. Adequate support through macro economic policies without of course creating conditions of monopoly and captive market which might blunt the sharp edge of competitive efficiency;
6. Selection of personnel on the basis of objective criteria;
7. Objective system of performance appraisal and promotion;
8. New philosophy of labour management which could ensure motivation on the part of entire work force;
9. Progressive planning for continued development and diversification of public enterprises.

# Annexure-I

## Syllabus for the Course on Management of Public Enterprises

Public enterprises have come to stay as a very important part in the national economy in terms of huge capital investments and their growth potentials. Flexible approach in management has been adopted to suit the needs of those enterprises. For obtaining proper returns from these investments within the framework of their defined objectives, there is an increasing need to familiarize senior and middle level executives of these enterprises with concepts of modern management.

The programme on 'Management of Public Enterprises' aims at providing a framework with which senior and middle level executives will be able to fit in their problems of planning, coordination, control. The programme will expose participants to methods of problem identification, formulation, analysis, and solution within constraints imposed by the environment.

Contents

I. **Corporate Management**

Role of Public Sector

Corporate policy Formulation and Planning

Project Identification, Formulation and Appraisal

Management of Projects

II. **Organisation Design**

Behavioural Science approach to structure, decision-making and motivation.

III. **Functional Systems**

Financial, Personnel, Material, Production and Marketing

IV. **Systems of Managerial Control**

Management Information Systems

Monitoring through Networks

Performance Budgeting

V. **Managerial Aids**

**Quantitative methods:** Linear Programming, Forecasting Techniques, Discounted Cash Flow, Game Theory, etc.

VI. Interaction with experts of Bureau of Public Enterprises on' Role of Bureau of Public Enterprises in a two-day seminar.

VII. Visit to Ministry/Public Enterprises.

# Annexure-II

## Syllabus for the Course on Economic Analysis for Public Sector Management

A basic familiarity with some important concepts of economic analysis is essential for those involved in the formulation of policy, as well as its implementation at various levels of government. Moreover, some important analytical systems have evolved response to the need for systematically delineating and assessing complex economic inter-relationship.

These analytical models have proved to be invaluable guides to the policy maker, specially in areas, such as location, industrial inter-dependence, forecasting and the evaluation of the alternative policy decisions. The wide applicability of such models at the national, regional, sectoral as well as the individual enterprise levels enhances their usefulness.

The objective of the course is to introduce participants to some of these basic concepts and analytical techniques, thereby reinforcing their abilities as decision makers, and also equip them with the tools of evaluating their own policy frame.

### Contents

The contents of the course broadly include Economic Interdependence, Elements of Input-output Analysis and its Applications in Forecasting, Multiplier Analysis, Employment Multipliers, Feasibility and Sensitivity Tests, Regional and Inter regional Impact Analysis and its relations with Economic Development. Furthermore this course will briefly cover the Location of industry and Infrastructure, as well as Cost Analysis and Pricing of Public Goods, Planning Models and Plan Implementation.

# INDEX


Administrative challenges in development, 33-34
  Employment and income generation, 216
  Increasing food production, 33
  National integration, 33
  Stopping population increase, 33
Administrative Reforms Commission, 33
Administrative Staff College of India, Hyderabad, 216
Administrator role in changing environment, 77-81
  After independence, 78-79
  Before independence, 77-78
  Manager and bureaucrat, 80
  Role as agents of change, 79
  Role as manager rather bureaucrats, 79-81
Advanced Professional Programme in Public Administration, 178, 218
Africa, 83, 162
Agnelli, 205
Aid Consortium, India, 129
Ambedkar, B.R., 125
Appleby, Paul, 35, 147, 150, 273
Armstrong, Robert, 201, 244-46, 251
Asia, 83
Ataturk, Kamal, 24
Australia, 83, 84, 202, 243
Ayub govt., 7
Balogh, Thomas, 251
Balwant Rai Mehta Committee, 42
Bangladesh, 3-5
Basham, A.L., 44
Belgrano, 244
Bettleheim, 147
Bhagavat Gita, 28
Bharat Sevak Samaj, 168
Bhutan, 3
Brayne, F.L., 78
Buddha, 24, 30, 160
Bureaucracy, 187-95
  Administrative reforms, 189
  Apparatus of, 191-92
  As rational institution, 191
  Citizens point of view of, 189
  Commitment of, 194
  Corruption in, 190
  Criticism of, 192-93, 195
  Definition of, 187-88, 191
  Features of, 187-88
  Military, 188
  Need in democracy of, 192
  Political neutrality of, 193-94
  Proliferation of, 188-89
  Quality of, 189-90
  Westminster model of parliamentary democracy, 193
Bureaucracy vis-a-vis political executive, 243-53
  Accountability of civil servants to ministers, 247-48
  Bureaucratic behaviour, 244
  Change in practice and thought between, 251-52
  Civil servants cannot carry ministers orders, 245
  Code of conduct for civil servants, 248
  Committed bureaucracy, 252
  Constitutional protection of, 247
  Division of labour between, 250-51
  Duties and responsibilities of, 246-47
  Political executive appointment, 252-53
  Political executives, 248-49
  Ponting case in U.K., 244
  Relationship between, 243, 253
  Remedies to, 245-46

Role of, 243
Role of civil servants in India, 247, 250
Special Assistant to Ministers, 252
Transfer of civil servants, 249
Burma, 161, 162
Calvin, 26
Canada, 83-84
Carter, 16
Centre for Urban Studies of Indian Institute of Public Administration, 220-21
Ceylon, 6, 160-61, 162
Chagla, M.C., 145
Chandra, Satish, 67
Charles, I., 84
Chetty, Shanmukham, 145
China, 24, 31, 37-38, 41, 126, 130, 148, 161-62
Chou En Lai, 162
Civil Service, 71-75, 192-202
Above all rules, 197-99
Domestic servant, 199-200
Honest advice, 200-01
Plight of, 74-75
Process of, 71-74
Public interest, 201
Commonwealth, 163
Curzon, 78
Dalyell, Tam, 244
Daring, Malcolm, 78
Denmark, 243
Department of Personnel, 216-17
Deshmukh, Durgabai, 172
Dey, S.K., 167
Dharma Vira, 67, 249
Efficiency in civil service, 53-58
Cost and benefit concept of, 53-54
Joint investment, 54
Morale and motivation, 57-58
Parkinson's law in reverse, 55-57
Promoting of, 53
Welfare of State depends on, 53
Excellence in administration, 13-18
Competence, knowledge and skill, 15
Courtesy and consideration, 14-15
Fairness and objectivety, 15
Punctuality in operation, 14
Quickness in dealing, 13-14
Sensitivity and concern for citizens problems, 14
Understanding new projects and schemes, 15
Field administration, 45-51
Administration power and authority, 46-48
Apex administration, 45-46
Formulation of policies and implementation, 50
Goals of, 49
Higher and lower administration relationship, 50-51
Pay lip service, 46
Priority to communications, 48
Reality of field problem, 50
Stereo type scheme, 49
France, 83, 243, 252
Gadgil, D.R., 131
Galbraith, John Kenneth, 45
Gandhi, Indira, 89, 177-84, 206, 277
Gandhi-Indira and public administration, 177-84
Administration relevant to Indian situation, 81
Development and change, 179-80
Discarded old rules and methods, 182
Disparity in development, 183
Forests, 184
India's diversity, 182-83
Land reforms, 183-84
Monopoly growth, 184
Positive atmosphere, 181
Social discipline, 180-81
Strong and self-relevant India as goal of, 179, 182
Thinking people, 183
Unemployment, 184
Gandhi, Mahatma, 24, 88, 128, 129, 143, 144
Gandhi, Rajiv, 23, 29, 202, 247
Generalist vs specialist, 203-06
Academic and agitational, 204
Controversy on, 203-04
Generalist need in specialist field, 205-06
Generalist with general administration, 204-05
Specialised, 205
Talent of, 206

George, Lloyd, 65
Gopalswami Ayyangar, 150
Gorbachov, 129
Gorwala, A.D., 150, 275
Govind Narain, 67
Green Revolution, 38, 131
Grow More Food, 130, 165-66
Gulick, Luther, 250
Hamilton, Alexander, 116
Heath, Edward, 136
Hindu Code Bill, 172
House of Commons Committee, 245, 246, 251, 252
India, 3-4, 6-7
Indian Administrative Service Staff College at Shimla, 212
Indian Administrative Service Training at Metcalfe House, 212
Indian Audit and Accounts Service Staff College, 212
Indian Civil Service, 59-63
  Accountable to elected govt., 62
  Bureaucratic structure of, 63
  Decline of European elements of, 61
  Definition of, 59
  Leadership role of, 60-61
  Protection of terms and conditions of service, 61-62
  Recruitment to, 62-63
  Role of, 60
  Traditions of, 59-60
Indian Civil Service and Indian Administrative Service, 65-70
  British members of, 66-67
  Constitutional protection of, 66
  Deterioration after first generation, 68
  Factors affected performance, 69
  Reputation for, 65
  Towering personalities, 67-68
Indian Institute of Management, Banglore, 203
Indian Institute of Public Administration, 177, 190, 216, 218-22, 229-34, 239
Indian Postal Service Officers, 212
Indian Revenue Service Officers, 212
Indonesia, 162
Institute of Development Studies, Bangalore, 216
Institute of Economic Growth, Delhi, 216
Institute of Management, Ahmedabad, 216
Institute of Secretariat Training and Management, 215
International Monetary Fund, 226
Jaitley, J.C., 199
Japan, 17, 24, 39, 148
Jha, L.K., 66
Jinnah, M.A., 153
Johnson, 203
Kaldor, Nicholas, 251
Karma theory, 27
Khub Chand, 67
Kripalani, M.K., 67
Krishnamachari, T.T., 145
Lal Bahadur Shastri National Academy of Administration, Mussoorie, 212-15
Lasswell, 109
Lindblom, 105, 113
London School of Economics, 25
Lugard, 85
Macaulay, 85
Mahalanobian model, 129
Maine, Henry, 65
Major, 90
Malaysia, 162
Maldives, 3
Malthusian, 39
Marxist-Leninist principles, 119
Mathai, John, 129
Mayer, Albert, 167
McNamara, 205
McNichols, 109
Montague-Chemsford Reforms, 60
MRTP Act, 129
Myrdal, Gunnar, 27, 90
Naipaul, V.S., 195
National Academy of Public Administration, 239
National Agricultural Commission, 102
National Institute of Banking Management, 240
National Institute of Community Development, 240
National Institute of Health Administration, 240
National Institute of Labour and Employment, 240

National Institute of Rural Development, 219
National Institute of Urban Affairs, 221
National Productivity Council, 22
Nehru, Jawaharlal, 35, 67, 87, 89, 125-29, 131-32, 143-75, 177, 249
Nehru and public administration, 143-75
  Adaptation to changing world, 147
  Administrative reform, 149-52
  Africa, 162
  Appointment and role of governors, 157-58
  Appointment of ministers, 158
  Astrology, 174
  Backward caste, SC and ST, 174
  Broad outlook—no single pattern, 145-46
  Burma, 161
  Cabinet system, 158
  Centre-state cooperation, 148-49
  Ceylon, 160-61
  China and Tibet, 161-62
  Christianity, 153
  Civil liberties vs repressive investors, 154
  Commonwealth, 163
  Communication importance to, 148
  Coordinated administration, 168
  Culture, 172-73
  Defence policy, 164
  Development projects, 166-67
  Eagle eye on administration, 146
  Economic policy, 164
  Economy in expenditure, 171-72
  Educational policy of, 173
  Environment, 171
  Food and Agriculture, 164-65
  Foreign policy, 158-59
  Foreign Service and missions, 163-64
  General elections, 158 .
  Grow More Food, 165-66
  Health and Medical policy, 173
  High standards of, 144-45
  Housing, 169
  Idealism and realism, 146-47
  Indians in neighbouring countries, 162
  India's peace keeping force, 163
  Industrial policy resolution, 168-69
  Indonesia and Asian Solidarity, 162
  Judiciary, 157
  Labour, 171
  Land reforms, 167
  Law and order, 154-55
  Linguism, 155-56
  Mahatama's ideals in, 144
  Media and development, 157
  Nehru's dedication to India's progress, 143-44
  Nehru's letter to Chief Ministers, 143
  Nepal, 160
  Open diplomacy, 163
  Open windows, 147-48
  Pakistan, 159-60
  People's Agencies, 168
  Planning and controlled economy, 169-71
  Policy and implementation, 166
  Political policies-unity and stability, 152
  Press freedom, 156-57
  Prohibition, 173
  Provincialism, 156
  Railways, 169
  Right policies and right means, 144
  Science and technology, 174
  Secular approach of, 152-53
  Sikh communalism, 153
  Social policy, 172
  Social welfare, 172
  Sports, 174
Nepal, 3, 4, 7, 160
Nixon, 161
Non-Alignment, 158-59
Office of the Comptroller and Accountant General, 275
Official Secrets Act, 201
Operation Black Board, 39
Orr, Boyd, 147, 166
Oxford English Dictionary, 104
Pakistan, 3, 4, 5, 7, 159-60
Panchayati Raj, 42
Pant, Govind Vallab, 67
Parkinson's Law, 55-57
Patel, Vallabhbhai, 61, 66, 67, 249
Patil, R.K., 166
Peter, The Great of Russia, 24
Pillai, Krishna, 203

Planning Commission, 35, 111, 136, 170, 275
PL 480 Programme, 131
Policy formulation in govt., 95-113
Administration and, 120-21
Analysis of, 102
Analytical process of, 108-13
Analysing the situation, 109
Formulating plans and strategies, 109-110
Implementing through organisation and control, 110-11
Limits to, 112-113
Selection of major problems, 109
Skill required for, 111-12
Balance view of, 119
Definition of, 104-05
Factors determine policy, 106-08
Holistic perspectives in, 123
Ideological policy, 98-99
Ideology and, 119
Implementation of, 102-04
Information and, 121
Innovation and environment, 105-06
Institutional and organisational instruments, 123
Macro economic and development policies, 99
Models of, 105, 123
Policy analysis and, 123
Model of policy delivery system, 121-22
Monitoring, 104
Policies related to social sciences, 100
Policy environment, 122
Policy making, 95-97
Decision making and, 95-96
Functions of administration and, 95
Importance of, 95
Planning and, 96
Process of, 100-02
Projects and programme formulation, 97
Political process of, 113-19
Administration, 117
Cabinet Committees, 116-17
Citizen participation, 113-14
Independent commissions, 117-18
Judges, 117
Parliamentary system, 115-16
Parties, 114
Proximate policy, 118
Proximate policy makers, 113
Public interest and, 121
Sectoral policies, 99-100
Symbolic policy, 106
Uniqueness of, 119-20
Who formulates the, 97-98
Policy making in India, 125-41
Agricultural policy, 138-39
Defence and foreign policy, 128-29
Deficiencies in, 133
Economic policy, 129-33
Agriculture, 130-31
Centralisation and decentralisation, 132-33
Liberalization policy, 130
Mass production, 129
Planning, 131-132
Population control, 130
Education policy, 140-41
Framework after independence, 125-26
Govt. machinery place in, 133-36
Law and order, 127-28
Political policy, 126-27
National unity and integrity, 126
Secularism, 126-27
Technology policy, 139-40
Ponting, 201, 244
Population, 33
Family planning, 34
Illiteracy, 34
India's density of, 33-34
People below poverty line, 34
Potter, 59
Preventive Detention Bill, 154
Public accountability and ethics in administration, 255-58
Accountability of, 255
Administrative executive to political executive, 256
Attitude of public servants towards public, 258
Enquires in administrative lapses, 257

Holding public servants responsible to, 257-58
Mechanisms of, 255
Parliament enforces the, 256
Public Accounts Committee on, 256
Public enterprise accountable to Board, 257
Subordinate legislation watch on rules and regulation, 257
Vigilance authorities on, 257
Public administration for 21st century, 35-44
Achievements after independence, 36
Agriculture modernisation and poverty alleviation, 38-39
Changes in economic system, 37-38
Democratic system—Panchayati Raj, 42-43
Environment preservation, 43
Inadequate growth rate, 37
Materialism and consumerism, 43-44
Refashioning administrative system, 42-43
Science and technology, 41-42
Task after independence, 35-36
Universal education and health facilities, 39-40
Urbanisation, 40-41
Public administration in India, 17-22
Contrary attitude in, 18-21
Exercising authority, 20-21
Illustrations on, 18-20
Waste of time in, 19
Improve productivity, 22
Noise pollution, 21-22
Smooth running in, 17
Public administration in South Asia, 3-12
Administration and citizen relationship, 10-12
Bureaucrats and politicians relationship, 8-10
Decentralisation, 7-8
Functions of, 3
Planning and its impact on, 4-5
Restructuring civil services, 5-7
Trends in, 3-4
Public enterprises—state policies and managerial improvement, 263-80
Bureau of public enterprises, 272-73
Cabinet on, 272
Changing role of state as economic agent, 263
Commercial criteria vs sub serving, 269-64
Economic development patterns, 263-64
Govt. influence on, 273-75
Appointments, 274
Circulars or office orders, 274
Meetings, 274-75
Powers to issue directives, 273-74
Prior approval, 273
International public undertaking, 277
Legal instructions on, 271
Managerial improvement for, 277-80
Objectives of, 269
Office of Comptroller and Accountant General, 275
Parliamentary control on, 271-72
Planning Commission on, 275
Political parties on, 275
Prime Minister on, 272
Rationale of, 269
Scope for, 264-66
Sectoral ministers, 272
Type of control on, 275-76
Typology of, 266-68
Public sector enterprise, 261-62
As a means of economic development, 261
Economic philosophy and, 261
Goals and criteria of, 262
Management-worker relations, 262
Philosophy and ethics of, 262
Relations with public, 262
State and, 262
Radhakrishnan, 163
Radhakrishnan Committee, 173
Railway Staff College, Baroda, 212
Rajagopalachari, C., 30, 67, 249
Rajendra Prasad, 67, 88, 249
Rayner, Derek, 251
Russia, 24, 37, 163, 263
Rustomji, Nari, 73

Sahay, Vishnu, 65
Salisbury, Robert, 119
Sankaracharya, 24
Sardar Vallabhbhai Patel National Police Academy, Hyderabad, 212
Self, Peter, 105
Sharda Prasad, 102, 178
Sharkansky, 105
Sharpe, Myron E., 45
Shastri, Lal Bahadur, 67, 190
Shrikant, M.L., 174
Simon, Herbert, 53, 110, 250
Singapore, 17
Smith, Adam, 98
Smith, Thomas, 103
Socialism, 130
South Korea, 39, 40
Sri Lanka, 3-5, 8
Sunderji, 135
Sweden, 148, 243
Switzerland, 17, 18, 148
Tanzania, 85
Tara Singh, 153
Tawney, R.H., 26
Thakkar, M.P., 199
Thatchar, Margaret, 136, 201, 202, 251
Tibet, 161-62
Training division, 217-22
  Indian Institute of Public Administration, 218-19
    Advanced Professional programme, 218-19
    Conducted by Institute, 218
    New courses at, 219
    Sponsored programmes at, 218
  Training and civil service development, 221-22
  Training in local self govt, 219-21
Training for transformation, 223-28
  Agenda for administrative action, 223-24
  Deficiencies in, 225-27
  Development and decentralisation, 224
  Organisation, 224
  Priority areas of, 227
Training in public administration, 229-34, 235-40
  Courses on, 229
  Dimensions of, 235-37
  IIPA courses, 231-34
    Administrative leadership, 233
    Computers courses, 232
    Economic analysis for public sector, 232
    Financial management, 233-34
    Innovation course at, 234
    Management information system, 232
    Man management, 233
    Material management, 233
    Project management, 230-31
    Technique of administration, 231-32
  Trainers and their training, 238-40
  Training arrangements, 237-38
Training system of civil servants in India, 209-22
  Development of Personnel by Training Division, 216
  History of, 209-10
  Institute of Secretarial Training and Management, 215
  Lal Bahadur Shastri National Academy of Administration, 212-15
    District training, 214
    Foundational course, 213
    In-service training programme, 215
    Professional course, 213-15
  Methods of training, 210
  New civil services, 210-11
  Size and calibre of civil service personnel, 211-12
  Specialised Autonomous Institutions, 216
  Specialised National Institutions, 216
  State training institutes, 215
Transplanting British administrative institutions, 83-86
  Africa model, 85
  Decentralization model in India, 85-86
  Maintenance of law and order, 83-84
  Monarchy to aristocracy, 84
  Patterns of, 86
  Recruitments in Canada, 84-85
  Self-governing territories of Australia, 84

Trone, 147
Turkey, 24
Twenty point programme, 54,97
U.K., 130, 202, 243, 247, 252
USA, 85, 183, 243, 252
USSR, 126, 130
Vaikunth Mehta National Institute of Cooperative Management, 240
Vellodi Committee Report on Administrative Reorganisation in Kerala, 24
Weber, Max, 26, 79, 80, 187, 188, 191
West Germany, 148, 243, 253
Westminster model of parliamentary democracy, 193, 243
Wheare, 84
Whither Indian bureaucracy, 87-91
  Bureaucratic limitations, 88
  Committed, 89
  Lacking objectivity and impartiality, 89-90
  Planning and control mechanism, 88
  Political neutrality, 88-89
  Privatization and politicisation, 90-91
  Reformed, 87
  Role in maintenance of law and order, 87
  Rural developn.ent and poverty alleviation, 87-88
Wildavsky, 105, 108, 111
Wilson, Harold, 115, 251
Wilson, Woodrow, 250
Work ethic in government, 23-32
  Administrative reforms, 23-24
  Alien to Indian tradition and religion, 27-28
  As genius of people, 23
  As work ethic of people, 23
  Backward sloping supply curve of labour, 25-26
  Communication role in, 29-30
  Indian traditions, 28-29
  In times of crisis, 31
  Management by objective, 30
  Morale in administration, 31-32
  Origin of, 26
  Revival of, 29
  Work to rule vs, 24-25
World Bank, 111, 129, 226, 230
Yugoslavia, 148
Zambia, 85
Zamidari System, 167